Rescue
THE
Captors

Russell Stendal

DI016847

The Voice of the Martyrs

PO Box 608, Streetsville
Mississauga, Ontario L5M 2C1
Phone: 1.888.298.6423
Fax: 905.670.0246
E-mail: thevoice@persecution.net
Website: www.persecution.net

Questions?

Comments?

www.lifesentencepublishing.com

Visit our online forum to discuss this book!

Printed in the United States of America
by LIFE SENTENCE Publishing, LLC
404 N 5th Street
Abbotsford, WI 54405
Ask questions and discuss this book on our forum at
lifesentencepublishing.com

Library of Congress Cataloging in Publication Data

Stendal, Russell, 1955-Rescue the Captors.
    1. Colombia—Politics and government—1974-
2. Guerrillas—Colombia. 3. Kidnapping Colombia.
4. Stendal, Russell, 1955-   I. Title.
F2279.S75 1984 986.1'0632 84-17826
ISBN 978-0-9832016-0-1

Acknowledgments

Special thanks to my wife, Marina, and brother, Chaddy, who risked their lives to negotiate my release; to my two sisters and my mother, who all worked so hard for my release; to my dad, who wouldn't give up until I was free; to all the many thousands of people who prayed for me and supported our family during this most difficult time; and above all, thanks to God who answered our prayers.

Preface

I am not a "professional" writer. I used to get good grades in high school except in English composition. If I had not been placed in such an unusual circumstance, this book would have never been written.

The pressures and the setting under which I wrote this manuscript greatly affected both content and style. In one sense it was kind of like playing *Arabian Nights* with the guerrillas. It was of utmost importance to hold their attention long enough to explain to them my real motives for being in Colombia before they killed me thinking I was something I wasn't.

As I edit this manuscript prior to publication, I am tempted to go back to the drawing board and write a whole new book. Somehow most of this book seems to be about my most spectacular mistakes and failures, and the lessons I learned from them. These were the stories that impressed my captors, causing them to consider their own failings. I could have written about experiences that might have painted me as a big hero with a white hat all the time, but it would have defeated my purpose.

You may not agree with everything I have written in this book; in fact, I am even a little shocked as I look back on some of the things I wrote while in captivity. The viewpoint of a prisoner writing in a guerrilla camp is definitely in a different plane of thinking compared with average life in the U.S.A.

6

I have gone against the advice of some of the literary experts I have talked with and have turned down several flattering offers by publishers wanting to take my experience and commercialize it. Instead of having a professional ghost writer take my story and wrap it around a "theme that will sell," I have presented it as it happened, in my own words. I trust that what I lack in literary style is made up for in sincerity and authenticity. The following story is true to the best of my knowledge. Names, places, and dates have not been altered in any way. You, the reader, are the ultimate critic.

To Manuel

The fulfillment of a boyhood dream—my first landing as pilot at a Mamarongo airstrip. Being a jungle pilot is a very thrilling occupation; but there are times when it can get a little too exciting.

Photo by Pat Stendal

Chapter One

August 14, 1983, 6:00 a.m.

It was a beautiful morning, not a cloud in the sky. My Cessna 170 Taildragger accelerated smoothly down the runway and rose swiftly into the crisp morning air. The old airplane's performance had been noticeably improved by the installation of a Bush Short Takeoff and Landing (STOL) kit the night before. In the copilot's seat on my right was my Colombian friend, Gilberto, who had come along for the ride on his first visit to the plains country, what we call *llanos* in Spanish.

As we departed from our hometown of San Martin in southeastern Colombia, Gilberto was fascinated with the beautiful hills and onrushing streams as they rolled by underneath our wings. Our first stop was the town of Mapiripan on the mighty Guaviare river where we left a packet of mail for my brother-in-law Raul, who was the flight dispatcher for the local airline in addition to being the town school teacher. We took off from there for a ten-minute flight to Chaparral, a ranch belonging to my family. We went into the ranch house to chat with my brother Chaddy, who reminded me that Carlos, the town council president of neighboring Canyo Jabon, was expecting me to attend a meeting with their local businessmen and fishermen. They wanted to buy a large cold storage room and other equipment related to my wholesale fishing business which had become inoperative the past year when communist guerrillas invaded the area. Because I was American they had singled me out as a target for their terrorism. They had shot up our other airplane, a Cessna 182, nine months before right at our ranch as my father was taking off with a sick Indian woman and some other passengers. Fortunately no one was hurt, though the plane had been hit in the right fuel tank, receiving several bullet holes in the cabin section as well. Dad continued the take-off and managed to escape to San Martin using the left fuel tank. After that, we knew we couldn't operate the fish business anymore since that would involve flying into the area on a scheduled basis, making it easy for another ambush. Being forced to leave the area, I was in the process of moving to an apartment in Bogota, the capital of Colombia. I had received the apartment as partial payment for the Cessna 182, which had been sold to pay off business debts.

My future plans were to give my business activities second priority while spending as much time as possible working with Colombian friend and partner, Ricardo Trillos. Ricardo was starting a non-profit organization in Bogota to work in the area of family counseling and reconciliation. We both believed very strongly that family problems were at the root of Colombia's tremendous social and moral problems. The country was slowly drifting out of control towards total anarchy as terrorists, mafia groups, government forces, and rightwing factors battled for control in a never ending, many sided, forever escalating war that was destroying the country and making it impossible for any honest businessman to make a living and the people to find jobs.

My wife Marina had been against my going on this trip. Today was Sunday, and she wanted me to stay home with her and our nine-month-old daughter, Lisa. She had pleaded with me earlier this morning, saying that she felt a premonition that something would go wrong and that I should cancel my plans. I had replied that the trip I was making with my friend Gilberto was to be my last trip to this area. I had given my word that I would be at the meeting in Canyo Jabon and had been hoping that I would be able to reach an agreement with the local businessmen and fishermen in order to keep the wholesale fishing business in operation, providing jobs for some 250 fishermen on the river who now were out of work. The only other economic alternative for these people was to work in the *coca* fields producing cocaine. I was going to offer to sell them the business on credit, allowing them to operate while providing me with a source of income to live on in Bogota.

Gilberto and I took off from Chaparral, arriving a few minutes later in the small river town of Canyo Jabon. We landed in less than 400 feet, thanks to my new STOL conversion which I thought was very impressive. Taxiing over to the ramp I noticed my "friend" Carlos waiting for me. "What took you so long?" he asked, "We've been waiting all morning for you. Come on down to my store and I'll call all the people together."

The three of us were walking the six blocks to his store on the waterfront when we heard some shooting. I asked Carlos what was going on. "Oh, it's just some of the guys having a little target practice on the other side of the airstrip," he replied casually. Reassured, I continued on into the store. After entering the store I noticed that some sort of commotion was going on at the other side of town. Moments later I could see armed men running down the streets. Women and children were screaming and fleeing in all directions. "It's the law," said Carlos. This was a logical conclusion since the authorities would at times dress in plain clothes while making raids on drug towns. I hesitated. The 20-gauge double-barreled shotgun in my hand gave me the option of shooting the two men who were blocking the side street should I need to make an escape to the jungle. I was mighty suspicious that something fishy was going on. Who were they? I suspected they might be communist guerrillas, but even then I wasn't sure what they wanted. Maybe they were just taking the town to impress the people so they could spread their propaganda and replenish their supplies as is their custom. By this time I could see more armed men converging on all sides of the town, some carrying what looked like handgrenades. Whoever they were, I decided I had no choice but to sit tight. If I started to fight, the odds were in their favor.

When they ordered all the townspeople out into the street, Gilberto and Carlos went out, but I stayed inside. I overheard the men arguing for awhile. Then Carlos came back into the store and told me that I had to come out too or Gilberto might get shot. "It's OK," he said, "these men just want to talk to you. Come with me, and I'll make sure everything turns out all right." Hiding the shotgun in the store, I followed Carlos out into the street.

As I stepped out into the open sunlight, I looked up and blinked, staring into the barrels of three machine guns. The gun's owners glared at me as they said, "Hands up! March!" As they marched me up the street towards the airstrip, suddenly I heard a pistol shot. My abductors stopped. One kept his gun centered on me as the other one fired a burst of bullets back down the street. "Faster!" they commanded. "Keep moving!" They marched me past the airstrip and into the jungle. I wondered if they had shot my friend Gilberto. A dark, mustached guerrilla, whose name I learned later was Manuel, told me to lay down on my stomach there in the jungle. I wondered if they were going to shoot me. Manuel repeated the order in a harsher voice so I obeyed. "Well, I guess I just have to trust you!" I exclaimed as I lay down. Manuel pulled my arms behind me and I felt him place a rope around my neck and arms, joining the three loops with a central slipknot. Manuel stepped back and ordered me to get to my feet. I held my breath thinking about the .38 Smith and Wesson revolver that I always carried strapped to my left ankle. My pant leg had come up while I was on the ground, exposing the revolver. The guerrillas must have been blind not to have seen it. Rolling over and getting to my feet, I gave my pant leg a tug and breathed a sigh of relief when the cuff of my pants dropped down over the gun.

They proceeded to march me into the jungle. After about 10 minutes we came to the banks of the Guaviare River. Guerrilla soldiers were milling about on the riverbank. I noticed there was a large pile of military equipment and backpacks on the ground; tied to the bank was a large dugout canoe. A young man in his early twenties came over to me introducing himself as their leader. "You have been kidnapped to raise money for our cause," he announced. "If you follow our orders you won't be harmed." His name, I found out later, was Jaime and that he was only 22 years old. Jaime looked at me for a minute and sized me up. I did likewise. He was thin and dark with Indian-like features. A fuzzy mustache was trying to grow on his upper lip. I was bearded and blond. We were both about the same height. I was very scared, but tried not to let it show. Jaime had previously ordered his men to search me, but being a thorough and methodical commander, he also asked if I was armed. Looking him in the eye, I flatly denied having a weapon. I lied.

About this time another guerrilla walked up carrying my flight case and Gilberto's blue bag which had been taken from my airplane. I later learned that they had chopped off the door of the plane with an axe even though I had given them the keys. They then machine-gunned all three of the airplanes at the airstrip, including my beautiful Cessna 170, in an effort to make it impossible for anyone to get away and inform the authorities of my kidnapping. They rummaged through my flight case, coming up with some .38 bullets. My heart sank. At that moment the guerrilla squad's nurse walked up carrying a stethoscope and a blood pressure cuff. She was about 28 years old and her name, I learned later, was Nancy. She was short, stocky, and not very pretty, but she appeared to be a very efficient and well-trained nurse. The young guerrilla rummaging in my flight case turned around and held up the .38 shells, demanding to know where the gun was. Nancy had hooked up her equipment and was checking my blood pressure and listening to my heart. I told the young guerrilla that the shells were for my brother's gun and that I didn't have one. My heart pounded as I felt the gun in my ankle holster. I frantically racked my brain to come up with a story that would get me off the hook. My heart thumped wildly as I tried to think up a lie that they would believe. My pant leg was too short to completely cover the holster. Nancy's face showed a worried frown as she listened to my heartbeat with her stethoscope. An idea came to me: "Don't bother me anymore!" I exclaimed. "I have a heart condition that comes and goes. You're putting too much strain on my heart. Just leave me alone for a few minutes and I'll be OK." Nancy gave them a worried look and motioned them back. Signaling me to sit down on a log, she asked me if I wanted something to drink. I sat down with a sigh of relief. A few minutes later she came back and asked me how I felt. I announced that I was recovering nicely from my "heart condition." The guerrillas by this time had finished loading their equipment into the dugout canoe. They dressed me up in a blue plastic rain poncho and put a military "Fidel Castro" style cap on my head. This was to insure that no one would recognize me as we traveled up river. The large canoe was powered by a 40 hp outboard motor. There were eight guerrillas in the canoe. Five were behind me and three in front. A second boatload followed us a few minutes later. We traveled up river for about an hour until we approached the bend where our ranch, Chaparral, was.

Suddenly, coming around the bend, a speed boat appeared heading right for us. "It's the police!" hissed one of the guerrillas. "Pull over right here!" Jaime ordered the young motorist. Quickly beaching the canoe in a banana patch on the left river bank, Manuel ordered me out of the canoe and proceeded to herd me to the back of the banana patch while the rest of my captors took up positions on the river-bank and prepared to ambush what they thought were the police. I got Manuel to take me back further into the banana patch, telling him I had to go to the bathroom as I was feeling sick to my stomach. I crouched down underneath the poncho facing the river and acted a little embarrassed. Since Manuel was interested in what was going on down at the river, he turned his head. I decided to frustrate the guerrilla's impending ambush of the police by trying to escape. Since Manuel had his sub-machine gun pointed right at me with his finger on the trigger, I knew better than to just point my little revolver at him and threaten him. I quickly drew my gun and aimed at his right shoulder to disarm him and free the rope so I could get away. He caught my motion out of the corner of his eye and lunged forward just as I squeezed the trigger. The SuperVel hollow point bullet mushroomed into the upper right side of his chest. The impact of the round knocked him over backwards, still clutching the rope with his good hand. Pulling hard on the rope, he tightened the loops around my neck and shoulder, cutting off the circulation and my breathing. I tried shooting at the rope in Manuel's left hand. Realizing I was losing precious time, I aimed directly at Manuel's head and pulled the trigger. Blood streamed from Manuel's mouth and chest, splattering everywhere.

Up until this point the guerrillas thought they were being fired on by a police ambush, not recognizing where the shots were coming from. A tall guerrilla named Giovani sized up the situation correctly and came running to help Manuel, who was struggling on the ground. About twenty yards away, he threw his German assault rifle to his shoulder. With a terrible look of hatred on his face, he aimed and pulled the trigger. His gun went "click." It had misfired. Quickly raising my revolver I sighted on his chest and pulled the trigger. The hammer fell on a spent cartridge—I was out of bullets! Giovani, seeing my gun, hit the dirt, falling behind a tree. I could hear him trying to chamber a new round, but he seemed to be having trouble with his gun. I frantically tried to break the nylon cord, dragging Manuel a few yards in the process. I threw myself down on the ground behind the only cover I could find—a clump of banana trees. The rope was tight around my right arm and neck, choking me. I clawed frantically in my pocket hoping to find more cartridges and reload my revolver. I knew the banana trees wouldn't stop the bullets that the guerrillas would soon be shooting at me.

As I lay there, literally at the end of my rope, I wondered what it would feel like to die. It appeared to me that my life would end in just a few seconds. I was powerless to do anything about it, so I lowered my head and waited for the end to come.

In front of jungle clinic, ready to hit the trail with my dad.
Photo by Pat Stendal

Chapter Two

Grand Rapids, Minnesota, 1957

My father was a civil engineer in charge of large construction projects in Minnesota. By the time I was two years old, I had learned to talk fluently. I was a fast developing kid and always seemed to be one jump ahead of my parents. My mom spent a lot of time reading me Bible stories and teaching me about God. Being an inquisitive child, one day I asked, "Mommy, where does God live?" My mother thought for a moment before replying, "God lives in heaven but He can also live in peoples' hearts." I asked, "Does He live in your heart?" Mother said, "Yes." I asked, "Does He live in Daddy's heart?" Mother said, "Yes, God lives in Daddy's heart too." I asked next about Stuart and Eleanor, who were friends of my parents. My mother answered that yes, God lived in their hearts too. Then I asked about Dennis and Terry, the sons of Stuart and Eleanor Watson. My mother said that while she was sure that God lived in Dennis' heart, she wasn't sure about Terry. He was even younger than I was. She explained that in order for God to come into a person's heart, that person has to ask Him in. I thought about that for a minute and then asked, "Does He live in my heart?" My mom started getting a little flustered at this point because she thought I was still a little too young to handle such deep spiritual matters. She replied that when I was older, I could ask God to come into my heart too. At this point I climbed down off of her lap and knelt beside the bed. I prayed in a loud voice, "Come into my heart, Jesus. Come into my heart, God." Then I stood up and jumped up and down exclaiming, "He's in there!" My mother was flabbergasted.

Six months later my grandmother came over and gave me a potted plant. She told me that if I took care of it and watered it every day, some day it would blossom with beautiful red flowers. I was very attentive to the plant for several weeks, but much to my dismay, no flowers were forthcoming. It was wintertime. My parents continued teaching me about God. They told me that God could be everywhere, that He could see everything, and that He could do anything. They taught me that God answers prayer. One Sunday morning, my dad asked me to say grace at breakfast. I prayed, "God, please bless this food and please let there be red flowers on my plant when we get home from church." My father was shocked. He started explaining to me that he didn't think God could answer a prayer like that. I insisted that I was sure God would do it for me. I was only three years old, and I didn't know that according to my dad's theology, God couldn't work in this day and age; although he believed all the Bible stories about God working in the past.

Dad fidgeted all through the church service. He thought, "We've gotten this kid off to such a good beginning, teaching him about spiritual matters. Now his little faith in God is going to be shattered. When we return home from here and there are still no red flowers on his plant, he probably won't believe anything else we tell him about God. Dad had checked the plant out before we left the house and he hadn't even found a bud on it. Dad decided to take us out to a restaurant before returning home. Maybe I would forget about my prayer. Then he drove us home by way of the park, stalling around. I began to get real impatient. When we got home, I rushed right over to the plant. I was delighted! There wasn't just one red flower; the plant had blossomed into dozens of little flowers. It looked gorgeous. I admired it for about five minutes and returned to playing with my toys. I had expected God to come through for me; I didn't know any better. My dad just sat there for the rest of the afternoon, staring at the plant with all its beautiful red flowers. My father's theology started to undergo some radical changes that Sunday.

Minneapolis, Minnesota, 1959

I was four years old. Our life was very comfortable. We had a nice home, two cars, and my father made very good money. He had just been offered a promotion to be one of the principal engineers building a 30 million dollar lock and dam complex on the Mississippi River at St. Anthony Falls.

One evening after my father came home from work, he sat down in the living room with me on his lap and started showing me a colorful picture book about Indians in South America. Dad thought he would broaden my horizons a little and show me how people lived in foreign countries. The picture book, however, turned out to be a little more candid than Dad realized. It showed the Indians working and producing handcrafted articles to sell in town on market day. They were selling their handmade artifacts and receiving the money. On the next page it showed the Indian men drinking up the money, and the women and children waiting outside. The men got into a drunken argument which led to a bloody machete fight. The last scene showed an Indian woman patiently trying to help her drunken husband home so he could sober up and start the same cycle all over again.

I was shocked. In all my sheltered existence I had never even dreamed that people could live like this. The fact that the setting for all this was the beautiful Andes Mountains made it all the more shocking. I turned to my father, and I asked, "Why do they live like this?" Dad replied, "Well, Russ, I guess it's because they don't know any better." I became very indignant and said, "Well, why don't they know any better?" Dad said, "I guess it's because no one has ever taught them or shown them a better way." I became more indignant, and so I asked, "Well, why hasn't anyone gone over there to help them?" Dad said, "I guess it's because no one really cares about those Indians, Russell." I looked at Dad, and I said, "Well, you care, don't you, Dad? Why don't we go?" Dad started to get a little uncomfortable. "Well, Russ, a person can't just take off for a foreign country. Why, that would be missionary work. God would have to call you. God would have to provide the finances and prepare the way. Maybe when you grow up you can be a missionary."

Dad looked pleased with himself and thought he had slipped nicely off the hook by putting all the responsibility on God. He didn't notice that I wasn't listening anymore and that I had slipped off of his lap. I was kneeling by the side of the couch praying aloud. I prayed, "Dear God, please call my parents to be missionaries so I won't have to wait until I grow up." Dad looked a little thoughtful the rest of the evening.

Four years later, after God had done many other things for us, we were on our way to Colombia, South America, as a family; going out as missionaries with the Wycliffe Bible Translators. My dad had resigned from his job, sold his house, and received linguistic training. Now he was ready to study a primitive Indian language and translate the New Testament of the Bible into the Indian language.

On January 3, 1964, we were on a four-engine airplane flying over the Caribbean Ocean on our way to Colombia. The Jim Walton family, also missionaries from Minneapolis, were traveling with us. As we winged our way over the Caribbean, a beautiful sunrise colored the eastern sky. My little brother and sister were asleep, but I was wide awake. I turned to my father who was seated beside me and said, "We're really having fun now, aren't we, Dad?"

Chapter Three

August 14, 1983, 1:00 p.m.

"Throw down your weapon!" shouted the guerrilla leader. I threw down my revolver. It was empty. "Now stand up!" he ordered. I couldn't! The best I could do was to roll over and sit up. Manuel, the guerrilla I had wounded, was still struggling on the ground, trying to get his weapon into his good hand in order to shoot me with it. I was relieved to see one of the other guerrillas take it from him. Two more came forward and grabbed me, pulling me to my feet. Jaime, the leader, strode forward. He walked right past me and over to Manuel, who still was on the ground, bleeding. "Why didn't you search the prisoner good like I told you to? This is what you get for failing to obey orders!" Then he turned to me and said, "Why did you do this?" The atmosphere was very tense. I knew that if I showed fear by cringing or begging for mercy, I'd probably be killed. These guerrillas respect courage and valor, and very little else. I thought for a moment, knowing my reply would be crucial, and then said, "Put yourself in my spot. If you had been captured by an enemy, and if you had a weapon with the chance to use that weapon to escape, would you?!" Jaime thought for a minute and then said, *"Tiene razon!"* which means, "You're right!"

They emptied my pockets and took my wallet, my money, my comb, my watch, and my gun holster. Then they tied me up good and threw me in the bottom of the canoe, covering me up with a tarp. All I could see through a crack from under the tarp was Manuel's face. I wondered if he was going to die. The shot I had aimed at Manuel's head appeared to have missed. The blood coming out of his mouth seemed to be from a punctured lung. He was in bad shape.

The people in the speedboat had turned out not to be the police. We continued upriver. The ropes were so tight around my arms that the circulation was cut off. There was a nail protruding from a board in the bottom of the canoe where they had thrown me that was digging into my back. It began to rain. The water collected in the bottom of the boat making me wet, cold, and miserable. As a jungle pilot I had seen a lot of gunshot wounds over the years and it looked to me like Manuel wouldn't live more than four or five hours. He didn't look too good. When he dies, I thought, they'll kill me for sure. What if they hang me by my heels for a day or so, with my head in an ant nest, and torture me for awhile before they finally kill me! I began to pray that Manuel wouldn't die and that I would get out of this awful situation alive.

After about three hours we turned off the main river and up a small stream. After awhile we stopped and my kidnappers ordered me to get out on the bank. Three of them ushered me about 50 yards back into the jungle while the others started unloading their equipment and setting up a mosquito net for Manuel. I could vaguely see some people milling around Manuel's mosquito net. They appeared to be working on him. The three guards who were watching me gave me a Coke they had taken from the plane to drink but appeared to be rather uptight and somewhat angry with me. I continued praying silently that everything would turn out OK.

After awhile, Nancy walked over to where we were and announced that Manuel was going to live and that he wouldn't be permanently maimed or disabled. The tension began to ease. The guerrillas started speaking with me and pretty soon we were telling each other stories, even a few jokes.

Soon darkness fell. The guerrillas began putting on their packs, and we were off. A serious looking guerrilla named

Arnuval had the other end of my rope. I later learned that Arnuval had been a university psychology student prior to joining the guerrillas. Jaime came over and loosened the loops around my shoulders and arms so I could walk better. We moved single file into the darkness.

I was in the middle of the column. First three guerrillas, then me, then three more. Nancy had stayed behind with Manuel. We were marching down the twin tracks of a jeep road through the Colombian llanos when we saw the lights of a vehicle coming toward us. My abductors herded me into a clump of bushes where we crouched down, hiding until the car had passed. Later I learned that this car removed Manuel to a guerrilla field hospital where they operated on him and removed the bullet.

As we continued to march, the moon came up. At the same time we could see flashes of lightning on the horizon, but it didn't rain on us. When we stopped for a drink and some rest at a small stream, I found myself sitting beside Giovani, the guerrilla who had tried to kill me. Giovani spoke Spanish with a coastal, Caribbean-sounding accent and was missing two front teeth. He said that he had never had a misfire like that before. I told him that I was glad that I had been out of ammunition and had not been able to kill him either. We both agreed that God had His hand in the situation and had kept us all safe. I remarked that I was surprised that the guerrillas hadn't beaten me or tortured me for shooting Manuel. Giovani replied that he was surprised by this too. He said that Jaime was an exceptional commander and since it had been Manuel's job to search me, which he hadn't done, that I probably would not be punished physically. Manuel had assumed that I was unarmed when he just checked my waist. It was hard for the guerrillas to imagine anyone carrying a gun in an ankle holster because of the mud and water they had to hike through all the time. If they were to carry a gun there, it would get wet in very short order. Giovani warned me, however, that if anything else were to happen in the future, I would be disciplined very severely. I made a mental note to respect the inner motives of the guerrillas as much as possible; thanking them and making them feel good about not having mistreated me after my shooting Manuel. I felt this was important in order to head off any trouble in the future. I thanked them for anything they would do for me, such as bringing me a drink of water. This made them feel important and valuable as individuals.

We continued on into the night. After several hours we were met by a Russian-made Gaz jeep. We all got in and went down the road for another hour. They kept me on the floor with my head down so I couldn't see where we were going.

Finally we came to a halt and got out. My captors marched me over to a nearby clump of trees and prepared camp. This consisted of unpacking their hammocks, pitching them between the trees with mosquito nets and tarps in such a way as to provide a dry, mosquito-proof place to sleep. Jaime motioned me into one of the hammocks and told me that there would be a guard on me all night. If I needed anything, I was to call out to the guard. I lay shivering in the cold, damp jungle, being all wet with only a light sheet to cover up with. Due to sheer exhaustion, I fell asleep.

Chapter Four

Sierra Nevada de Santa Marta, 1967

My parents had been working for several years with the Kogi Indians in the rugged Sierra Nevada mountains of northern Colombia. These mountains rise from sea level to 19,000 feet in only 35 miles and are separate from the famous Andes mountains. The Kogi Indians lived practically in the Stone Age even though they had been among the first Indians contacted by the Spaniards over 400 years ago. This contact had been bitter, bloody, and brief, resulting in the retreat of the Kogi Indians up into the mountains where they isolated themselves to the present day from the outside world. It is a crime punishable by death by poisoning for a Kogi Indian to give out language or cultural information to an outsider.

Dad came across a Kogi man named Santiago who was bilingual. Santiago wasn't under the control of any of the main Kogi chiefs because he lived too far away, a two-day walk from the nearest village of Mamarongo. Santiago agreed to help my dad study and learn the Kogi language. My parents spent two years living in a house Santiago had built for them next to his. It had mud walls, a dirt floor, and a thatched roof They made steady progress learning and analyzing the language. Then disaster struck. Santiago was poisoned. It looked like he would die as he began to bleed internally. My father felt terrible knowing that he was indirectly responsible. My parents went down to Santiago's to pray for him where they got an idea. Giving Santiago a laxative called Metamusil absorbed the poison, moving it on out of his body. Santiago recovered! My dad's fame as a doctor spread throughout the mountains where some 10,000 Kogis were living without any medical help. Even though Dad had no formal medical training, he had a couple of good medical texts along with a supply of medicines. People would come from miles around with their problems. Dad would treat them the best he could with modern medicines, while at the same time he would pray for them. To my knowledge they all recovered.

One day Kogi runners arrived from the village of Mamarongo. The chief, Mama Nacio (in Kogi "Mama" means "chief," I guess in English it does too!), was dying. He had been slowly getting worse and now he was nearly dead. As a last resort he was sending for my dad. Talking it over with Santiago, they both went. This was a noble gesture on the part of Santiago as this chief had probably been involved with Santiago's poisoning. He had earlier threatened Dad's life also if Dad should ever try to enter Mamarongo. Two days later they arrived in Mamarongo after crossing five treacherous mountain rivers which were swollen by the rainy season.

Dad examined Mama Nacio finding him just skin and bones with a raging fever. The diagnosis was probable advanced tuberculosis coupled with pneumonia and parasites. Dad told the chief, "Medically speaking I think I've come too late. You should have called me sooner. However, God can still heal you, and if you will agree to give God the thanks when you are healed, then I will pray for you." The old chief agreed to this, so Dad prayed. Even though he didn't have the right ones, Dad got out his medicines and he did the best he could. The Kogis then escorted him down the mountain into a house across the river. "Now we're in bad trouble," Dad said to Santiago. "If the chief dies, we probably won't get out of here alive because the people will blame us."

They spent an anxious night. In the morning, lo and behold, here came Mama Nacio down the trail towards the house. He was leaning on a staff with a Kogi man to support him on either side in case he fell. He walked up to my dad, who was flabbergasted to see him, and said, "God has given my life back to me." Mama Nacio kept his promise and thanked God for making him well. Dad checked him over a second time and could hardly believe it. Though still very skinny, Mama Nacio was clinically well! The chief gave Dad an open invitation to come and live in the Kogi village of Mamarongo. This was exactly what Dad wanted to do! He spent several days in the village treating the sick before returning to Santiago's farm.

Dad had to wait until the next dry season to visit Mamarongo again because some of the large rivers could only be crossed in dry season when they weren't quite so deep. The Kogis took him to a site where they were building a new village, and he noticed that out behind the village was a flat piece of land being used for a pasture. In these mountains, where it was difficult to find a flat area big enough on which to build a house, he hadn't hoped for an airstrip. But there it was, a flat stretch almost 1300 feet long, perfectly shaped and slanted for the rain to run off. Dad decided that as a civil engineer he couldn't have designed a better airstrip.

The next night in the Kogi men's council house. Dad told them about his idea to make an airstrip. Dad knew that it would be nearly impossible for his wife and little children to make that long, overland journey on the narrow Kogi mountain trails. An airstrip would solve the problem. The flight would only take 15 minutes.

The Indian men didn't share his enthusiasm. "It's bad enough for us to let you come in here," some of the old ones said. "If an airplane were to land here, it would be the end of the world." They refused to allow the airstrip location to be worked on.

After a few more days it was time for Dad and Santiago to return home. They were a little late getting started and Santiago was in a hurry. They would really have to move fast in order to make it to the spot where Santiago wanted to spend the night. It started to rain. As they were leaving the Kogi village, Dad saw an old woman sitting on the doorstep of the last round Kogi house. She was very old, and she appeared to be in great pain. Dad stopped to find out what was the matter, but Santiago came back arguing that they needed to keep moving because they were late. Dad felt compassion for this lady and felt inside that he should do all he could to help her. He reached over and pulled the slip knot that held the bag of medicines onto the back of Santiago's donkey, letting it fall to the ground. This ended the argument with Santiago. Dad turned to examine the old woman, finding a severe infection in the left side of her face. She couldn't see out of her left eye or hear with her left ear. After Dad gave her ear drops, eye ointment, an antibiotic and some pain medicine, he prayed for her. Finally convinced that he had done all he could for her, Dad helped Santiago load the donkey again, and they continued on their way.

Dad arrived home with mixed emotions. He was excited about the fact that Mama Nacio was well and had invited him to live in Mamarongo, although he was depressed when he thought about the perfect airstrip site that he couldn't utilize. For the next two weeks my parents couldn't seem to get this situation out of their minds. Then one day Kogi runners from Mamarongo arrived. They walked over to my dad and announced, "We're ready for you to come and show us how to build the airstrip." Dad was surprised. "What made you change your mind?" he asked. One of the Kogi men replied, "Do you remember the little old lady that you helped as you left town? She is my mother. She is well now, and she can both hear and see perfectly. The land that you want to build that airstrip on belongs to her. She says you can come and build that airstrip anytime you want, and all the rest of the village agrees."

Dad went back to Mamarongo with them and soon the first 600 feet of runway had been finished. The situation of the Kogi Indians in Mamarongo was critical. They had only two old axes and a dozen old machetes with which to work and raise food for almost 400 people. The Kogis are almost pygmy Indians, averaging about 5 feet in height. This is partially due to malnutrition and the fact that all the Kogi men chew coca leaves. They mix them with lime in their mouths, producing a powerful drug, namely cocaine.[1] This practice over a period of time wrecks their teeth and destroys the mucous membranes in their noses, sinuses and throats. The Kogis were plagued with numerous diseases such as tuberculosis, hookworm, amoeba, and other intestinal parasites. Infant mortality was extremely high. One woman had given birth 13 times and had lost all her babies. Another woman birthed 10 children and only one was still alive. I have heard anthropologists lecture on university campuses about how the Indians live in their little tropical paradise and how the white man ought to just leave them alone. This was not the case with the Kogis. They had had little or no contact with the white man for over 400 years, living in relative isolation from the rest of the world. Yet they appeared to be living in hell, not the garden of Eden like the anthropologists said.

My parents rolled up their sleeves and went to work. Tools were obtained from the government and given to the Kogis. Medicine and vaccinations were brought in by the case. Seedlings of fruit trees were flown in. Vegetable seeds were given them, and we showed them how to balance their diet. My parents did nothing to destroy the Kogi culture. Instead they encouraged the Kogis to wear their white hand-woven clothes and long black hair. Since the Kogis did not have God in their lives yet, it was extremely important that they feel pride in their own culture and language. This would give them the will to live and do better than the society around them.

One day Mama Nacio presented my father with a chief's hat, called a *numtu,* and made him an honorary chief of the tribe. Dad sprayed it against head lice when the Kogis weren't looking and then wore it down to the men's council house that night.

My parents got ahold of several cases of dog flea spray in an effort to eradicate the fleas and lice that infested the Kogis' long black hair. This campaign was fairly successful. I can remember picking up one of the empty cans and reading on the side, "For the best loved pets in the world."

---

[1]   Kogi men have a life expectancy of over 10 years less than Kogi women, who do not use cocaine. The norm for most Indian tribes is for the women to have shorter lives than men due to the dangers of childbearing in primitive conditions.

My mother learned to pull teeth and help the Kogis with their dental problems. Some of these Indians had been living with three or four simultaneous toothaches.

Dad worked every day on the language analysis and soon began translating parts of the Bible into the Kogi language. When he finished translating the Gospel of Mark, Dad took it over and read it to the Kogi men in their council house. Mama Nacio got up afterwards and made a speech. "This is the real truth!" he said. "We have passed our mythology down by word of mouth from father to son for so many generations that we have lost the truth, and things have become twisted. We have countless versions of the same story. They can't all be right. This written book is accurate and contains the real truth that we have lost."

My parents continued to help the Kogis and to help train young Kogi men for leadership positions such as teachers or medics. I was with my parents studying by correspondence. In my spare time I would go hunting with the Indians. On weekends all the Indians would get together, and we would all work on lengthening the airstrip. As I dug rocks and stumps out of the airstrip, and later as I watched the airplanes land and take off on the little mountain airstrip, I decided I was going to be a pilot when I grew up.

Chapter Five

August 15, 1983, 6:00 a.m.

I awakened to the screams of colorful parrots in a nearby palm tree; it was a few seconds before I realized where I was. Yesterday's events seemed like a dream until I sat up in the hammock and saw a young man about 20 feet away holding a G–3 assault rifle across his knees. The other end of the nylon cord tied to my neck was in his hand. The young guard noticed the welt around my neck and whistled, "Boy, you almost choked to death yesterday!" he exclaimed.

Giovani came over and offered me a cup of coffee. They led me over to where they had improvised a kitchen and served me fried sausage, eggs, and corn patties for breakfast. In spite of the excellent breakfast, I wasn't hungry. There was too much adrenalin flowing through my veins. I wasn't used to having people point machine guns at me with their finger on the trigger at all times. What if they slipped and shot me by accident? I managed to force down about half of the breakfast.

My guard put a piece of plastic over a damp log and told me I could sit there, which I did. Surveying the camp, I noticed that most of the men seemed to be cleaning their weapons, which they kept spotless. Some of the men began to include me in their conversation. They even began to joke with me. I was surprised to see their spirits so high after I had shot Manuel the day before. They said things like, "This unit has fought the Colombian government for four years without casualties, and then we run into you. You did us more damage in five minutes than the whole Colombian army did in years." Then they would laugh and laugh. One of them said, "Boy, you sure didn't hand over that revolver of yours until it was empty, did you?" They chuckled some more. It seemed like the idea of my standing up to their eight machine guns with a little five-shot revolver tickled their sense of humor. It caused them to treat me with respect, almost as an equal. They wanted to know why I had started shooting like that. I told them I was a Christian and that Christians had to stand up for what they believed in, even if it was dangerous. I told them that kidnapping was morally wrong, and that if I had just passively gone along with it, I would have considered myself to be an accomplice to my own kidnapping. If I had "chickened out" and not used the gun, I would have had a hard time living with myself for the rest of my life. I hadn't fired at them with the shotgun in Carlos' store because I wasn't sure who they were or what they wanted. Once I knew what they were doing, however, I had a moral obligation as a Christian to resist what I knew to be wrong. I pointed out that it had been my initial decision to shoot Manuel in the shoulder instead of the head, which ended up preventing me from escaping. I had valued Manuel's life, not wanting to kill him if it wasn't necessary.

It began to rain, so we took cover under the tarp that the guerrillas had hung over their hammocks. The weather cleared that afternoon, and about 3:00 p.m., three strange guerrillas walked into camp. A tall, muscular guerrilla with the walk of a born leader strode up to me and held out his hand. "Hi!" he said. "My name is Vicente, and I'm in charge of negotiating your release. If you will cooperate with me, it will make things much easier for all of us." "Well, I'll do the best I can," I replied, "but there are certain things I can't morally go along with because I'm a Christian." I proceeded to explain to him about my parents' mission work and about the fish business I had been trying to get running again in Canyo Jabon that would provide work for 250 people. I said, "If you think I am a rich capitalist just because I'm an American and fly an airplane—

think again! I'm not a wealthy person and my plane is a 1952 Cessna 170. It looks nice, but it's not worth much. If you are really interested in the welfare of the people of this area, let me go, because that's what I'm interested in too." Vicente was very courteous and cordial to me but said he would have to talk everything over with his superiors, and they would make the decisions. Later I learned that Vicente was a company commander in the guerrilla organization in charge of almost 80 men. Vicente, and another man who came with him, left, but the third man, Javier, stayed behind. He was the replacement for Manuel. At 29 years old, Javier was the oldest man in the group. He was tall with scars on both sides of his face and carried a huge Ml rifle along with a Colt 45 automatic. Since he looked like a seasoned fighter and crack shot with a rifle, I made a mental note not to try to escape while he was on guard duty.

Nancy rejoined us at dusk with a happy look on her face and announced that Manuel had been operated on and was recovering nicely. As soon as it was dark we moved out again. The guerrillas like to travel at night and hole up in the daytime. We hiked single file until we came to the edge of some virgin jungle. Entering the jungle, we came to a stream and waited while two of them cut logs and made a crude bridge to span the ten foot wide gully. We crossed over on the bridge and set up camp along the riverbank. It was about midnight when Jaime motioned me over to one of the hammocks and told me to sleep there. The air was clouded with mosquitoes as it began to rain. I climbed into the hammock and tried to sleep. These guerrillas certainly knew how to pitch a hammock in the jungle. It was nice and dry with no mosquitoes under the mosquito net. The rain beat down upon the black plastic tarp above me.

In the early morning it began to get very cold. I spent several hours shivering until morning finally dawned. It was still raining when Giovani came over and gave me a cup of coffee. Later he returned to serve me breakfast right in the hammock. The weather started to clear, and soon I could hear the ring of machetes chopping all around me. The guerrillas were preparing a semi-permanent camp. After a couple of hours Jaime appeared. "Come with me," he said as he ushered me over to a place he had prepared for me. He had cleared a small area of underbrush where in the middle he had built something resembling a park bench, using living trees, cut poles, split palm, and vines to tie it all together. Waving me over to the park bench he told me to sit down.

Another guerrilla, named Alfredo, was busy building me a table. I found out later he was only 14 years old though he carried an Ml carbine. Working cheerfully, he soon had made a handsome table using forked sticks and split palm. Giovani came over and hung a hammock for me, complete with a large mosquito net. All this time Arnuval, who was the guard, stood off to one side holding the other end of the nylon cord that was looped around my neck and arms. He had his gun leveled in my direction.

Towards evening Jaime came over and handed me a wool blanket. "I noticed you were shivering last night," he said. "Here, use this." I gratefully accepted it, learning later that this was Jaime's personal blanket that he was sharing with me. It made me feel better that these guerrillas were people, just like me.

A few days passed. I began to get to know my captors better. There were eight of them assigned to guarding me. I was surprised to see how well they got along with each other. I hadn't even heard a cross word between them. I would converse with the guards when they were on duty and sometimes they would come back when they were off duty and play chess with me. Jaime and Nancy maintained themselves fairly aloof, but the others opened up as time went on. My discussions with my abductors would be friendly and easy-going until we started discussing politics or world issues. It became quite clear that the guerrillas hated "capitalists" with a passion. They also hated the United States of America. When I would stick up for the United States our discussions would take a nasty turn, with the guerrillas threatening to shoot me if I said anything else. One time, Mariano, the 21-year-old gunsmith for the guerrilla unit, said to me, "I wouldn't mind your being an American if you would just admit how awful America is and be ashamed of it." I replied that I wasn't trying to say that America was perfect, but that even with its faults, the American system and way of life was head and shoulders above any other system in the world today. The very fact that we have a free society opens us up to being exploited by those who would abuse their freedom. I had to admit to the guerrillas that yes, it is true that in the United States there is drug addiction, homosexuality, pornography, prostitution, and other things going on that are not right. There are also many selfish individuals who care only for themselves, who care not the slightest about the fact that a lot of suffering is going on in the Third World countries around the world. Our American system of checks and balances, of government for the people, with participation and representation of the people through all levels of government, turns out to be the best way to limit and contain the activities of selfish, corrupt individuals. There is more true individual freedom in America than in any other nation on the face of the earth. We were interrupted at this point by Giovani, who came over and served my dinner. I could sense, however, a tremendous underlying current of bitterness and hatred on the part of the guerrillas towards the United States and Americans in general. I began to wonder how this had happened. There appeared to be many underlying factors. I tried to sort these things out in my mind as I ate supper. What motivated each of these guerrillas to leave the comforts of civilization to run around in the jungle fighting for what they thought was true freedom? Thinking back over my conversations with various guerrilla warriors, one theme seemed to stand out. Social injustice was the major factor that was fanning the flames of rebellion in these young hearts. They had grown up in a country where corruption, kickbacks, and blackmail are a way of life; a country where corrupt politicians were stealing a high percentage of the money destined for roads, schools, and hospitals; a country where corrupt policemen extort drug growers and shake down anyone passing through their road blocks, or *retenes* as they are called in Colombia. In fact, most people cheat so badly on their income tax in Colombia that it is estimated that most of the population pays less than half of the taxes they are required to pay by law.

According to one estimate, in Colombia, 20% of the women are or have been involved in prostitution at some point in their life. Illegitimate children make up over 50% of the births. An honest government official is an exception—not the rule. In Colombia there are thousands of children who live roaming the streets of the large cities, eating out of garbage cans. As they grow older they learn to live by stealing and armed robbery. Wages are very low and jobs are difficult to find. This is what the guerrillas have reacted against, what they call "corrupt capitalism."

In their minds, this rotten, corrupt capitalism is responsible for all the trouble. They are taught by their leaders, according to communist ideology, that the roots of capitalism are in the United States. They think that since Colombia is a capitalistic country, and since the United States is capitalistic, that the two systems are the same. Going a step further, they say that the United State's capitalism is worse than the Colombian version since it is on a worldwide scale. They proceed to blame all the Third World problems on the United States, which seems very logical and extremely plausible to the average guerrilla; or even to the average high school student in Colombia. They have never been to the United States and been able to witness how life actually is in our country. It is very easy for them to conjure up in their minds an image of a huge, powerful monster nation exploiting all the Third World countries—ripping off all the developing nations' natural resources. They are thoroughly convinced that the world would be a decent place to live in if they could only get rid of the United States. It never even occurs to them that the roots and causes of many of their problems might be found a little closer to home. It doesn't dawn on them that basic human selfishness is at the root of our problems around the world. We can't have better society until we have better individuals. If a majority of the policemen, government officials, and businessmen were honest instead of corrupt in Colombia, their present political system would work just fine. The state of Colombian society reflects the state of the Colombian individuals who make up that society. The same is true for the United States.

After supper I laid down in my hammock under the mosquito netting and continued to think about all these things, and gradually two things became clear to my mind. The first was easy to explain but the second more complex. I will do my best to relate them to you here.

First, the United States of America was founded on Christian principles; from the very start our motto was "In God We Trust," and it is still inscribed on our coins to this day. We don't often consider the connection due to division of church and state, but Christianity has greatly influenced and modified the capitalism that goes on in America. Our country has a great moral Christian heritage that many Third World nations do not have. This has greatly influenced the way we do business in our country. Therefore, our American way of doing things is not always the same as the way businesses are run in other countries where there is no moral heritage. To lump everything together in one basket is not correct and is very naïve.

Second, people tend to evaluate someone else's position and performance on the basis of what they would do if they were in the other person's spot. Latinos tend to build up an image of the tremendous military might and economic wealth of the United States. Then they transpose themselves into the equation and think of what they would do if they had all that power at their disposal. They assume that the United States is doing what they would do in any given situation of foreign policy. It is totally alien to them to think that the U.S. might be intervening in a given country out of a genuine concern for the people of that country. In Latin America it is extremely rare for anyone to help someone else unless there is something in it for himself. They just automatically assume that this must be the case with anything the United States government does. They then commence to hate the United States and Americans in general. This is further accelerated by a feeling of inferiority on their part. They basically resent the fact that Americans are more affluent than they are, and that American industry and standard of living is much better than theirs. These feelings leave them wide open to admit and accept charges that American wealth, affluence, and industrial superiority has been obtained by illegitimate or criminal means. This forms a vicious circle for their thinking, resulting in their building up a tremendous hatred and bitterness against Americans. But what they are really hating is their own motives and problems that they have transposed on America in their mind's eye.

This helped me to understand the guerrillas' reasoning regarding myself. They liked to think of themselves as social Robin Hoods, restoring social justice by force. They were financing their revolution in part by kidnapping wealthy capitalists who they felt had been exploiting the common poor people. However, unlike Robin Hood, they spent the money on weapons and terrorism instead of giving it to the poor. In their line of reasoning, if anyone deserved to be kidnapped—a dirty, rotten, corrupt American capitalist (me) deserved it. As I lay there in the hammock listening to the sounds of the jungle at night, I wondered, "How in the world can I present to these guerrillas the truth about who I am and what I am doing in Colombia in a way that they can understand?" Just before I fell asleep, I decided that I would ask for pen and paper to begin writing this book in the morning. For some time now, prior to the kidnapping, I had felt very strongly that I should write a book about my life and relate some of the extraordinary experiences that had happened to me over the years, along with a few of the lessons I had learned through them. I had even promised God that I would spend an hour each morning working on the book, a promise I had never kept. Now I had the opportunity to write the book at machine gun point!

Chapter Six

Finca Chaparral, 1975

I had just returned to Colombia after two years at the University of Minnesota studying agriculture. During my time in the States, I had managed to obtain a private pilot's license. A friend of mine in Minneapolis, Mike Zaske, gave me the flight instruction free of charge. Meanwhile, back in Colombia, my father had been appointed Tribal Coordinator, in charge of all of Wycliffe's Tribal teams, working in about 40 Indian tribes. As he visited the various tribal locations, he soon became very concerned that the translations being produced would not be adequately distributed and utilized by the Indians. He decided to try and enlist the help of Spanish-speaking Colombian national churches from various missions and denominations. There were no funds available to support these workers, so we decided to try to help them become self-supporting. This type of work was not permitted under Wycliffe's government contract, so my father obtained a separate visa and secured a large tract of undeveloped land in the Llanos Orientales, or eastern plains of Colombia. Since my parents had their hands full with continuing their work among the Kogi Indians, I was to be managing this farm project. Our goal was to use modern agricultural techniques to improve the traditional slash and burn farming that was going on in the area. My father had hoped to use revenues from this project to support Christian Colombian literacy workers needed in rural and Indian areas. We also hoped to be able to help the poor *campesino* people in the area to improve their lifestyle.

I had grown up in the Colombian *llanos* and had many friends in the area. Deep down inside I felt extremely uncomfortable with a missionary effort that told the people about God but turned its back on the terrible poverty and social problems in Colombia. To me, an important part of being a Christian is to help those in physical need.

When I arrived at Chaparral, my brother, Chaddy, was already there with a new Ford diesel tractor and implements that a local bank helped us to buy. Some Christian national workers had been handpicked to work with me on this project.

We got this land very cheap because of its distance from civilization. We had to build roads, houses, an airstrip; and had to fence the boundaries ourselves because the land had not been developed at all. In order to get to our farm from San Martin, we had to endure a 16-hour truck ride followed by a 2-hour river trip by boat. Arriving with lots of enthusiasm, I rolled up my sleeves and went to work.

There were many things that had to be done, and done quickly, for soon we would have to begin making payments on the loan for the tractor. We were also trying to buy cattle to start a herd on a 3,000-acre plot of grassland located on the property.

Several months went by. Then some problems began to develop. The "Christian" national workers that we had employed could sing and pray all night if need be, however, when it came to manual labor they just wouldn't work very hard. They loved to sleep in late and then go hunting or fishing for the rest of the day. After awhile I went out and traded all the hunting shotguns we had for cattle but they still didn't get the picture. Matters came to a head one day when the leader, a man named Juan, decided he shouldn't have to harvest rice by hand. I was out in the field harvesting rice the same as everyone else did, setting an example. Some of the men followed me, and some followed Juan. It seemed that they were of the persuasion that anyone with any kind of an education shouldn't have to do any type of manual labor. Especially if the person was a pastor or Christian literacy worker, he shouldn't have to get his hands dirty. I told them that the apostle Paul had said, "If a man doesn't work, neither should he eat." About half of them left the project. I felt badly about it, but our project was certain to fail with a bunch of freeloaders involved.

Imagine my consternation when these people turned around and threatened to sue us in court for back wages. Although they had done little or no work, while causing us to spend a lot of money on food and supplies, we were required by law to pay them the going wage for all the time they had spent at the farm, plus vacation and severance fees.

Dad thought that a mistake must have been made in the selection of these people, so he went to some other churches and selected some more personnel that were supposed to be of better quality. We had more trouble yet with the next crew. They started having trouble even among themselves. They were very strict in their Christian principles. In fact, they would very zealously watch each other's lives and be very quick to point out what they would consider "sin." If someone were to be accused of drinking or smoking, a general hue and cry would go up for this person to be thrown out. Then, later, some of the same ones who were the most critical would wind up in a really serious problem which would end up totally destroying their whole family situation. This caused the farm project to struggle along for several years. I never had any problem handling the strenuous physical work, but the personnel problems were killing me.

As we began to work very closely with the various Colombian Protestant churches, I was amazed at the amount of envy, jealousy, strife, and gossip that went on among them. No wonder they weren't growing. It wasn't just one church denomination either. Of the three major denominations working in our area, it was difficult to determine which one had the most problems. These churches seemed to fight as well within their own ranks as they did with each other. It would make me sick to see a young pastor, fresh out of Bible school, arrive to take over a small, struggling church and see him doing everything possible to milk as much money as he could from the poor congregation. The young pastor's main goal in life would be to live just like the missionary. The missionary had a nice house on the hill in the better part of the city with a car, refrigerator, stereo, and TV. I could hardly believe some of the things I saw happening. In one major denomination the pastors would actually refuse to baptize a new member into their church until the new believer had paid his tithe for six months. The pastor would keep accounting records on each member and let them know exactly how much to pay. Most of the intellectual upper and middle class people in town would have nothing to do with these churches. It was as if these churches with their hard-nosed attitude, treating God's kingdom like a business franchise, were giving the majority of the Colombian population the equivalent of a vaccination against God. After an inquiring person had an experience with one of these churches, he often would never want to see another church again. Although the condition described here was the norm, there are many notable exceptions in Colombia of churches and missionaries who are doing an excellent job and being used very effectively in God's kingdom.

I didn't understand how a church denomination that seemed to do just fine in the United States could have so much trouble in Colombia. They had the same doctrines, the same statement of faith, similar church structure, but what a difference! Was it that some important part of Christianity had been left out or had been filtered out when the missionaries translated all the church procedures, including the hymns, from English to Spanish? Did the fact that we were dealing with a different culture require a different approach to church organization than in the United States? Or did the problem lie deeper than that? Are some of our churches in America dying slowly? Are our churches just kind of coasting along on the tremendous moral heritage and the great economic wealth of our country? If hard times were to come upon some of our North American churches, would serious problems surface similar to the ones in the Colombian churches?

As I think back over those many years of heartbreak while we were trying to train, send out, and support national workers to help the Indian tribes of Colombia through a farm project, a central theme began to impress itself upon me: these churches that were causing so much trouble seemed to be made up of individuals and not close-knit family units. When someone accepted the theology of a church and joined it as a new Christian, they would be immediately taught to go home and preach to their families. The families would not always appreciate this, or the holier-than-thou attitude that this new "believer" would sometimes take. The church, then, would be ready for this and tell their new "convert" that they had to suffer "persecution" for the cause of the Gospel. The end result would be a terrible split in family relations. The new Christian, instead of becoming a better father, a better mother, a better sister, or a better brother to his family, would become a Pharisee instead. His family would soon take note of all his defects and call him a hypocrite.

Most of the problems in the churches, or among the Christian workers, appeared to have their roots in a broken family situation. The problems that didn't start here were many times made worse by a lack of family support and understanding for the person having the problem. I began to realize that if these churches could be made up of close-knit family units, they would be much stronger and much more effective. Ricardo, my Colombian friend, felt the same way. He felt so strongly about this that he resigned his position as an evangelist for a major Protestant denomination and joined the Catholic Charismatic movement as a lay worker. The Catholics weren't perfect by a long shot, but they were placing an emphasis on the family. Ricardo's move branded him as a heretic in most Protestant circles, but I still continued to treat him as a friend. Ricardo began to be more and more impressed with a verse from the Bible, Malachi 4:4, which says: "Remember the law of Moses, and before the end comes I will send the prophet Elijah unto you and he will cause the hearts of fathers to return to their children, and the hearts of the children to return to their fathers lest I come and destroy your land completely."

I remember myself thinking, "Well, if anybody can reconcile all these split marriages, families, and churches it's going to have to be God. I sure don't know what to do."

I began to feel the need to have an airplane at Chaparral. To send a sick person over the road on a 20-hour, bumpy truck ride to the hospital was torture. Various mission organizations that had airplanes would sometimes fly for us, but it was expensive and difficult to coordinate things. Most of these air operations took a very hard-nosed view point as far as finances were concerned.

I can remember one case where a flight was needed for a friend who was injured. The airplane operator required payment in advance before he would move the airplane. This caused a day's delay and my friend almost died.

One day I was working in the new river town of Mapiripan. My brother, Chaddy, and I had just started operating a saw mill. We were trying to open up a market for wood in the newly developing area, so I was building a model wooden house in town. I wanted to show the people that they could use wood in construction instead of cement blocks like the rich, or mud like the poor made do with. As I worked on the model I remember thinking about having an airplane and saying a silent prayer to God asking Him to provide me with an airplane. I thought, "If I ever get a hold of an airplane, I'm going to do mercy flights on the basis of necessity and trust God to provide for the financial costs. If the people who need an air ambulance flight are able to pay, then I will charge them. If they can't pay, and I see a real emergency, then I'll do it anyway."

I was thinking these things over to myself when I heard the sound of an airplane engine. I thought, "That's funny. It sounds like that plane is headed straight for Chaparral." After a few minutes I heard the plane again. This time it was headed right for me. The airplane landed and we all ran out to the town airstrip to see who it might be. In those days airplanes were few and far between in that part of Colombia. Imagine my surprise when I saw my dad climb out of the pilot's seat and my old friend Ricardo Trillos climb out of the passenger's side. I ran up and shook their hands and asked them whose airplane it was.

"It's ours," Dad said.

It was an elderly Cessna 170 that Ricardo had helped Dad negotiate in Cali, the city where Ricardo was working. They had obtained this plane real cheap because it was underpowered for mountain flying, and Cali was in the middle of two ranges of the Andes mountains. Out here in the flat plains country it ought to do OK.

Dad asked me if I wanted to take it for a spin. I looked the old airplane over; it was in rough shape, but everything essential to safe flight seemed to work, so I climbed into the pilot's seat. Dad got in on the other side. I took off and climbed to a safe altitude over the town and practiced some maneuvers and stalls since I hadn't flown for two years.

When we landed, we found the town in an uproar. They weren't used to airplanes, and it turned out they had never seen an airplane stall before. When I cut the power and the plane pitched downward they thought that we were going to crash right on top of their town. Panic-stricken women and children had run screaming into the street. Now they all started chewing me out for giving them such a scare.

Dad and I walked into town and found Ricardo and my brother Chaddy having a Coke in one of the local stores. I hadn't seen Ricardo since he had joined the Catholics so I started asking him how he was doing. He said his work with Catholic young people was doing very well, numerically speaking. He was having trouble, however, reconciling himself to some Catholic practices. Sometimes he would feel like resigning, but then he would become enthusiastic again, seeing his ministry help many young people to pull their lives back together. Ricardo said that the Charismatic Catholic movement was changing a lot of things in some of the old, dead, cold traditional churches of Colombia. He felt God wanted him to let some light into some of those dark spiritual shadows. Ricardo had become very interested in the Sermon on the Mount as related in Matthew chapters 5–7. He told me a story of how he had been praying and asking God to give him a message to preach to Colombia that would bring about family reconciliation like God promises in Malachi 4:4–6. In the middle of his prayer he claimed that his wife, Jenny, had started to see a vision. She had seen something similar to a TV screen with red letters flashing across it. The letters had said, Matthew

5–7, Matthew 5–7, and had continued repeating themselves for quite a while. This had led Ricardo to the conclusion that Matthew 5–7, Jesus' Sermon on the Mount, was the message for family reconciliation.

Later on I looked up the passage in my Bible, but it didn't look like a sermon on family reconciliation to me. I decided that maybe I would just have to take some of the things Ricardo was saying with the proverbial "grain of salt."

My dad said that he was leaving for the United States in a couple of weeks to go on a speaking tour of American churches, telling about his work in Colombia. I asked him if I could use the plane while he was gone. He replied that if the Colombian authorities would issue me a pilot's license, he would leave me the plane. I went up to Bogota, the capital city, and with much fear and trembling, applied for a pilot's license. Colombian law required 100 hours of flying time and an instrument rating in order to qualify for even a private pilot's license. I had less than 70 hours and no instrument rating. Imagine my joy when they issued me a provisional license which was good for one year. I considered this to be a miracle, given the strict legalistic attitude of the Civil Aeronautics Department.

I thought back to another miracle that had made it possible for me to be a pilot in the first place. Back in Minneapolis, Minnesota, in 1959, several months after I had prayed and asked God to call my parents to be missionaries; a terrible accident had happened to me. I had been playing in the basement with my cousins. I dove head-first onto a pile of old cardboard boxes and a metal staple in one of the boxes caught me in the eye. This resulted in a jagged, three cornered tear right through the pupil of my eye. My parents took me to the hospital, where the doctors told them that I was in danger of losing my eye. The damage was too great to repair and if infection were to set in, I might lose the other eye also. It was Saturday. I was sent home with my eye bandaged shut. My parents were to bring me back to the hospital early Monday morning.

By now my dad was starting to feel that maybe God really could work supernaturally in this day and age. He was troubled, however, because the church he was attending was teaching that now we are in the dispensation of grace and that the age of miracles is past. My parents called up all of their friends and asked them to pray for me. We had a time of prayer in our home as well, and Dad asked me to pray. I prayed and I told God that if He would heal my eye, that I would always use my eyes for Him.

On Sunday, Dad took me to the home of another eye specialist to get a second opinion. The doctor put orange dye in my eye to check the damage, just like the doctors at the hospital had done. He looked at my eye for a minute and then announced that he couldn't find anything the matter with it. He didn't even put the bandage back on!

My dad couldn't believe it. He thought it was too good to be true. My mother told the specialist that there had been a triangular tear right through the pupil. The specialist became angry and said to her. "Did you see it yourself?" She replied that when the first doctor had put the dye in, he had shown her the tear in the pupil. The specialist was incredulous and did not believe my parents. The first doctor had said that even if that jagged gash had healed, there would still be a line of scar tissue across the pupil of the eye, obstructing vision.

To this day I have perfect 20/20 vision. I have never had any trouble passing my flight physicals.

The day after the Colombian government issued me a license to fly in their country, I returned to San Martin and fired up the Cessna 170. The first place I flew was out to our farm, Chaparral. I arrived at Chaparral just as a rain squall was moving in from the side. I attempted a crosswind landing on our short, narrow runway and scared myself pretty bad as the airplane zig-zagged out of control in the violent wind. My flying career almost ended right then and there. Somehow I managed to get the Cessna 170 Taildragger back into the air before we ground looped.

I flew over to a neighboring farm where I found a runway that was lined up into the wind. There I landed and waited until the wind died down before resuming my journey to Chaparral. Badly shaken, I decided that I would have to impose some severe restrictions on myself until I learned the ropes of jungle flying.

On the return flight, I landed in San Martin and picked up my mom, who wanted to go into Villavicencio with me. Villavicencio was the capital of the department of Meta. It was at its airport, Vanguardia, that my dad had decided to base the 170. He had contracted a local shop to provide maintenance and tie downs.

Mom and I took off from San Martin for the 20-minute flight to Vanguardia. We were almost half-way there when all of a sudden, Blam! The Cessna 170 began to shudder, and our airspeed fell off a little. I checked the mags and the engine seemed to operate smoother on the left mag. We had lost a substantial amount of power and the engine vibrated severely. I radioed the tower and said it looked like we had lost a mag. Then I revised my ETA and told them we'd be a little late. They asked me if I wanted to declare an emergency. Since we weren't having any trouble maintaining altitude, I told them it wasn't necessary, although I did ask for a straight-in approach.

When we landed, I was surprised to see a fire truck and an ambulance out on the ramp waiting for us. As I taxied past the fire truck the firemen made frantic gestures for me to shut off the engine. This I did. As I got out of the plane, I noticed a lot of black smoke coming from beneath the engine. There was also a dent and a hole in the engine cowling. We examined the engine and discovered the problem. One of the lower spark plugs had apparently been installed cross-threaded. The result had been that the spark plug had departed from the cylinder and continued right into the cowling, making a dent in the side of the airplane. Airplanes have dual ignition (two spark plugs per cylinder). Thus the top plug had continued to fire, sending a jet of flames out the lower hole every time it ignited. The old Continental C-145 engine had numerous oil leaks. This spilled oil had collected in the bottom of the cowling and streamed back down the belly of the airplane. All this oil had been smoldering, causing the smoke. In a few more minutes the whole business might have caught on fire with disastrous consequences.

It took several days to fix the plane, so my mom returned to San Martin by bus. As soon as the 170 was repaired I took off. Everything went fine until the right brake failed on landing in San Martin. I checked it out and found a loose brake line. All the brake fluid had drained out. I began to have serious misgivings about the manner in which the airplane was being maintained. In fact, I even began to wonder about the old airplane's log books. The engine was supposed to have only 400 hours on it, but knowing human nature, who knows what the real total was.

The next day I flew over to a large mission station. I had known most of the people there since childhood. They operated three aircraft there and had very good maintenance facilities. I landed and taxied over to the hangar. I felt real proud as I climbed out of the old 170. I was eager to impress all my friends there with my new role as a jungle pilot. My friends greeted me with open arms, and I felt great until the head of their aviation department and their chief pilot invited me into their office. With very sober looks on their faces they informed me that aviation in Colombia was for "professional" pilots flying well-maintained aircraft in a "professional" flight program. Given my limited experience and the deplorable mechanical condition of my airplane, they said the chances were that I would kill myself in three months or less. They said it was bad enough for me to kill myself, but what was really terrible was that I would probably kill a whole plane load of innocent passengers too. They told me of many fly-by-night operations that had had fatal accidents in the jungle. They wanted to wash their hands of me and my flying operations. I was welcome to buy aviation gasoline from them, but this was all they could do for me.

I felt terrible as I left the office. As soon as I was out the door, I began to think of all kinds of responses I could have made. I felt like going back there and asking them how they got started in aviation. Experience is nice to have, but no one is born with thousands of hours of flying experience. For a fledgling aviator, good advice and practical help from old timers can literally make the difference between life and death. I walked out of that interview with a burning desire in my heart to prove the "professionals" wrong.

Chapter Seven

September 7, 1983

    The treading of my captor's booted feet, together with the incessant rain of the jungle, has turned this campsite into a sea of ankle-deep mud. I have now spent three weeks in captivity. The guerrillas have me under very tight security. Three of them are on guard duty around the clock. They still keep me tied up with the nylon cord ending in a slip knot around my neck. The rope drags in the mud and gets my clothes and bedding dirty. It is extremely hard for me to get used to living with absolutely no privacy. I am required to be in my hammock under the mosquito net by 6:00 p.m. It is sweltering hot in the evening, and the hammock is made of wool. The mosquito net is made out of drapery material and doesn't admit much air. I lay inside and sweat for hours until about 10:00 or 11:00 p.m., when the temperature drops to the point where I can get some sleep. The guard takes away my shoes when I get in the hammock, presumably to make it harder for me to try to escape at night. Escape without shoes would be difficult since the jungle is full of sharp stickers. Sometimes he will tie a string to my hammock which he will tug from time to time to reassure himself that my weight is still in the hammock. The guard will shine his flashlight on me any time he feels me move or turn over in the hammock. At night, whenever a guerrilla shines his flashlight on something, he lays it alongside his gun barrel in order to be able to shoot if he decides to. Every time the guards shine their flashlights on me, I can be fairly certain that their gun is pointing at me also. There are many sounds in the jungle at night. Every time a dead branch comes crashing down, or a dead palm leaf falls to the ground in a gust of wind, the guerrillas jump and click off the safeties of their weapons. Some nights it is rather hard to get to sleep. I am beginning to wonder what my chances are of being shot by accident by a nervous, jumpy guard.

The guerrillas all get up at 4:00 a.m. and take down their hammocks, rolling them up in their packs. They are always ready to be off at a moment's notice. I am allowed to get up at 6:00 a.m. Giovani always brings me a cup of coffee and then some water with which to brush my teeth. This is followed by breakfast at about 7:00 a.m.

After breakfast I sometimes do exercises. Alfredo, the 14-year-old guerrilla, made me a chin-up bar by tying a pole between two trees. My captors have given me two old gunny sacks to spread on the ground so that I can do sit-ups and push-ups without getting muddy. I also spend a lot of time pacing back and forth as far as the nylon cord will allow me to go. This is about ten paces in either direction. The guards have taken to tying the other end of the rope to a tree.

I am very alert for a chance to escape, but no easy opportunities have presented themselves so far. I find that I have to carefully control my thoughts in order to avoid going into a severe depression. If I let my mind think about my wife and little ten-month-old daughter, I feel terrible all day. The baby had just learned to walk prior to the kidnapping and the high point of my day had been when I would come home from a hard day's work, pick her up and play with her. Now my wife, baby, family, and friends seem to belong to another world. My chances of seeing them any time soon seem very poor.

If I let my thoughts dwell on avenues of escape or on the possibilities of snatching a weapon from the hands of a guard, adrenalin will start to flow in my veins. Then I will soon find myself unable to eat or sleep. I go over the probability or chances of success for a given escape plan. Would it be better to make my move in daylight or at night? In fair weather or in foul? Should I just run, or should I try and incapacitate the guard first? If I do manage to break free from the guerrilla camp, what are my chances of finding my way home from here with no equipment, no matches, no food, and no weapons. I can envision my baby daughter growing up without a father. I had better not do anything foolish that I will regret later, or worse yet, not live to tell about. If I can't come up with an escape plan that will have at least an 80% chance of getting me home in one piece, I had better stay where I am.

I have begun to carefully calculate all my words and actions in an effort to lull the guerrillas into complacency with me. Maybe they will give me a chance to escape. Unfortunately, the incident of my shooting Manuel has caused them to handle me with much more security than would normally have been the case. They aren't taking any chances with me.

I fight depression by forcing my mind onto positive issues. This kidnapping is giving me a whole new perspective on my life and the world. How can I use this new viewpoint to my advantage? What can I learn from this experience? Is it possible for anything good to come out of this kidnapping? I begin to make a list of the answers that come to my mind. I am beginning to wonder if I can have a beneficial effect on my abductors. How can I relate to them?

As I explore positive viewpoints, my feelings improve. I remember a verse from the Bible that says: "All things work together for good in the lives of those who love God and are called according to his purpose."[1] Can God have a purpose in allowing me to fall into the hands of these guerrillas? If I were to relax and trust God to get me out of here, will He work everything out for good?

My mind tries to tell me that this viewpoint is crazy. In my wallet the guerrillas have found papers linking me to the Colombian government and identifying me as the previous head of the Civil Air Patrol for our area. My captors have been interrogating me and sometimes they insinuate that I must be a

---

[1] Rom. 8:28

government agent, maybe even a CIA agent! I have tried to explain that my job had just been to fly search and rescue missions for downed civil aircraft, but they continue to hassle me. My mind keeps telling me that I am trapped and that the guerrillas will never let me go alive.

Still, deep inside my spirit I feel that God might really have a purpose in this kidnapping. As I think over my situation, I have decided to look at it as an opportunity to have a positive effect on my captors. I am starting to preoccupy myself with how to present the truth to the guerrillas in a way that they can understand instead of just condemning them outright. I have decided to tell them about some of the mistakes I have made in my life and about some of the lessons I have learned "the hard way." Maybe they can relate to me this way. Hopefully they will eventually be able to evaluate their own lives and admit their own mistakes too. I have started telling the guerrillas stories about the wonderful things God has done for me in my life. God has always come through for me whenever I have found myself in trouble. All I have to do is just be honest with God and be willing to admit my problems and failures in order for Him to be able to help me out. I keep telling them that God can help them out of their problems too.

Nancy is bitter towards Christianity. One day she said to me, "I don't believe all this Christian garbage about mercy and love, and you don't either. You shot Manuel and therefore you must have hated him." I replied, "No, I didn't hate Manuel, even though I shot him. Kidnapping is wrong and I didn't want to let you people get away with it. I had nothing personal against Manuel. He just happened to be standing in my way to freedom. Be honest with yourself, Nancy. You wouldn't have thought very much of me if I would have just cowardly handed over my gun without using it. I do feel that I made a big mistake, however. The error I made was when I lied to Jaime about having the gun in the first place. A Christian shouldn't tell lies, no matter what the circumstances. There were many other things I could have said in answer to Jaime's question about the gun. I didn't have to lie. I even invented a fake 'heart condition' that I didn't have. Look at this guerrilla camp. Most of what you guerrillas tell me is lies. Most of what your leaders tell you is lies. You can't trust anybody. If I claim to be a Christian and tell lies too, it puts us all in the same boat, doesn't it? I have placed my life under God's authority from a very early age. Therefore, He is much stricter with me than with someone who doesn't even acknowledge His existence. If I had been able to escape, utilizing my revolver after having lied to Jaime about it, I would have come to an erroneous conclusion. I would have concluded that, yes, it is necessary for a Christian to lie under difficult circumstances when he is in a tight spot. After I lied about the gun, there was no way God could let me get away with using it. Instead, He very mercifully kept Giovani safe and He made sure I didn't kill Manuel either. Now, thanks to God, we can all sit here and discuss what happened and learn from our mistakes."

Nancy didn't reply. She left to go about her business without saying a word. I think she was remembering back to an incident several days before. It was my 20th day of captivity and Manuel had returned to camp. He was weak from his gunshot wound but he could talk. He came over and glared at me without saying a word. His left hand fingered the butt of a 9mm pistol stuck down the back of his pants. I greeted him and we spoke back and forth for a few minutes. It was clear when he left that he held a desire for revenge against me. I had prayed for Manuel that night, and I asked God to change his attitude. I prayed that Manuel might be able to forgive me and that I would be able to shake his hand. The next afternoon, Manuel came back. We talked for three hours. By the time he left I knew that he held no resentment towards me for shooting him, nor did I feel bitter toward him for kidnapping me. Manuel told me that he was personally against kidnapping, but that he was a member of a military organization and he had to follow orders even if he didn't agree with them. I told him that I had nothing personal against him, and that I shot him only because I deemed it necessary in order to escape. When Manuel rose to go, he held out his hand. We shook hands and he said, "It's okay; there is nothing between us." The next day Manuel was transferred up river to the main guerrilla camp to recuperate. I didn't see him again for over a month.

One day a guerrilla asked me if this experience was the worst thing that had ever happened to me. I thought back over my life and I had to say, no. There have been several times in my life when much worse predicaments have befallen me. In fact, several times the terrible predicament has been entirely of my own making. This time the predicament I am in isn't even my fault. I am feeling a growing conviction inside that God is in control of this situation. If God has intervened in my life before and spared me when the problem has been entirely my fault, I am convinced that He will have all the more reason to work everything out now.

I am beginning to enter into meaningful dialogues with my captors. I find that if I talk with them on a personal, one to one basis, that they will open up to me to a certain extent. If I speak to a group of them, they just clam up as individuals and simply parrot their communist indoctrination. They appear to be astounded that an educated person like myself can believe in God instead of evolution.

Today I got into a discussion with Giovani. I found out that atheism is the basis on which the communistic ideology is built. I have been noticing that each morning all the guerrillas not on guard duty have to attend a two-hour long ideological meeting. Giovani told me that God and religion are clever falsifications thought up by very clever individuals to obtain power and money.

"Prove God's existence!" he demanded of me. "I can surely prove that evolution is true."

I told him to go ahead and prove evolution to me. He said, "Well, everyone knows about the fossil record and there are examples of evolution throughout nature. Man is the product of his environment, and the next inevitable step in the evolutionary process is to overthrow the capitalistic governments of the world by force and impose a new order of world socialism. Cuba and Nicaragua have already been 'liberated.' El Salvador is now in the process of being freed from capitalism. Right now, we are still too weak to be able to 'liberate' Colombia, but we are helping our brothers in El Salvador by sending them as many men and as much money as we can spare. After our brothers triumph in El Salvador, then the full resources of our friends in Cuba, Nicaragua, and El Salvador will be concentrated on the liberation of a new country, which will probably be Colombia. Mexico and the other Latin American nations will follow. Ultimately we will win and it is inevitable that the United States will finally fall. Then our new world order will quickly clean up all the world's problems. We will redistribute all the world's resources and completely eliminate hunger, disease, illiteracy, and poverty. We will also try, convict, and eliminate all the corrupt capitalists; especially everyone found perpetrating this terrible religious hoax about God. We consider 'religion' to be a crime against the 'people'."

"Give me an example of evolution in nature," I asked him.

"How about a caterpillar turning into a butterfly? For sure that's evolution," Giovani replied.

I said, "If the butterfly could lay eggs that would hatch directly into little butterflies, then you might have a point. However, the truth is that the butterflies' eggs hatch back into caterpillars, which spin cocoons and turn into butterflies again. This process is called metamorphosis, not evolution. Evolutionary scientists have a hard time explaining how metamorphosis evolved. On the other hand, a creator would delight in designing a life-cycle like that. As for the fossil record, its evidence is far from conclusive. For example, if the fossil skeletons were to show a large monkey or ape with a shorter and shorter tail, finally turning into a creature with no tail at all, it would be stronger evidence. As it is, they show us skeletons of progressively larger and larger apes with complete tails, and then jump over to skeletons of small men with no tail at all and show skeletons of larger and larger men.

"Take the Kogi Indians for example, who average less than five feet tall. If an archaeologist were to dig up one of their skeletons without ever having met a real live Kogi, he might think he had the missing link. Knowing the Kogis, however, it is easy to see that they are just as intelligent and human as we are even though they are very small.

"Another thing that is messed up is the dating system. I heard about one major archaeological find that was sent to two different laboratories for dating. One laboratory reported the bones to be one million years old. The second lab reported two million years old. The precision of the dating techniques, using analytical mathematics in this case, is one million years, plus or minus a million years for the first lab report. In other words, the specimen could be anywhere from 0-2 million years old.

"The more you study things like genetics, microbiology, ecosystems, and food chains, the more difficult it becomes to defend evolution. The smaller things get, the more complex everything becomes. A seemingly simple, single-celled animal such as the amoeba, is just as complex as any of the cells making up the human body. When a person begins to grasp the tremendous complexity of the inner working of just a simple amoeba, the odds of all this coming together by chance seem impossible. It is easy to see how a given species can adapt to its environment to a certain extent within its gene pool. The genes for a given species however, are usable only to that species and cannot be transferred to another species. Every species of plant or animal is genetically locked into a given range of size, color, and other attributes. Thus a dog breeder may breed large dogs, small dogs, long-haired dogs, short-haired dogs, or vary any of a number of characteristics; but it is genetically impossible to breed a dog into a cat, or into some other animal. As scientific research goes on in genetics and microbiology, evolution keeps getting harder and harder to defend instead of the other way around. Of course, if we initiate our search to discover how we happened to come into existence with the dogmatic assumption that God doesn't exist, well, then we are forced to believe something like evolution."

Giovani was stunned; he had never even dreamed that evolution could be questioned in such a way. He was still sure that what I was saying was pure heresy, but he was at a loss to respond, so he said nothing.

I continued speaking. "Let's examine things from your point of view," I told him. Arnuval had joined us, but I went on with my chain of thought. "If evolution is true, we are going to have a very difficult time reconciling it with your argument about social justice as being your main motivating force. If 'natural selection' and 'survival of the fittest' are causing the overthrow of the capitalistic governments of the world by force as the next level of evolutionary 'progress,' then let's not confuse the issue by talking about social injustice being the cause. Evolution by its very nature is cruel. 'Survival of the fittest' means that the one with the most strength or force survives and replaces the weaker or more pacific animal. The fact that the stronger animal kills and replaces the weaker animal has got nothing to do with justice. If we throw God out of the equation, then justice is simply what pleases us at the moment, and injustice is what we do not like. In order to even be able to discuss justice and injustice, we must have a supreme good being on which to moor our standards. Otherwise everything becomes relative."

Arnuval and Giovani were silent for a few minutes as the full implication of what I had just said began to sink in. All of a sudden they were being faced for the first time with the possibility that maybe there really was a supreme, good being named God, who had really created all things. What would this "God" have to say about some of their guerrilla procedures and activities?

Arnuval broke the silence, "Well, we rank and file guerrillas are just members of a military organization. If our leaders order us to kidnap someone, or try to kill someone, we have to obey our orders. If we are 'just obeying orders,' then whatever happens isn't our fault. We don't like to kidnap people, but our leaders say it is necessary in order to finance the revolution."

I replied by saying that sometimes it is necessary for a person to take a strong moral stand on a given issue no matter what the consequences. If it were true that Arnuval and Giovani had joined the guerrilla movement in the first place due to a desire to fight social injustice, and to stand up against the corruption in present Colombian society, then why weren't they standing against what they knew to be wrong within the guerrilla organization? They both appeared rather sober for awhile and Arnuval looked a little wistful. Finally he said, "Well, you still haven't proven God's existence to us, although I will admit that you have given us a lot of food for thought on all these matters."

"The first place we can look for God," I answered, "is in His creation. I don't think that the beauty and artistic designs that we see in nature could have happened by chance. The earth is just the right distance from the sun to provide optimum temperatures for human life. There is just the right amount of oxygen in the air. The balance between land surface area and water surface area are optimum on this planet for the weather and rainfall needs of most areas. The earth spins on its axis and has just the right amount of tilt to provide days, seasons, and optimum utilization of a very high percentage of the earth's surface area. The way everything interacts in nature seems to point to a master plan made by a creator. The probabilities of all this coming together by chance are so remote as to seem utterly ridiculous. The Christian explanation that this world was at one time a perfect creation and that basic human selfishness has somehow caused this world to 'go wrong' becomes more and more plausible if we are willing to set wishful thinking to one side and each of us be prepared to accept our share of the blame for the mess we are all in. If we stick our heads in the sand and refuse to admit our own mistakes, we can make no progress whatsoever towards discovering God. We only become more and more bitter as we see the mistakes that other people are making around us and feel frustrated when we can't change them. This can lead to our taking the law into our own hands and trying to set things right by use of force. The use of force in private hands will nearly always backfire since the people taking the law into their own hands are far from being perfect individuals. Their personal imperfection will interfere with their ability to wield force in a just manner, and the end result may be way worse than the start."

Giovani scowled darkly at me at this point and remarked that I had better watch what I was saying because he could kill me whenever he wanted to. I decided to not pay too much attention to this threat, because I now understood what they had been saying about "just following orders," and I knew Giovani couldn't just shoot me on the spur of the moment because those weren't his orders. If I were to try to escape, however, that was a different story.

"You know, if God is really out there like I am telling you He is," I continued, "if He really made this earth and all that is in it, if God really loves each one of us as individuals and has a plan for each of our lives, then I don't have to prove God's existence to you. If God exists, then He can prove himself to you. All you have to do is talk to Him and authorize Him to intervene in your life and control all of life's circumstances affecting you. I am convinced that God himself is capable of proving his own existence in a much more convincing way than I ever could. What have you got to lose? You have everything to gain."

The previous day we had moved the location of our campsite a few hundred yards through the jungle onto higher ground. The guerrillas had made me a desk out of split palm. Jaime rigged a spare tarp over the top, so that I could write even when it rained. Mariano, the gunsmith, set up his tools, using an old fallen log for a workbench. His 'workshop' is about 20 yards from my 'desk.' Today Mariano came up with, wonder of wonders, a typewriter. Arnuval announced that I am to type my book out in Spanish for all the guerrillas to read. If I do this, then they will let me take a handwritten English version home with me when I leave. I typed most of the day, translating this book into Spanish for my captors to read. I look up every now and then and watch Mariano work. He is fitting a new stock to an M2 automatic carbine. I am amazed at the quality of his work in spite of the limited tools available to him. He has to carry everything in his backpack along with his bedding, food, and personal belongings.

I was fairly tired when I climbed into my hammock that night. It is nice to be in a new campsite without ankle-deep mud. The guerrillas have washed my bedding, too. Due to the recently cleared campsite, there is an abnormal amount of mosquitoes. An enormous black and white bodied mosquito with huge oversize blue fuzzy legs descended onto my arm like a little miniature lunar landing vehicle. I quickly swatted it and checked the inside of the mosquito net for more. The guard shined his flashlight at my movement, and I took advantage of the light to make sure the opening of the mosquito net was secure. I then settled back into the hammock to relax, thought back over the day's events, and said my prayers before drifting off to sleep. Thinking back over my conversation with Arnuval and Giovani, I began to chuckle to myself as I remembered another time when I had suggested to someone that God was perfectly capable of defending himself and proving His own existence to us humans.

Four years ago, I had been flying fish from an out-of-the-way jungle airstrip named Tomachipan. My friend, Fernando Suarez, had built a fish trap on the falls of the Inirida River. There was a volcanic ridge, flat on top, that stuck up out of the jungle. On top of this flat lava rock an airstrip had been built. Fernando had built his fish trap in such a way that some of the fish trying to jump the falls would wind up in the trap. All he had to do was clean out the fish trap every morning and store the fish in a cold storage room he had built by the side of the airstrip. He sold me the fish at the airstrip and I flew in all his supplies and diesel fuel for his cold storage unit. I used to like to spend the night at Tomachipan, because it was a lovely spot. There were few mosquitoes, and the water was clear. The falls were beautiful, descending in several easy stages, making a lot of noise.

One day I flew in at about 5:00 p.m. Fernando came down to the airstrip landing and picked me up in his outboard motor-powered dugout canoe. This same day a professor from a high school located on the headwaters of the Inirida River in a major town had made a day-and-a-half boat journey down the river with a boat load of high school boys. They said they were on a field trip to study the volcanic rock formation, the falls, and the fish trap. While we were all waiting for the supper to be prepared and served, I got into one of these classic evolution-versus-creation debates with the professor. The professor was about 45 years old, almost bald, and he was really putting on a show in front of his students. The debate got hotter and hotter. As we were really getting into the high decibel range, Fernando came out and tried to reconcile things, saying he thought that both sides had a point and that now it was time to forget the debate and have supper. I made a closing statement and told the professor that I didn't need to defend God. If the professor would authorize God to intervene in his life and reveal himself, I thought that God would be happy to do so and convince the professor beyond the shadow of a doubt in a much better way than I could in the debate. The Bible says that God is a Spirit and that we must worship Him in spirit and in truth. If we have no concept of God and are unable to conceive of a spiritual world invisible to our physical senses because we have not developed our spiritual senses, then we must be honest and look for the truth. If we follow the truth, then our search will ultimately end in God's revelation of himself to us in a way that we can perceive and understand. I told the professor that if he wanted to be honest, we could ask God himself to settle our little debate.

The professor drew himself up to his full stature and replied, "Well, I authorize God, wherever he is, to reveal himself to me, if he can, but until then I will continue to believe evolution!"

All the school boys laughed at this and thought it was very funny. There were a few more things I could have said, but I decided to leave matters be and get on with the meal.

The next morning I left early with my load of frozen fish. I didn't return to Tomachipan until two days later. Fernando met me at the airstrip, and he looked a little pale.

"What's the matter, Fernando," I asked. "Don't you feel well today?"

"You aren't going to believe what happened to the professor," he replied.

"What happened?" I responded.

"The other morning after you left," Fernando continued, "we all went back to the falls and the school boys helped me clean the fish that were in the traps on the far side of the river. When we got done, we started to go home. I ran my canoe well upstream along the banks to a safe distance above the falls before crossing the river, like I always do. The professor and the high school boys didn't do that. They tried to cross in the very mouth of the falls. Their motor quit halfway across and before they could get it started again, they were sucked over the falls. There have been thirteen people that I know of prior to this go over those falls, and they have all been killed.

"Fortunately, I also keep a boat and motor on the lower end of the falls, so I ran down there. The old outboard motor that normally takes 15 minutes to start because it has no compression, started up on the first crack. I headed out into the rapids below the falls and began fishing out the schoolboys. Soon I had all seven of them in the boat, and they were all alive. We searched both banks of the river below the falls but we couldn't find the professor anywhere. The boys told me that the professor couldn't even swim, so I figured he must have drowned. Then we noticed something in the water far downriver. When we got closer, we just couldn't believe our eyes. It was the professor, perched on top of the capsized canoe. He was hanging on for dear life, digging his fingernails into the slimy, moss-covered bottom of the dugout canoe as it went down the rapids.

"It turned out that he had gone down one chute of the falls. The canoe had taken another. At the bottom of the falls there is a tremendous geyser. This jet of water had hurled the professor into the air just as the large dugout canoe had passed by from the other chute of the falls at right angles. The professor had landed on top of the water-logged canoe and had hung on for all he was worth. He was completely exhausted when we finally pried his fingers loose from that canoe.

"We spent most of the next day dragging the large canoe up the portage on rollers. I dried out their motor, which we found still bolted onto the transom of the canoe. I went through all my clothes and gave them each a pair of pants in which to return home because all their clothes were lost in the river. I fixed them up with an old gas tank of mine because theirs had been lost also. They left this morning to go home. It's too bad that you missed them. The last thing the professor said before they left was: "Tell Martin (I am called Martin in Spanish) that now I believe in God, too!"

"The school boys didn't laugh this time either," continued Fernando. "They all left here this morning just as sober as judges. I guess a person had better be very careful what he says about God."

As I thought back over this incident that had happened four years previously, I began to seriously pray that some of my captors would have the courage to be honest with God. I thought about Giovani and something stirred in the back of my memory. His face was familiar but I couldn't quite place where I had run into him prior to the kidnapping. There was something about Giovani's manner of speaking. His speech had an accent to it that I couldn't quite place. Maybe he wasn't even a Colombian. I continued to run this all around in my brain trying to place him. Giovani's Spanish accent was almost Caribbean. Could he be a Cuban? Then I remembered that early in my captivity he had asked me if I remembered him. He said he had conversed with me at a remote jungle airstrip several years ago. I had pressed him as to the exact time and place, but he wouldn't come clean.

All of a sudden a cold shiver ran down my spine and everything fell into place. Giovani had been in that group of high school boys that had gone over the falls at Tomachipan four years ago! What a coincidence! Wait a minute, maybe it wasn't a coincidence. What if those high school boys hadn't really been on a field trip? What if they were actually being recruited by the guerrillas, right out of high school? Was Giovani a Cuban agent? How old was he? I made some rapid mental calculations and came to the conclusion that we were now less than twenty-five miles from Tomachipan. The next morning I told the guerrillas the story of the professor and the high school boys. Then I looked straight at Giovani and asked him how the "professor" was getting along, and if he still believed in God. Giovani gave a start. Visibly flustered, he replied that he didn't know what I was talking about. Giovani began to appear more and more thoughtful as the days went by. These thoughtful periods were punctuated with abrupt bitter tirades against me and Americans in general. He would rant and rave about President Reagan, calling him every filthy name he could think of. Every time I started to defend our President, he would threaten to kill me. I would then get mad instead of scared. As I would think about the tremendous moral character and quality of our 72-year-old President, I felt an overwhelming urge to defend him, and not see him misrepresented in such a manner. When I would ignore Giovani's threats, he would turn livid and tremble with hatred and rage.

Chapter Eight

April, 1978, Finca Chaparral, Colombia

I was putting the finishing touches on a large walk-in freezer I was building on the banks of the Guaviare River at Chaparral. My plan was to buy fresh fish from the local fishermen on the river. The big catfish would be frozen, and then I would fly them to market in the airplane. We should be able to make enough profit on this wholesale fish operation to pay for the costs of doing all the public service and missionary flying that urgently needed to get done but no one could pay for. With the help of my brother, Chaddy, we had made an airstrip along the riverbank using an old D2 Cat bulldozer and our Ford 5000 tractor. This would enable us to load the fish in the plane directly from the walk-in freezer.

I had designed the cold storage facility for maximum freezing ability coupled with low diesel fuel consumption after analyzing various fish wholesaling ventures in the jungle that had failed due to high fuel costs. I used a Lister 750 RPM diesel engine with a band drive to Tecumseh 10 H.P. Freon compressor turning at 450 RPM. I used 100% manual controls, eliminating delicate electrical systems that can sometimes break down in the jungle. The result was a very efficient, reliable facility that could store about six tons of fish at temperatures ranging all the way down to 30 degrees below zero.

If I ever got homesick for my native Minnesota, some time spent inside the freezer would take care of the problem.

The local people became very excited about the project. It would provide them with a source of much needed income. My enthusiasm grew as we went on, and I borrowed heavily from the bank and from private individuals in order to finish the walk-in freezer and airstrip.

When the facilities were finished, I had to borrow more money for operating capital in order to be able to buy fish and to stock food, fishing supplies, and fuel for the fishermen. Many of the fishermen needed equipment or supplies on credit in order to be able to start fishing. Boats and motors had to be bought and run back and forth on a daily schedule picking up fish as they were caught and transporting them to the freezer before they spoiled.

Soon I was in debt way over my head. At first I didn't get too worried, because I figured that since my motives in doing all this were to produce funds for doing air ambulance flying, missionary work, and to provide jobs so that poor people could better their lifestyles, that God would automatically be very pleased with me, and bless our business so that it would be no problem to pay all these debts. I wouldn't have gotten into all these debts if the business had just been for me personally. But since this business was really for God, I took out as much money as I could borrow, because I was counting on God to pay it back.

It turned out that there was a tremendous amount of logistics involved in an operation like this. There were over 50 full-time fishermen selling their catch to us, and about 200 part-time fishermen. That meant we had to handle about 250 separate accounts. Some of the fishermen had outboard motors. They all looked to us for fuel, parts, and service. Many of the fishermen wanted to buy motors or upgrade their present one (all on credit, of course). My brother and I took out a Johnson motor distributorship, and soon we had a big debt with Johnson, also.

By now I was flying fish as fast as the little Cessna 170 could haul it. The 170's engine began to complain. One morning it quit three times on me on the way to the farm. This resulted in three different forced landings which fortunately all turned out okay. I checked the engine over and replaced some intake manifold hoses which were rotten and broken. I also found some sediment in the fuel screen. Thinking I had taken care of the problem, I loaded up with fish and set out for Villavicencio. Half-way there, the engine began to act up, and when I arrived in town, the engine temperature gauges had gone past the red line and buried themselves into the high end of the scale. I decided it was time to retire the old engine. It had run faithfully well past its recommended overhaul time.

At this point I made another mistake. Instead of just buying a new engine for the 170, I listened to a local Cessna dealer who wanted to sell me a whole new airplane. I was under a lot of pressure because the cold storage facility was full and overflowing at Chaparral, and I needed to move fish immediately because my bank debts were coming due. I also needed to receive more fish from the fishermen in order to recover the money I had lent them. The Cessna dealer showed me a nice, one-year-old Cessna 182 worth $50,000 U.S. He said not to worry about a down payment; I could take care of that later.

It was a beautiful airplane, able to carry 50% more load than the 170 at about a 40% increase in speed. This, coupled with a greatly extended range, due to much larger gas tanks, made the new airplane ideal for my needs. I took it without thinking twice about the implications of this new debt at very high interest.

The next month after I bought the 182, we entered the dry season. Unknown to me, fishing gets very slow in the dry season. The fish sink down into the cool mud at the bottom of the river and kind of hibernate until the rainy season comes. If the river is shallow, as is the case in other areas of Colombia, this makes for excellent fishing. The Guaviare, however, is very deep (over 90 feet in some places), and our main fishing season is the rainy season. We went through three very slow months, in which we lost money and were unable to meet our obligations.

In April, when the rainy season started, it was of absolute necessity that everything go well with the fishing season if our business were to survive. I decided we needed help selling the fish, to make a bigger profit margin. My old friend, Ricardo Trillos, had left his job with the Catholics and was presently employed as a salesman for a large hardware store. I talked him into coming and working with me in the fish business as a partner in marketing. We started working hard, and soon we were beginning to catch up on our payments. I started trusting in Ricardo's marketing expertise to pull us out of our financial mess. Unfortunately, Ricardo wasn't any better at managing finances than I was, although he was a very excellent salesman.

About this time I made another mistake and wound up learning a lesson in Colombian politics the hard way. I got caught up in a small town fight between different political factions and wound up thrown in jail on trumped up charges. Ricardo did everything possible to get me out and finally succeeded after about a week. During the week I was imprisoned, one of our employees rolled our jeep and demolished it, losing a load of fish he was carrying.

Immediately after this, my father returned from the U.S. and sized up our financial situation. We were right on the verge of going bankrupt. Any further incidents could push us over the edge. Dad blamed Ricardo for some of the financial problems and sloppy bookkeeping and fired him to cut overhead. I was really the one responsible for our financial situation, but I didn't accept my share of the blame.

I went back to work harder than ever, trying to make up for lost time. We were about half way through the rainy season, and the fish were really coming in. One morning I took off from San Martin in the 182 with a load of supplies for the fishermen. As I turned final for the fish house airstrip, I was surprised to see a large, twin-engine airplane on the ground at the far end of the strip. I landed and taxied cautiously up to the house. Guillermo, my employee in charge of the fish buying operation, met me and told me the story. The large, twin-engine airplane (it was a Howard 350 with 2500 H.P. engines) had landed at dusk the day before. It had run out of fuel and been unable to land anywhere else due to bad weather. Four Americans had been aboard. The pilot had announced that he was a retired colonel from the U.S. Air Force, and that he and his crew worked for the Drug Enforcement Agency (DEA). Due to the short runway, the large airplane had run off the end of the strip and halfway into a plowed field at the end of the runway. It was now hopelessly stuck in the wet, plowed ground. My brother, Chaddy, and Guillermo had worked most of the night with the tractor, trying to get the airplane out of the mud, but to no avail. Early in the morning, a speedboat with what appeared to be mafia personnel came and picked up the pilots. They had left just before I arrived.

"Guillermo," I said, "I think that this airplane probably belongs to the mafia,[1] and those pilots told you a lie so that you would help them. I had better go and get the police so that we won't be blamed for the appearance of this United States registered plane on our property."

Fortunately, the "mafia" airplane was empty inside and not carrying drugs. They had probably been coming down empty to pick up a load of marijuana or cocaine. I quickly flew to the new police station in Mapiripan, 15 minutes flight time away. I told the local police commander the story and asked him to set up a checkpoint on the river and stop the mafia speedboat. He appeared more interested in the airplane, so I took him and one of his men back to Chaparral with me in the Cessna 182. I was relieved to have him take over the responsibility for this huge airplane on my property.

We were just walking from the 182 over to inspect the big airplane, when all of a sudden a T-33 jet fighter plane appeared out of nowhere and began shooting its six .50 caliber machine guns at us. I told the policemen to stand out where the fighter pilot could see their uniforms. They did so, but the T-33 continued making passes at us, and the policemen were forced to run for cover. Some bullets went right past my new Cessna 182, and I thought, I'm not going to let them shoot up my $50,000 airplane; it's not even insured against something like this.

---

[1] The word "mafia" is used in Colombia and for the purposes of this book to denote anyone involved in narcotics trafficking and does not refer to ethnic Italians.

I knew it would take the jet fighter plane a minute or so to turn around and make another pass on us, so I climbed into the 182 as soon as the T-33 was past us and started it up. The police commander hopped in the other side. As soon as the engine caught, I firewalled the throttle and took off. Unknown to me there was a second fighter plane on top of us at 30,000 feet. This second T-33 dove at us as we made our take-off. We were almost 100 feet in the air when I saw the fighter. It was coming at us head-on. Its machine guns were blazing. Six faint red lines of tracers were converging somewhere under my left wing. Instinctively I lowered the nose and made a hard turn to the right. The fighter tried to follow my movements. I could see the wings of the T-33 tremble as the jet approached a high-speed stall in its efforts to turn with me. Puffs of smoke came from the machine guns in the fighter plane's wings. Fortunately the six lines of tracer bullets were now converging behind us, as we could turn much faster than the T-33, and the fighter's tremendous speed carried it past us. I leveled the 182 out about three feet above a large swamp. I couldn't believe we were still alive.

All of a sudden, Whump, Whump, Whump. The original T-33 had turned around and was now firing at us from behind with machine guns and possibly rockets. Something hit the swamp just under our tail and blasted debris up into the air, doing minor damage to the 182's tail. I started to zig-zag the 182 as sharply as I could while I headed for the edge of the jungle.

The police commander was screaming something at the top of his lungs. I told him to shut up and look out the back window and tell me when the fighter got back on our tail. This he did.

The T-33's made several more passes on us until we either lost them, or they ran out of ammunition. I flew all the way into Mapiripan zig-zagging at low level. When I went to reduce power for landing, I found the power levers all in the full forward, full power position. I had been so upset by the fighters that I had forgotten to pull the power back to cruise after take-off. Fortunately, the 182's engine is rated for continuous full power operation.

I landed and pulled off the runway to park. It was only after I shut the engine off and started to climb out of the airplane that the full shock of all that had happened began to set in. The police commander was in worse shape than I was. His knees were knocking together so badly that it was several minutes before he could even walk. He wasn't used to riding in airplanes, let alone the maneuvers I had been using to keep the fighters from hitting us. Most of his remarks about the Colombian Air Force were unprintable.

We hurried back to the police station and used the police radio to inform headquarters of the situation, requesting that they call off the Air Force before they killed someone at Chaparral. The other policeman had remained at Chaparral when we had taken off.

We learned later that the Air Force pilots thought that the pilots of the mafia airplane were being evacuated in the Cessna 182. That's why they had attacked me. The next day I went down to the Air Force base and talked to the commanding colonel. He said that he was sorry about what had happened and that the offending pilots of the fighter planes that had fired on us were now locked up in the brig. He claimed that he had given them permission just to fire a warning burst into the river. It wasn't clear to me if the pilots were locked up because they got carried away with themselves, or if it was because of their poor marksmanship! I decided to accept the colonel's apology and leave it at that. The colonel was worried that I might sue the Air Force, but I assured him that I wasn't going to do that.

Later that week, the colonel sent a whole company of paratroopers to mount a guard on the mafia airplane and to repair the damage done by the fighter planes to our runway. They filled in all the holes and began to widen and lengthen the runway in preparation for flying the Howard 350 super Ventura from Chaparral to the Air Force base. Soon we had an extremely nice runway, courtesy of the Colombian Armed Forces.

When they were finished with the runway, an Air Force pilot came out to fly the big mafia plane out. He looked at the airplane and measured the runway. Then he looked at the place where he would have to pass our house with less than three feet of clearance between his wingtip and the roof of the house. He said this wasn't enough safety margin for him. The runway length was marginal, and if anything were to go wrong, there would be an accident. He said the big Lockheed Howard 350 was a very nice airplane, but that as far as he was concerned it looked like an elaborate, 5000 horsepower coffin.

The paratroopers were withdrawn and replaced by a squad of six Air Force guards. I had been impressed with the discipline, training, and manners of the paratroopers, but these new guys were different. They decided to set up a checkpoint on the river. If a boat didn't stop, they would fire their guns at it as a warning. If the boat owners didn't rapidly come up with either some cigarettes, money, or liquor for the guards, they would be in for a long delay. Our fish business began to suffer. Most of the fishing was done at night. These Air Force guards were very nervous at night, so they would fire their weapons at anything that moved. After a couple of close calls, the fishermen quit bringing in fish at night. Many of the fishermen didn't have I.D. cards or draft cards, living way out in the country, so they were scared to come in at any time for fear of being hassled by the guards. Fish production went down to about 25% of what it had been previously. I began having trouble making my payments to all my creditors. I was now so far behind in my airplane payments, it was a wonder they didn't foreclose on the 182.

A whole year went by with this situation going on, and I had to look for other avenues of income to avoid going bankrupt. I started flying supplies and meat into small jungle towns that could be reached only by air. I would haul dried fish on the return trip. It was during this period that I lined up the contract to buy the fish production of Tomachipan. By now I was so far in debt that it was difficult for me to even meet the interest payments on all that I owed. Many of the fishermen that owed me money had entirely given up fishing and were now farming marijuana. Unfortunately when they sold their lucrative crop, they would forget to pay their debts. It was a case of easy come, easy go. In spite of the seriousness of the situation, it was amusing to see some of the things that these poor people would spend their money on when all of a sudden they had a large amount of money in their hands for the first time in their lives. Many of the poorer people would get into drug cultivation because it seemed like a wonderful opportunity to have things they had only been able to dream about before. Now they would be able to feed and clothe their families adequately. They might even be able to send their children to high school. If a family member became ill, now they would be able to pay for doctor bills and hospitalization. It seemed to me to be a terrible paradox that the money spent by some affluent American kid on drugs (with probable disastrous consequences on his life and character) could actually wind up down in Colombia being used to pay for the education of a poor kid who had never had a chance to get an education before.

However, when these poor people actually got a hold of the money they had always dreamed of having, a disappointingly small percentage of it seemed to get spent on worthwhile projects that would help them in the future. They spent their money on portable generators, fancy speedboats, video equipment, and all kinds of junk that was completely useless to them after the marijuana bubble burst, and they were poor again.

At this time, the marijuana business was so profitable that almost everyone in our area began scrambling to get a piece of the action. They would say, "If the rich Americans want to buy pot, that's their problem. We aren't hurting anyone. What's the matter with us making a little money for the first time in our lives? We aren't using the drugs here in Colombia."

We were among the last holdouts in our area, trying to make a living by honest means, and we were about one inch away from bankruptcy. All my friends would come and argue with me. They would say, "It's impossible to make a living in this area if a person doesn't participate in the drug trade."

I tried to warn them of the negative consequences of what was going on. I would tell them of the terrible damage drugs were doing to North American youth, but it would fall on deaf ears.

The drug business started having some negative effects on Colombian culture as well. The local law enforcement officers were soon corrupted by the drug traffickers. A high percentage of the drug bonanza was spent on liquor and vice. The very worse elements of Colombian society began to descend on the area in search of easy money. Bodyguards and hired gunmen were in demand by rich mafia figures. Fighting and violence began to erupt as different mafia[2] factions battled for turf and the right to buy marijuana in a given area. Communist guerrillas began moving in on the most lucrative areas, levying a tax on the drug growers to finance terrorism and revolution. Since growing marijuana was illegal, the poor *campesino* families growing the pot were open to extortion from all sides. They were forced to pay the crooked law enforcement personnel, the mafia, and the communist guerrillas. The dreams and illusions that had brought the average Colombian farmer into growing marijuana began to turn into a nightmare.

At the same time, my financial condition steadily deteriorated. Instead of accepting at least part of the blame for my predicament due to my poor planning and over-borrowing, I blamed everything on the "mafia." It was all their fault for flying that airplane onto my fish house airstrip, I also blamed the mafia for the lucrative marijuana industry that was attracting the fishermen and causing them to plant pot and forget about the money they owed me. I wanted to make the mafia pay for all the damages they had caused me. I was at my wits end trying to get rid of the mafia airplane parked at Chaparral with its Air Force guard disrupting my fish business. It seemed to be in limbo; the Air Force wouldn't fly it out, but they wouldn't abandon it either. I considered flying it out myself and the Air Force at one point authorized me to do so, but pilot friends of mine cautioned against it, and as I think back on it, I'm glad I took their advice. At that point in my flying career, I just didn't have the experience to fly something like that out of such a short, narrow runway.

One day I heard a rumor that the mafia was negotiating with the government to pay the fine they owed for violation of

---

2   Instead of having organized crime, the proper term for Colombia would be disorganized crime. There were over 25 major drug rings operating in our area.

Colombian air space in a U.S. registered airplane. The Howard 350 would be turned back over to the mafia upon payment of the fine. I figured that by law they should be liable to pay for all the damages they had caused me. I was talking this all over one afternoon with my friend, Pedro. Pedro was head of the Civil Defense for eastern Colombia. He had named me head of the Civil Air Patrol for our area several months before. The two of us had been on several daring search and rescue missions together that were the talk of the town. I used to stay at Pedro's house when I was in Villao. Unknown to me, Pedro was also very involved with the mafia. Pedro remarked that he "just happened to know" the people who had landed that airplane at Chaparral. He offered to arrange a meeting with them.

The guy from the mafia looked cruel and ruthless. His bodyguard looked even worse. Yes, he was sorry his airplane had caused me so much inconvenience. Yes, he would pay me damages as soon as he regained possession of his plane and was able to remove it from my property. He would appreciate it if I were to do him some small favors like fly some mechanics out to work on the plane before his pilots picked it up. Of course, I was to understand that I must be careful to keep my mouth shut about all this. If I were to breathe a word about any of this to the press, or the authorities in Bogota, or to the U.S. government, he would have me killed right away. Our meeting lasted less than five minutes. I shuddered and asked Pedro if these guys really would kill someone at the drop of a hat over some minor misunderstanding or rumor. Pedro replied, "Don't worry about it; those guys always talk like that." I did feel uneasy, though. Something about those two mafia characters made cold shivers run up and down my spine.

At this point, I decided I had a moral obligation as a Christian to do something to try to stop the drug traffic. I had tried in the past to work with the Colombian authorities on this, but corruption was rampant throughout all the law enforcement agencies and it was extremely dangerous for me to give them any information. From time to time I would find an honest Colombian law enforcement officer, but I could never be sure that there wasn't a bad apple around, who would repeat anything I said to the mafia.

I decided to contact the American Drug Enforcement Agency (DEA) in Bogota. I had a Colombian police officer, whom I respected, introduce me to an American DEA agent. I told him the story of all that had happened in our area, and invited him to come with me and see for himself. He rather coldly informed me that he didn't have time to check out all the rumors that people told him in his office.

Trying to convince him that I was speaking the truth, I told him of the meeting that Pedro had set up for me with the "mafia" figures, and I told him their names. The DEA agent said, "I'm real busy right now; I have a lot of paper work to take care of. Why don't you go out and gather more information, and then come back and see me. If these "mafia" people ask you for a flight that doesn't involve your having to haul any drugs, go ahead and do it, and see what you can find out."

Now I come to a part in my story that I would rather forget about and not tell. If it wasn't for the fact that I am writing this in a guerrilla camp, with armed guards watching my every move, I would be tempted to leave this part out. Most people wouldn't believe this story anyway. My chances of getting out of here alive don't look good right now. The guerrillas have been extremely interested in this book. All those that aren't on guard duty stand around my typewriter waiting for the next page of the book to be finished. Some of them read over my shoulder and ask me questions, which I sometimes type right into the book and answer.

A guerrilla named Elkin, a 19-year-old explosives expert, just asked me if I have ever been involved in marijuana trafficking. I decided to tell the truth. Maybe these young guerrillas could learn something from my mistakes. They really enjoyed the story about my being shot at by the T-33s.

The truth is I never actually participated in the marijuana trafficking. I did get a little too close to it one time, and this is what happened. Boy! Did I ever learn my lesson.

I was taking a nap in a comfortable hammock at Pedro's place one nice Saturday morning when the telephone rang. Pedro went over and answered it; I was too sleepy to pay attention to what he said. After a while he came over and woke me up.

"Would $10,000 be enough to keep the Cessna people from foreclosing your 182?" he asked me.

I sat up in the hammock and perked up my ears.

"It might be enough," I answered.

"Well," Pedro replied. "My friend from the mafia just called, and he wants me to take care of some urgent business for him. If you will do a flight for us in your 182, there is $10,000 in U.S. money in it for each of us."

"Come on, Pedro," I answered. "You know I have a set policy against flying drugs in my airplane. You'll have to get someone else."

"You don't have to fly any drugs to make the ten grand," Pedro explained. "It's like this. An airplane from the U.S. is on its way down for a load of pot. The plane is headed for the wrong airstrip. Since it is already in the air, it can't be recalled. All you have to do is fly me out there. I'll climb on it and guide it to the right airstrip where the load is ready and fuel is available. I'll make sure it gets loaded and refueled. You can pick me up again the next morning after the drug plane has already left. It's too late for me to get someone else. We have to leave right now. If you don't go, that poor pilot will lose his airplane and go to jail. There isn't even any gasoline at the airstrip he is headed for. Look at it this way; all you have to do is just transport me to one location and pick me up the next day at another. It's just a simple air taxi flight, and you make ten grand. You've lost a lot of money lately, and it was due to that mafia airplane that landed at your farm. Now's your chance to get some of it back. You really have this money coming to you. Let's take advantage of this situation."

Pedro finally convinced me after an hour or so of argument. I thought, well, maybe I'll be able to obtain some real conclusive evidence for the DEA. Then they will believe me and start cracking down on all this drug traffic. We left directly for the airport where I had left the Cessna 182. As we took off, I felt very uneasy about this situation, but it was too late to chicken out.

We headed for the right airstrip first, so I would know where to pick Pedro up the next day. Pedro told the men there to get ready to load and to light a large bonfire at each end of the runway in case he got there after dark. It was already quite late. We continued on to the airstrip where the other plane was supposed to arrive. There it was. A Beechcraft Queen Air. The pilot's name was Joe and he was glad to see us. It was now 6:00 p.m. and getting dark. I started to tell Pedro that it wasn't a good idea to fly after dark, and that he should wait until morning. But he insisted that they had to go to the other strip right away and asked me to fly along in my plane. He wanted me to guide Joe to the other strip, because he couldn't find his way there in the dark. I was used to the area so I shouldn't have any trouble. All of a sudden a young kid ran up and said, "There's an army patrol boat coming up the river. If you don't leave immediately, you'll be caught."

I didn't want to sit around and explain to the army what I was doing in a clandestine airstrip without a flight plan. I just barely had time to synchronize a radio frequency with Joe, the pilot of the Queen Air, and we were on our way. Pedro was on board Joe's plane. I asked Joe how he was fixed for fuel, and he said, "Fine." He had over two hours' worth.

We were flying wingtip to wingtip with just our rotating beacons on, flashing in the growing darkness. In five minutes it was completely dark. I began to see some lightning flashes on the horizon, and I had a gut feeling that this was going to be a bummer. We started picking up some turbulence, and then some light rain. The lightning was flashing much closer now. I descended to about 200 feet above ground level and flew along shining my landing lights on the ground below. Joe followed, above and behind me.

I found the airstrip we were looking for. The storm had almost reached it, and great gusts of wind would blow me off course every time I tried to line up on final. I couldn't see it very well because the bonfires hadn't been lit on the ends of the runway. I decided to buzz the house and find out why no one was at the airstrip. It was an hour's walk or ten minutes in a jeep from the house to the airstrip. There was a Coleman lantern lit in the house, and I headed for that. Unfortunately, Joe and Pedro got the same idea at the same time. The house was on top of a high hill. At night it is impossible to tell where another airplane is going by just looking at a rotating beacon with no position lights. When I finally realized that the Queen Air was heading for me, it was right on top of me. It came in at an angle, very difficult to see in the driving rain. They seemed to be a little above me, so I went down as far as I could. It was a very near miss. The prop-wash of the larger airplane shook the 182, and blew me lower still. I hit something. It turned out to be the radio antenna from the house. A piece of the wire was looped around my landing gear, making a whistling sound in the slipstream. I pulled up and turned my position lights on. Joe did the same. Both of us were shaken. Down below, the men from the house were heading for the airstrip in a jeep. The driver looked up at the airplanes instead of at the road and ran over the side of a steep hill, rolling the vehicle. That put them out of commission for several hours.

Back in the house was a lady with her two children. She was so scared to death when the two airplanes buzzed her home, she grabbed the Coleman lantern and threw it over the side of the hill, putting it out, and causing Joe and me to lose our point of reference. At that moment, the main wave of the storm hit. Joe and I had all we could do just to keep track of each other. It was a severe storm and the lightning flashed very close. It would blind me and several times almost caused me to lose Joe.

I still had enough fuel left to fly to the Air Force base and make an instrument approach. I mentioned this to Pedro, and we decided we would have to go to the Air Force base. Pedro would use his status as head of the Civil Defense to get us off the hook. He would have to say that he had captured Joe and was bringing him in for a citizen's arrest. Poor Joe would lose his airplane and go to jail, but that was better than crashing in the jungle, out of gas in the middle of a storm.

We explained all this to Joe, but there was one problem. The Queen Air was too low on fuel to make it to the Air Force base. There were no other instrument approaches in eastern

Colombia. In that area, night flight was prohibited by law for obvious reasons.

I now had a tough decision to make. I could take off for the Air Force base and save myself and the 182, or I could stick with Pedro and Joe, using my expert knowledge of the area to find an airstrip outside the storm. If I left, what would I ever say to Pedro's wife? I decided to stay.

I radioed Joe and told him we would turn south. Maybe we could find a river and ditch the airplanes. This would be better than crashing in the jungle. The storm's intensity diminished by about half. I looked down and saw two lights. It looked like an airstrip, so I told Joe to circle overhead while I went down to check things out. Everything seemed fine and I prepared to land. I reduced power and applied full flaps. My forward-looking landing light picked this moment to burn out. My remaining landing light angled down vertically. I didn't see the house until I was right on top of it. I quickly applied full power just as my right landing gear grazed the ridge pole of the house. It took the airplane a few seconds to respond to the power. We continued down into the vicinity of the back yard of the house, heading straight for an old rotten split-palm fence with some palm leaves leaning up against it. The 182 was starting to fly again, and we were about three feet in the air when we hit the top of the palm leaves leaned up against the fence. I later deduced that this rotten palm lean-to must have been the local chicken coop. I don't know how many chickens went through the prop, but it must have been a few! One intact chicken body came through the prop and hit the windshield with a resounding blow. The rotten palm leaves gave way, and we were out the other side, flying again.

I checked for damage. The engine seemed okay, and the prop wasn't vibrating. I radioed Joe that there wasn't an airstrip, just two houses about a half mile apart.

I climbed up to where the big Queen Air circled, and we resumed our journey south. Joe was down to 15 minutes of fuel. I had a little over 30 minutes. It was still raining lightly, and our situation looked hopeless. Pedro took over the radio on the Queen Air so that Joe could give the airplane his undivided attention. Five minutes passed. I began to pray fervently to God. I told God that if He got us all safely down on the ground, I would never again in all my life have anything to do with a drug operation.

I checked my ADF and according to the San Jose beacon, we were hopelessly lost out over the jungle. I chose to ignore the ADF. Sometimes mineral deposits in the area caused it to read wrong. Pedro called me to tell me one of their engines had just quit due to fuel starvation. At this moment we flew out of the storm. I recognized the lights of Mapiripan ahead and the faint outline of the Guaviare River. Joe got the dead engine started again on another tank. He was using the last dregs in each of his tanks. The engine quit again and this time he had to feather it (which is an emergency procedure done to reduce drag by bringing the propeller blades of a dead engine parallel to the slipstream). I located the airfield we had taken off from almost three hours before and dove the 182 on it, hoping some-one would put some lights on it. A faint light appeared on one end of the airstrip, but Joe couldn't see it. I guided him around onto final. The Queen Air was low and to one side of the runway. It was hard to land at night with one engine inoperative. They ran through the top of a mango tree on short final, doing minor damage to the left wing. Finally, they were down.

I wondered why they didn't move the airplane off the runway. I waited for several minutes before finally deciding to land the 182, even though the Queen Air was in the middle of the runway. I landed and pulled off to one side of the strip. The 182 had less than 20 minutes fuel remaining. I started walking toward the house. There was an eerie silence and, I thought, that's funny! Where are Pedro and Joe?

It was now about 9:00 p.m. A three-quarter moon was beginning to rise on the horizon. The weather had cleared and I could see a few stars. There was a small house off to one side of the runway. I saw the faint glow of a dying wood fire in the open kitchen outside the house. Maybe that's where Pedro and Joe had gone, I thought. As I stumbled along through the bush-es to one side of the airstrip, I came across a path that seemed to head toward the house. It was uncanny; the runway had been lit, apparently with flashlights, but where were the people? I began to fear that something was wrong. It was too quiet. All of a sudden I heard the sharp clash of an M1 carbine slide being racked. A flashlight beam caught me square in the eyes. Five policemen stepped out of the bushes with their guns leveled in my direction. "Freeze where you are. Don't move," one of them yelled at me. My heart sank. After what seemed like an eternity of silence, although it was probably only a few seconds, the police commander called me by name. I recognized his voice. He was the same man who had been with me in the 182 the day the Air Force fighters had tried to shoot us down. Meanwhile, Pedro stepped out of the bushes behind the policemen. He had a huge Colt .44 magnum six-shooter. "You'll never take us alive," Pedro announced in a calm, smooth voice. "My men have you completely surrounded," Pedro bluffed. "Now let's be reasonable and talk this over." Back in the bushes, Joe coughed. The situation grew very tense. The policemen didn't know how to react. I expected shooting to start at any moment, with me in the worse possible position. I told Pedro that this police commander was my friend, and to put away his gun. The policemen, at a command from their leader, lowered their carbines. My friend came forward and gave me a big *abraso,* or hug. He then introduced me to his men as the man who had saved his life during the air attack. I introduced him to Pedro and everyone shook hands. Latin America runs on a friendship system and this incident was a prime example. I learned from my friend that they, the police, had been the ones to light the runway with their flashlights. They had received a report about our 6 o'clock takeoff and had been investigating the incident when we happened to return three hours later. My friend, who knew my family background, wanted to know how in the world I had gotten myself involved in what was obviously a drug deal, even though the planes were empty. All Pedro's suave logic, that I had accepted hook, line, and sinker a few hours earlier, seemed utterly stupid as I tried to explain to this police chief how I had gotten involved with this whole mess. I have never before felt so ashamed and embarrassed. My friend heard me out and finally he said, "Well, one favor deserves another, and I certainly owe you one. So, I am going to let you all go this time. You had better watch it, though. You're liable to get killed flying around at night like this." The policemen informed me that the army patrol boat that we had worried about earlier had left the area.

I heard someone swearing a blue streak in English. The voice wasn't Joe's. I took a few steps in the direction the voice was coming from and came face to face with another American named Peter. Peter was about twenty-five years old, and he was mad. He now turned his attention to me and included me in his expletives. "You may think that you're Blankety-Blank good pilots," he cursed, "but what you did tonight was Blankety-Blank-Blank-Blank stupid." It turned out that Peter was trying to use the airfield we had just landed on to dispatch a DC-7 in the morning, to be loaded with 25 tons of marijuana. His men had been moving bales of pot and drums of aviation fuel up to the airstrip from the river when we landed. He was extremely upset with our arrival. He said we had compromised his whole operation even though he had paid off the law enforcement personnel for miles around.

Peter wanted to get rid of us so bad that he gave us seven drums of Av gas to fuel our planes with. We lost no time in rolling them over to the airplanes. Joe examined the damage to the left wing of the Queen Air. His remarks were unprintable. We couldn't find any fuel at all in the tanks. I couldn't even get any gas to come out of the fuel drains on the side I checked. We pumped six drums of Av gas into Joe's plane. Then we fueled my 182 with the remaining drum.

Joe wanted to know about all the chicken feathers he found clinging to the tail and sides of the 182. I told him about the chicken coop and we both rolled around on the ground laughing, breaking the tension. Our nerves had been wound up almost to the point of exploding and now we released our pent-up frustration.

As soon as we finished refueling, Pedro announced that since the weather had cleared and the moon was up, that we could now fly over to the airstrip where the marijuana was. Joe said, "No way." He was finished. This was his first involvement in something like this. He had learned his lesson. He just wanted to get a few hours sleep and then fly home empty. Pedro turned to me and offered me an additional sum of money if I would make two trips in the 182 over to the other airstrip and bring back the load for Joe's airplane. I explained to Pedro about my prayer and my promise to God. I told him we ought to be thankful that God had spared our lives.

Peter had been listening to our conversation all this time. Now he turned to me and asked, "Who the hell do you work for, anyway?"

I didn't say anything. Instead, I just looked at him. Peter sized me up for a while and I guess he started to notice that I was different from the type of guys he was used to dealing with. "No, don't tell me," he finally said. "You work for God. All the other members of my family are dedicated to God and they all pray for me. I'm the only black sheep. Every time I try to do something like what I'm doing now, God sends someone over to mess it all up for me. Sometimes I get the feeling that God isn't going to lay off until I give in to Him and straighten out."

Peter then refused to give Pedro any of his marijuana on credit. Joe said he couldn't haul any pot even if Pedro managed to come up with some because the timing of his re-entry into the U.S. had been upset. The officials he had bribed to let him in would now be off duty.

Joe and I stretched out in the Queen Air and tried to get a little sleep. Pedro seemed to have a one track mind, however. He went out and hired a speedboat, spending the rest of the night trying to negotiate some pot to load in Joe's airplane, whether Joe wanted to haul it or not. Pedro's mission was unsuccessful. No one would give him a load on credit.

Joe took off at dawn. Pedro and I left a few minutes later in the 182. Pedro was still trying to talk Joe into landing at the other strip to load. Once Joe was in the air though, he left and headed straight home. He had learned his lesson.

Peter's prophecy was correct. His DC-7 came in the morning, and the pilots saw Joe and me taking off. Peter's pilots thought we were the law, so they turned around and went home empty. I found out later Peter decided he couldn't win, fighting against the prayers of all his family, so he gave up and went back to the States.

Pedro and I also went home. We stopped on the way to find out why the guys at the other airstrip hadn't lit the bonfires for us the night before. We found them all banged up from the jeep accident. Pedro wasn't very happy with them, and that's putting it mildly. We ate breakfast and took off for Villavicencio. Upon arrival, I ran the 182 into the hanger and had the mechanics check it over for damage. I collapsed into a hammock at one end of the hanger. I was extremely frustrated and upset. I began to think over last night's events. I was even a little angry with God. It wasn't fair. Everyone else in the whole area was making money hand over fist from the drug trade. Here I was in dire financial trouble, and God wouldn't even let me make a measly ten grand to save my airplane from being repossessed. I had gotten into debt in the first place because I felt a desire to start the fish business and do great things for God's Kingdom with the profits. I would have never gotten into such huge debts just for myself. The mafia had been responsible for the fish business not making a profit lately. In doing this flight, I had felt justified in that I was going to receive money that I really had coming to me. It seemed to be a chance to recover some of my losses. God had very clearly taken another viewpoint. I should have been killed several times over in last night's episode. Obviously, God didn't have me in the same category as everyone else. I had placed my life under His authority at a very early age. Now He had just given me a crystal clear object lesson that He didn't want me involved in the drug trade in any way, shape, or form; not even to gain information for the government.

At this point my chain of thought was interrupted. The mechanic had walked over with a smirk on his face. He wanted to know how come there were chicken heads and pieces of chickens under the engine baffles and on top of 182's engine cylinders. Was I trying to invent a new way of frying chicken? If I wanted to franchise my new procedure, I would have to learn to pluck and clean the chickens first, because just running them through the prop was a little too messy! I gave a rueful grin as I remembered last night's chicken coop incident. I told the mechanic to mind his own business and to get back to work.

Several days later I stopped by Pedro's house again. Pedro growlingly informed me that I was now in bad trouble. His mafia friend was not only refusing to pay us anything for our night's work, but he was accusing me of being involved with the DEA, and was threatening to kill me. Pedro had talked them into meeting with me first, instead of them just putting out a contract on me like they would have normally done.

The meeting was very tense and bitter. I tried to deny having any connections with any government agents. The mafia leader looked at me coldly and informed me that his organization "owned" several people in the government and that he had complete information on my meeting with them. Pedro intervened for me at this point and told them that I had been caused a great deal of inconvenience and was actually being blamed in some circles for the mafia's airplane that had landed at our fish airstrip. Pedro said he could understand how I would want to go around to the various government agencies and clear myself of any charges that might be leveled at me. I also indignantly told the mafia leader that he had been the cause of many problems for me, both financial and political. Somehow I managed to slip off the hook. I went home that night, sick inside with the shocking realization that not even the government agents were exempt from being corrupted by the tremendous amounts of money being moved by the drug traffickers.

The lesson I learned was to stand me in good stead over the next few years. I had no desire at all to get mixed up in any more funny business on either side of the law. It was now crystal clear to me that the moral of this whole story is that "the end does NOT justify the means."

Unfortunately Pedro didn't learn his lesson. He was killed a year later in a DC-6 drug-related crash in the Caribbean. The Howard 350 at Chaparral was returned to the mafia by the Colombia government upon payment of a fine. A mafia pilot flew the empty airplane out of our airstrip almost a year after it had originally landed there. They landed at Mapiripan, and began to do some mechanical repairs on it prior to returning to the U.S. Then one day they loaded it with 1400 gallons of gas and four tons of marijuana for the return trip. It crashed and burned on take-off, killing everyone on board.

During the rest of 1978 and 1979 the U.S. government seemed to take a very lackadaisical attitude toward drug enforcement. I was happy to see the Reagan Administration take a much tougher stance on drug related issues and make great strides of progress in dealing with these types of problems. The only real solution, however, would be for the American people to simply quit buying drugs. We, the American people, need to wake up and see and treat drug addiction as the horrible problem that it is. The fact that it takes place in slow-motion shouldn't be allowed to blind us to the reality of the consequences of drug use in our society.

Chapter Nine

October 1, 1983

I was seated at my split-palm desk in the jungle, pecking away at the typewriter my abductors had given me. The Spanish version of this book was coming along nicely. Yesterday Vicente had arrived in camp. He had taken some Polaroid pictures of me to prove to my father that I was still alive. It appeared that negotiations for my release were now underway. The guerrillas had asked my family to send a known article of clothing for them to photograph me in. My father sent a Bible instead. Vicente took a nice picture of me holding up the Bible. I also received a book of cartoons by Phil Saint, a book on bear hunting in Alaska, and some candy. As the next page of this book neared completion, the guerrillas gathered around to read it as soon as it came out of the typewriter. Realizing I had a captive audience, I decided to give them all a dose of their own medicine. I started to talk to them about the candy I had received. It was a package of Giant Sweet Tarts from the States. I told them that U.S. candy was vastly superior to anything they had ever tasted. The package contained three large candies, colored red, yellow, and purple. I took out the purple one and started to munch on it, smacking my lips and telling my audience all the while how good it was. Then I took out the red one and divided it into little pieces. I offered a piece to each one of the guerrillas. They eagerly accepted. I patiently waited until they had all finished eating their candy. Then I stood up with a happy smile on my face and exclaimed, "I won! That red candy had poison in it, and now you will all die in five minutes!" Nancy turned white as a sheet. Looks of pure terror flashed across their faces. One of them, I think it was Mariano, pointed his gun at me and told me if he died that he would take me with him. I gave him a weak grin and finished typing my page. After a tense five minutes had passed, I told them that it was okay and I was just joking with them. I told them, "Now that you know what it feels like, you can see that it isn't right to terrorize people." Then I laughed and laughed. They didn't seem to think my little joke was very funny though. I didn't get anymore candy for a while, but I figured it was worth it.

Jaime, the squad leader, had told me earlier that he had joined the guerrilla movement because he wanted to fight for peace and freedom. I told him now that it isn't possible to reap peace when we sow violence and terror. If we want peace we must sow mercy and love. The only way to do that is to end our rebellion against God. Jaime picked up the Bible and began to leaf through it. He told me he had always been curious about the Bible, but had never read it. Over the next few days, Jaime came over and talked with me from time to time. Sometimes he would even borrow my Bible and read it for up to an hour at a time.

One day Arnuval and Giovani came over and started asking me more questions about my beliefs. "If Christianity is the solution to all of man's problems," they questioned, "how come it hasn't worked? Christianity has had almost 2000 years in which to change the world. Obviously, it has failed. The world's problems are getting worse all the time. All this religious hogwash you're talking about only confuses the real issues."

I thought for a minute and then answered. "It seems to me that there is a difference between true Christianity and organized religion. Organized religion can go one of two basic routes: The first is when men take a concept of God and utilize it to build their own kingdom instead of God's Kingdom. In this type of religion, men decide what the essential beliefs about God are and organize how the church is to function. When carried to its logical conclusion, this philosophy results in clever men utilizing the church for their own gratification, be it money, power, or prestige.

The second is when the men organizing the religion or church really believe in God and want to be approved of and accepted by Him. They then proceed to think up their own plans to further God's Kingdom. Large quantities of time, money, effort, and talent are spent on these important projects for God. These devout people feel that God will be very pleased with them for all the big favors that they are doing for Him. It was in this category that I had started the fish business. I was sure God would bless my business because of all the wonderful favors I was going to do for Him with all the money I was going to make.

True Christianity is a little different. True Christianity is the Kingdom of God. The Kingdom of God can be defined as whatever God is the King of. In other words, if we want to function within this Kingdom of God, then we must receive Jesus Christ as the King. As King He has the right to make the plans, not us. He is the one who does the big favors for us, not the other way around. He can look into the future and we can't. God could have foreseen all the problems I was headed for when I started the fish business. I couldn't, so I had to blunder on through them. There aren't very many of us willing to let God be the King. We always think we can do things better on our own. This is why the organized religion we call Christianity hasn't worked. We can't blame all the world's problems on God if we refuse to let Him make the plans. Our world problems are the result of our own human short-sighted selfishness. We have no case against God whatsoever."

As the days passed, I began to notice subtle undercurrents of fear and terror within the guerrilla camp that had not been apparent at first glance. These young men and women who had appeared so good-natured and happy at first were really not that way at all. Every once in a while I would catch hints of something very sinister happening behind the scenes. Some of the conversations I had with various guards had been overheard by young Alberto. He had reported them in a twisted fashion to the powers that be. This had resulted in some of the guards being disciplined. I was informed that I could no longer speak to these guards. Several of the guards would still speak to me in whispers, but we had to be continually alert for the presence of "Rabbit Ears," as I nicknamed young Alberto. Alberto was too young at 14 to seriously question the guerrillas' ideology. He was involved in an absolute hero-worship of the guerrilla commander, Vicente, giving him unquestioning loyalty and obedience. The leaders relied on the younger guerrillas such as Alberto to keep them informed of anything abnormal occurring within the camp. Alberto was trained and encouraged to spy and tattle-tale on his own buddies. Discipline was so strict within the camp that no one dared to get into an argument with anyone. The consequences were too severe. Therefore, the only alternative for the average guerrilla was to superficially joke and jest, while deep down inside he was smoldering with bitterness, resentment, anger, and hatred.

Gradually I became acquainted with the real way in which the guerilla camp was being run. I was told in confidence by a friendly guard that capital punishment was employed from time to time among the guerrillas themselves. If one of the guerrillas had a drug or alcohol problem, questioned an order given to him by his superior or questioned the Marxist ideology ingrained into all of them, punishment for a first offense was severe discipline, i.e., no cigarettes, no trips to town, extra guard duty, etc. Punishment for a habitual or repeat offender was death. The person involved would be shot in front of the rest of the troops. This seemed to have quite a noticeable effect on any other would-be offenders. The rank and file guerrillas lived in fear deep down inside, never knowing when some young zealot like "Rabbit Ears" might decide to turn them in for some serious offense, be it real or imagined. As I had gotten to know my captors better and better, I was shocked at some of the stories they had to tell about their lives. My guards said it would be okay if I asked questions and let them talk, so I started asking each one about his family and his personal life. I don't have time to relate all that I heard, so one example will have to suffice.

Young 19-year-old Elkin, the squad explosive expert, had been the son of a Colombian army officer. His father had displayed a real *macho* attitude toward his wife and kids. During Elkin's early years his father had repeatedly abused and mistreated his mother. Finally, his mother's brother, inflamed by what he saw, had taken Elkin and his three brothers and turned them over to the guerrillas to be raised as terrorists as a revenge against the father. Elkin informed me, with a bitter frown, that he would shoot his father if he ever found him. His younger brother had been shot four times in the chest by a machine gun in an ambush set for the guerrillas by the government. He had recovered somewhat but was still an invalid, maimed for life. Tears of hatred ran down Elkin's cheeks as he told me this, and my heart went out to him. He had now been six years with the guerrilla rebels without ever hearing a word about his mother's whereabouts or well-being.

For a while I couldn't reconcile some of the negative things that were going on in camp with Jaime, the leader. All the men obviously liked the young leader and would follow him with great enthusiasm whatever the circumstances. It took me a while to figure out what was really going on. Another person, not Jaime, was responsible for squad discipline. I identified the disciplinarian as Giovani. Jaime was merely the military leader. Giovani wielded the real power behind the scenes. The men really liked Jaime. They displayed no emotion at all towards Giovani. I learned from one of the guards that this concept of dual leadership was in effect throughout the guerrilla organization at all levels. Gradually I began to learn the ropes, as to how to survive in the guerrilla camp. I had to be very careful what I said to Giovani and Alberto or I was liable to wind up in hot water.

It turned out that our camp was located in the jungle not far from several large coca fields. As many of the guerrillas as could be spared from guard duty or other camp chores were sent over to pick coca leaves for processing into cocaine. In fact, later on in my captivity, I was held for a while right in a cocaine lab that was being run by the guerrillas. This was all extremely interesting to me, given my college chemistry background. All the supplies for the coca fields—calcium bicarbonate, gasoline, potassium permanganate, sulfuric acid, and ammonium hydroxide—would come right past our camp on their way to a final destination.

One day I asked Giovani why the guerrillas were involved with cocaine. Wasn't this one of the corrupt, immoral problems that was causing social injustice? If they were really trying to make the world into a better place to live, why didn't they stamp out the narcotics traffic instead of trying to take over control of it? Giovani replied that the individual members of the guerrilla organization were prohibited from using cocaine. But, he grinned broadly, "If the corrupt capitalists in North America want to buy cocaine, we'll produce and sell them all they need. We will destroy your corrupt society with its own money. The revolution is being financed by Americans who use cocaine!"

Chapter Ten

Javier, the tall, scar-faced guerrilla who had replaced Manuel, was the strong, silent type. Under his rough exterior was a shy, sensitive personality. One day he opened up to me a little and told me he had joined the guerrillas after his wife had run away from him with another man. He had a young daughter he hadn't seen in three years. Having joined the guerrillas in a rash mood of depression, he now longingly remembered married life and his little daughter whom he would probably never see again. Rank and file guerrillas like Javier were not allowed to marry. Only high ranking commanders like Vicente were allowed to have a wife. I had a picture of my wife and daughter in my pocket. All the guerrillas were very interested in discussing marriage vs. their policy of having sex without a long-term commitment to the other person. Some of them showed strong homosexual tendencies. Most of them seemed to feel an intense loneliness deep inside. They would try to cover this up with frivolous banter and jokes, but every once in awhile I could see the need for fulfillment as an individual that each one kept guarded deep down inside. I decided the best example to use regarding personal happiness and inner fulfillment in a long-term marriage commitment was my own case.

Villavicencio, Colombia, 1979

Being an American carries a tremendous amount of social status and prestige in Colombia. I struck up a friendship with

a man named Carlos Herrera[1] who was a member of the social elite, his family having a lot of wealth and power. Carlos
owned a spray-plane company. He employed the best aviation
mechanics in town and his aircraft maintenance was first class.
I had flown into Carlos' crop dusting base in the 170 one day,
and a lasting friendship developed. Carlos took me under his
wing and provided me with excellent maintenance for the old
decrepit 170 at a very reasonable charge. He also taught me a
lot about flying in the jungle. Carlos was an excellent flight instructor with over 9,000 hours flying DC-3's, PBY's, and crop
dusters. He would sit down with me and patiently teach me
the ropes of jungle flying. If he ever caught me showing off or
horsing around in an airplane, his normally easy-going personality would become serious. He would say, "Aviation is not a
circus. Now shape up and fly right." By the time I bought the
182, Carlos had helped mold me into a smooth, professional
pilot, capable of staying calm even in the worst emergency.
Better yet, he had taught me to think ahead in order to avoid
most dangerous situations.

After a while, Carlos decided to do me yet another favor. He
decided I needed to marry into one of the wealthy, high society
families. Soon I was being invited to all the major social func-
tions. Carlos was hard at work spreading propaganda about
me to all the eligible, rich young ladies. I was soon the center
of attraction at all the parties. It became clear that whenever I
wanted to get married, I could choose from among several outstanding young ladies of very wealthy and powerful families.

Deep inside of me, however, was a dream. I could picture
a certain blend of physical, intellectual, and moral attributes
in my mind's eye of the girl I wanted to marry. None of those
high society girls seemed to fit that image. I would never seem
to get very far in my relationship with any given girl before
discovering some obvious defect that would cause me to think
twice about marriage, so I would terminate our relationship.
I hesitated to get into a marriage just for money and power.
My dad was very concerned for me at this time. He always

---

[1]   No relation to the Carlos mentioned in Chapter One of this book.

had some American girl he was promoting. Dad introduced me to many excellent girls, but none of them seemed to fit my dream.

I was now 24 years old. I began to lose hope of ever finding my "dream girl." Maybe I would just have to compromise and do the best I could. I narrowed the field of marriage prospects down to about four choices. Every evening I would spend some time praying that God would let me make the right choice. I felt uneasy and was scared to death of getting married to the wrong person. One night I thought to myself, "If God could create me with a dream in my mind of a specific girl who could completely satisfy my desire for a wife, then I think God could also make the girl who would be the personification of my dream and be perfectly compatible with me in every way. She might not seem perfect to anyone else; she would be designed especially for me." I thought, "If this is true, then I had better let God choose the girl I am to marry. If I make the choice and blow it like I am prone to do from time to time, my life will be miserable." I prayed again and told God I wanted Him to choose me a wife. I expected God would probably pick one of the four girls I had been considering as final prospects. I was astonished when thoughts of an entirely different girl flooded my brain. "Impossible!" I told God. "You can't mean her. Why, she is from a poor Catholic family. Her mother is even an Indian. I don't mind that, but it's just not socially acceptable in Colombia for me to marry into a family like that." An inner voice, deep inside me, seemed to say, "Well, you asked me to make the choice for you, and she is it. If I were you, I would get with it and court her before someone else gets into the act and takes her away from you. You haven't even been nice to her recently."

I continued to think about Marina, the girl that had popped into my mind. She really was extremely attractive. In fact, she was downright beautiful, far surpassing the other girls I had been considering. Still deep in thought, it suddenly dawned on me that Marina was the only girl I had ever gone out with who had never presented an obvious character defect, such as being stuck-up, or lying to me about something, or chasing me. I had never considered marrying her though. I just treated her as a friend. How could I have been so blind? That last part about not having treated her nice recently hit me right between the eyes. I remembered our last meeting.

It was November 10, 1979, during the annual festival in our town of San Martin. I had a date with Marina to pick her up at 7:00 p.m., and take her to a folk music contest. On the way over to her house I ran into some old acquaintances whom I hadn't seen for years. When I finally pried myself loose, it was 8:00 p.m. I hurried over to Marina's house intending to apologize to her for the delay. She answered my knock on the door, and I was surprised to see that she was wearing her nightgown. She then coldly informed me that if I expected to take her out, I would have to come back the next night at 7 o'clock sharp, and that now she was going to bed. With that she slammed the door in my face. "Women sure are funny sometimes," I thought as I left. The next night I arrived at her house at 6:55 p.m. Marina was all dressed up, and we left, heading for the town square where there was to be folk dancing in the streets. When we arrived at the town square, who should we run into but my friend, Carlos Herrera. He was accompanied by his wife, and several society girls who knew me. At this point they unfortunately decided to each greet me with a kiss. When I finally got myself untangled I turned around and Marina was gone. "That's strange," I thought, "I didn't even get to introduce her to Carlos. Well, if she wants to be like that, that's her problem," I muttered to myself.

Bob and Carol Geiger, an American couple who were down working with my father, joined us, and we settled down to watch the colorful folk festival. San Martin is a very historic little town that was established over 450 years ago. I was engrossed in conversation with Carlos and his friends when Carol leaned over to me and whispered, "What did you ever do to make that girl who came in with you (Marina) so mad. She just walked by with another guy and stopped right in front of you and gave him a big kiss. You were so engrossed in your conversation that you didn't even notice. She stomped out of here mad as hops."

A couple of weeks later I felt bad about the incident and wished I could apologize. Marina, however, had left with some relatives and was in the city of Cali on the other side of Colombia.

This had all happened several months before. Now I didn't know what to do. I might have to travel all over Colombia searching for her. What if she was still mad at me? I started getting depressed as I wondered what course of action to pursue. "It must not be impossible," I thought, "or God would have never brought this all up." I decided to go over to Marina's house the next night. Maybe one of her family could tell me where she was.

I felt some butterflies in my stomach as I headed over to her house at about 7:30 p.m. San Martin is a small town, and I was on foot. As I approached the last corner, I was astonished to see Marina and one of her girlfriends walking down the street toward me. With much fear and trembling, I walked up to them and said, "Hi, where are you going?"

"We're going to a party," Marina replied. I noticed they were both all dressed up. With my heart in my throat I asked, "Do you have a date?" "No," Marina replied. "I just got back from Cali last night and no one knows I'm back yet." It turned out that the girlfriend had come over to Marina's house with the sole purpose of inviting her to the party, which was at the girlfriend's house. I then timidly asked Marina if she would accept an invitation from me to the local ice cream parlor so that I could talk with her. Then I could take her to the party afterwards. The girlfriend said that she had to get right home, so we went by her house first, and then Marina and I wandered off in the direction of the ice cream parlor. I don't know if it was the effects of the full moon or if it was the lovely white lace dress that Marina was wearing, but we never made it to our intended destination. We meandered off into the municipal fairgrounds, deserted at this time of the year. All of a sudden she was in my arms, and I was telling her that I loved her. She told me that she had missed me. We spent the evening strolling around in the moonlight, talking. Then I escorted Marina back to her home and she kissed me good night. I went back to my house walking on air.

The next morning I woke up and mentally kicked myself. "Now you've done it," I accused myself. "You have really put your foot in it now. Whatever possessed you to say all those things to Marina last night? Now if you ever have to terminate your relationship, her heart will be broken." I began to wonder if Marina were really the right girl for me. As I meditated about this situation, I remembered two things my father had taught me about how to choose the right wife.

"First," my dad had told me, "take a good look at the girl's mother. If you can't stand your future mother-in-law, then think twice about marrying her daughter because in twenty years your wife will probably be very much like her mother is right now.

"Second, pay attention to how your prospective bride treats her father. If she still respects and admires her father, even though she knows his weak points and defects, the chances are that she will still respect and admire you even after she gets to know your weak points and problem areas."

I decided to apply these two tests to Marina's situation. I was tremendously impressed with Marina's mother after I got to know her. She was a wonderful example of a devoted wife and mother. Her figure was still trim and shapely even after having eight children. I thought, "If Marina looks and acts like her mother in twenty or thirty years, I will be more than satisfied."

I then turned my attention to her father. On the surface he seemed to just be a typical small town politician. Underneath, however, I soon began to see a very strong, moral, and family-oriented character. It was quite clear that Marina respected and admired her father. In fact, none of my future father-in-law's eight children had ever rebelled against him. They all felt the same way Marina did toward her father. I thought this was a re-markable feat on his part in this present age of parent-teenager conflict.

My parents were planning to leave in a week or so for the United States. They would be gone three or more months. My brother and my sisters would be going with them. I would be left alone in Colombia "holding the fort." I decided to introduce Marina to my parents before they left because I might be engaged to her before they returned.

Dad immediately called me off to one side and gave me a stern lecture about not getting involved with Colombian girls. "Why, no telling what their motives are," he said. "And no telling what her family's motives are." After Dad had taken this tangent it was impossible for me to explain my true feelings about Marina, so I said nothing. I did have a heart-to-heart talk with my mother before she left and she promised to work on explaining things to Dad for me.

During the school year Marina had been staying with her grandmother in San Martin. At about the same time my family left for the U.S., Marina moved to Mapiripan to be with her parents. This was not far from Chaparral. I was flying a lot of fish out of Chaparral and Tomachipan during this period. All day long my thoughts would somehow seem to center on Marina and at the end of each day's flying, the 182 somehow seemed to wind up in Mapiripan for the night automatically. I can remember trying to coldly calculate the pros and cons of my marrying Marina until one day it finally dawned on me that I was madly in love with her. In fact, I was so head over heels in love with her that I was having trouble eating, sleeping, and flying the airplane. I had several close calls with the plane. On several occasions I wound up flying through severe thunderstorms, just to visit Marina in Mapiripan. I finally decided that I had better ask her to marry me quickly before I killed myself. It was dangerous to fly around in a daze thinking about her all the time.

The next weekend I was invited to a picnic with Marina and her family. I had already talked with my future father-in-law as to my intentions toward his daughter, as is the custom in Colombia. He had given me his blessing, but of course the final decision was up to Marina. I called her off to one side after the picnic and asked her to marry me. She was shocked. Marina had just turned eighteen and she had been thinking of marriage in the distant future. I pressed her for an answer, but she wouldn't say yes or no. She wanted time to think about my proposal.

Two weeks passed. The suspense was almost unbearable for me. By now I had come to the conclusion that I couldn't live without Marina. She was one in a million. If I ever lost her, I knew that I would never be the same. I started presenting my case to Marina's sisters, trying to get them to intervene in my behalf and talk Marina into marrying me before I went insane. Matters came to a head when I was invited to a birthday party for Marina's younger sister, Clemencia, who was fourteen years old. It was an evening party, so I arrived at about 7:00 p.m. Unknown to me, another girl at the party had dreamed up a devilish scheme to break up my relationship with Marina so that she could make a try for me. This other girl had mixed up an Indian love potion named *chundu*. Since she was the one serving the refreshments at the party, it was easy for her to slip some *chundu* in my glass before she served it to me. She thought the love potion would make me love her instead of Marina.

I had finished about half of the contents of my glass when I started to feel funny. I got up, and left the living room, heading into the kitchen. By the time I reached the kitchen my sense of balance was severely impaired. There was a hardwood post in the center of the kitchen holding up one of the beams to the roof. I reached out and clung to it with one hand trying to clear my head.

My future mother-in-law entered the kitchen. I barely managed a weak grin. Inside I thought, "Oh, no, I wonder if she thinks I arrived drunk to her daughter's party!" She looked at me, and handed me a cup of coffee. I tried to drink it as best I could knowing full well that if I let go of the hardwood post I would fall down onto the floor. Finally, Marina's older sister, Rosario, came in and noticed my predicament. Noticing that I was very pale and dizzy, she asked me if I wanted to lie down. I told her what I thought had happened and she helped me into one of the bedrooms and put me to bed. The girl responsible for this little episode got scared and split the party when she saw Rosario put me to bed.

I lay there in bed, so dizzy that I could not sit up. Inside I felt as if my emotions were having a tug-of-war. I asked Rosario to call Marina. I felt a strong desire to be with her. Marina came in and spent a couple of minutes with me and then left. She was used to living in a small town and was scared to be in the bedroom for very long for fear of sparking gossip. Therefore, she decided to spend her time out in the living room with all of the guests and head off any rumors. My desire for Marina became more and more intense as I continued to feel worse and worse. This *chundu* was really bad news and I must have been given an overdose. I couldn't understand why Marina wouldn't stay with me. Suspicion flashed in my mind. What was she doing out in the living room? With whom was she talking? Was someone else trying to take her away from me?

It was almost midnight before my head finally cleared enough for me to be able to stagger back out to the kitchen. Most of the guests had gone home, but a few still lingered in the living room. I sat down on the kitchen table (all the chairs were in the other room) with my back up against the wall. The table was placed near the doorway leading to the dining room. Marina came through the doorway and I grabbed her, putting my arms around her in a bear hug. "Let me go, you're embarrassing me," she whispered to me. I said, "No, I'm not going to let you go until you give me a straight answer about whether or not you'll marry me." "You're holding me too tight," she hissed. "Let me go and we'll talk in the morning."

"I won't let go until you tell me if you will marry me." "You're drunk!" She exclaimed. "It's not my fault," I said. "Somebody fed me a love potion and it really spaced me out, but it's wearing off and I feel better all the time." "You just want to marry me because I'm pretty," Marina said sadly. "When you find out some of my problems and weak points, you won't want to have anything more to do with me. Why do you want to marry a poor half-breed like me when you can pick and choose among the very highest society?" I said, "I love you just the way you are, problems and everything. I can't face life without you. I think you are God's choice for me." She said, "I still think that you are drunk, but yes." "Yes what?" I asked sharply. "Yes, I'll marry you," she whispered. "Now will you let go of me and stop making such a scene?" I clung to her even tighter and started to cry. She broke down and started to cry too, and we really did put on a scene. I don't remember how long this all lasted, but the evening finally ended with one of my future brothers-in-laws hanging a hammock in the hall and helping me into it. Marina tucked a blanket around me and kissed me good night.

I woke up the next morning feeling like a heel. "No telling what my future in-laws think of me," I thought. Fortunately they all knew about the *chundu* and didn't seem to hold anything against me for last night's incident. Better still, I went for a walk with Marina and she confirmed her decision to marry me. "I really love you and wanted to marry you all along," she said. "Then why did you cause me so much grief?" I asked indignantly. "I just wanted to find out if you really loved me," she replied, smiling sweetly.

I told Marina that I thought we ought to get married right away. She was aghast at the idea of us getting married while my parents were still in the States. "Your family will never accept me if we do that," she worried. "Just trust me," I replied. "This is the way it has to be. I know what I am doing."

In Colombia there are only two ways of getting legally married. You can get married by a judge in court, a procedure that takes a good six months of paperwork. Or you can get married in the Catholic church. I knew that Marina's family would want the Catholic wedding. I also knew that my dad would want the legal wedding followed by a ceremony in a Protestant church. I knew that I could not take waiting for six months for the wedding while this type of explosive situation existed between the families. If we just went out and got married, I was fairly certain that my family would accept Marina and we would sidestep a problem that could bring lasting damage to the future relationship of the two families. After I convinced Marina of all this, I had even a harder time convincing her mother. After I convinced her mother, I ran into another problem.

I was informed by the Catholic priest I consulted that it was impossible for him to marry me to Marina because I wasn't a Catholic. There was a past history of friction between Catholics and Protestants in Colombia and this type of thing just wasn't done. I consulted several other priests and received the same answer. I could be married in the Catholic church only if I allowed myself to be baptized as a Catholic first. I felt my marriage vows should be directly made to God and not to any sectarian church. I felt that it would be wrong for me to join the Catholic church just so they would marry me. My dad was going to have a hard enough time accepting a Catholic wedding at all. There seemed to be no solution in sight. My parents were due back from the U.S. in less than four weeks. I began to pray. I told God that since this marriage seemed to be His idea in the first place, that He would have to work things out, because I couldn't seem to get anywhere.

I remembered that there was one priest I hadn't talked to yet. His name was Father Joel Martinez, and he presided over the parish of San Martin. He had a reputation of being very strict, so I hadn't even considered approaching him. I finally went to see him and found out that he was a dedicated Christian. He listened to my story and decided to help me. He felt he could convince the bishop to issue us a special dispensation for a marriage of mixed religion. It was Friday. Father Martinez promised me an answer on Monday morning.

Marina and I went to see Father Martinez early Monday morning and the answer was yes; all the paper work was in order. He then informed us we were required to take a pre-marriage orientation class. The next class was due to begin in three weeks. I nervously explained to Father Martinez that we didn't have three weeks. He eyed us suspiciously and Marina blushed. I hurriedly explained the situation with my parents and how I felt it was important to proceed with the ceremony as soon as possible. Father Martinez said, "Well, I have a very full schedule this month, but I do have one free night and that just happens to be tomorrow night. If you will come over at 9:00 p.m. sharp, I will give you a special marriage orientation class. Then I could marry you on Thursday."

The next day we feverously began to prepare for the wedding. Marina needed some things, so we went shopping in Villavicencio. On the way home, there was a terrible storm and the bus we were on broke down. It was 11:45 p.m. when we finally arrived in San Martin. It looked like we were out of luck. Father Martinez would be in bed and he was a stickler for rules. We had just missed our only opportunity for the marriage orientation class, and I knew Father Martinez would not make an exception and marry us without it. Our hopes were dashed.

Marina said, "Well, let's go knock on his door anyway. What have we got to lose?" It was with much fear and trembling that we knocked on the parsonage door at midnight. Father Martinez got up and opened the door. He invited us in and made us each a cup of coffee when he saw that we were wet and shivering. Then he spent from midnight to three a.m. giving us a special marriage orientation class. The sound advice of Father Martinez was to stand us in very good stead many times during our first year of married life.

The wedding was now set for Thursday, two days away, at the 5:00 a.m. mass. My financial situation was now a complete disaster. Many of my bank loans were now overdue. I was being hounded by lawyers from one of the major banks. I had taken to writing post-dated checks in order to obtain credit in the stores, so I could keep the fish business running. Some of these checks were overdue. In Colombia, a bad check can result in an immediate jail sentence with no bail. To top it all off our mechanic had started up the 182 to heat the oil prior to changing it. He left the plane running unattended on the ramp. The parking brake slipped, and the plane took off across the ramp and hit a parked car whose owner was threatening to sue me for damages. The propeller was demolished and the engine damaged. Repairs would cost almost $12,000.00. Fortunately I had rebuilt the 170 and had it running on an overhauled chrome engine that some of our friends in the United States had given us.

I now owed quite a bit of money. With my credit bad there was no way I could raise the money to repair the 182. Without the 182 I was doomed. The 170 didn't have the payload or the range to fly deep into the jungle where the money-making flights originated. It would only be a matter of time now before I would be foreclosed on and probably would be put in jail to boot for writing bad checks. If I could somehow get the 182 running, there was a faint possibility that I might be able to keep enough money coming in to stave off my creditors. The engine and the prop to the 182 had now been overhauled, but the Cessna Company wouldn't let me have them until I paid the full $12,000.00 because I owed so many overdue payments on the airplane. My insurance had refused to cover the accident.

At this precise instant, the day before the wedding, my friend Armando showed up. The last time I had seen Armando he had been the head of the secret police for our area. He informed me that he had resigned his job. He was now making a fortune smuggling marijuana and cocaine. He had heard that I was in financial difficulties so he came over to see if I needed some help. I told him about my problem with the 182. "No problem," he said. "If you had the money, how long would it take you to get the plane flying?" "Oh, about three days," I replied. "It's a deal," Armando said. "What's the deal?" I asked.

"I'll give you the money you need to get your prop and engine out of hock," continued Armando. "In four days I need you to fly a shipment of drugs up to the Guajira peninsula in northern Colombia and then we're even. I'll need more flights from time to time and I think I can advance you money against future flying if you need it. In fact, I have my brief case full of money right now. See, I'm not kidding. You don't have to worry about a thing. I'm representing some very wealthy and influential people. Security is no problem for us. It is impossible for you to get caught on this mission. Everything has been taken care of."

"I can't do it, Armando," I replied. "I'm getting married tomorrow, and besides, you know I have a strict policy against having anything to do with drugs." Armando didn't want to take no for an answer. He wanted me to put the wedding off for a week. He said, "What good will it do you to get married if you go bankrupt afterwards. Think it over and discuss it with your fiancée. I'll be back in two hours for your answer."

If I hadn't been under such terrible financial pressure, I wouldn't even have considered Armando's offer. Now I thought about the consequences of my going bankrupt, the embarrassment to our family, and of my new wife-to-be. Maybe I should do just this one flight for Armando, and get the 182 flying again. Then I would be able to continue my normal, legal jungle flying and pay my bills. Suddenly I remembered back to my night flight with Pedro several years before. I remembered that the end does not justify the means, and God had very clearly taught me that lesson. I knew what I had to do. When Armando returned, I firmly and forcefully told him that I couldn't accept his offer in any way, shape, or form. Finally Armando grew tired of arguing and picked up his briefcase and left. I breathed a sigh of relief. I began to feel a firm conviction that I had done the right thing. In fact, after Armando had left, it seemed silly to me to even have considered his offer. After experiencing what was clearly God's hand in lining up my marriage, I began to feel a growing confidence that God would see me through this financial crisis if I just kept my nose clean.

Marina and I were married on Thursday, August 28, 1980. Father Martinez performed the ceremony at 5:00 a.m. The ceremony seemed very significant to me. When we got to the part where Marina and I each held our two candles together, merging the two separate flames into one, I was choked with emotion. We both felt a strong commitment to one another and to God. The fact that we were both from different church backgrounds seemed irrelevant.

I had tried to keep the wedding a secret, but about 50 of my closest friends found out about it and gave us a breakfast wedding reception at a local motel. From there we rented a taxi for a five-hour ride over the scenic Andes Mountains into Bogota, the capital city of Colombia. Marina was happy, but very tired. She fell asleep with her head on my lap as we traveled over the winding mountain road. It was a clear day, and I was awed by the great beauty of the 14,000-foot high mountains. Crystal streams rushed by along the road from time to time. At one point I could see three spectacular waterfalls simultaneously. I looked down at the sleeping, almost angelic face of my new wife and a great sense of responsibility came over me. She trusted me completely. Would I be able to live up to that trust?

Would I be able to provide for her and for our future children? I decided to forget my financial troubles until after our honeymoon.

That evening we boarded a jetliner in Bogota for a two-hour flight to San Andres Island in the Caribbean. I had written another post-dated check to a friendly travel agent for the tickets. We spent a very enjoyable two weeks in this tropical island paradise. I had just received a new credit card, so I was able to charge all of our expenses.

On the third day of our honeymoon I was reading the newspaper when an item caught my eye. There had been a drug bust in the Guajira. The details weren't too clear, but it appeared to have been my friend Armando and a pilot he had hired. A special army patrol had caught them landing with a shipment of drugs. Their airplane had been confiscated and they were both facing the possibility of long prison terms. I began to praise God that I hadn't listened to Armando.

I sent a telegram to my sister Sharon that just said, Honeymoon/San Andres/Love Russ. Then I wrote a long letter to my parents trying to explain the situation. Back in the U.S. everyone thought the telegram was just a joke, but the letter really shook them up. My parents were shocked that they hadn't even been invited to the wedding, but they took it quite well.

Marina and I returned to San Martin. I began to work with renewed dedication in order to face my creditors. I landed several well-paying contracts with the 170. Money started to come in, and I was able to pay off the credit card and some of the past dated checks. I was amazed at how getting married changed my outlook toward financial matters. God began to deal with me on financial responsibility. I longed to be completely free of debt. I could see that I was really a slave of my debtors. I owed so much money, that prior to my marriage I hadn't even been able to produce enough income to meet the interest payments on all the loans relating to the fish business. Compound interest is very subtle in the way it can turn a seemingly stable financial situation into a nightmare if the business suffers a few unforeseen setbacks. The bank presidents who had been so friendly and eager to make me a client of their bank, showed no mercy now that I was in deep financial trouble. Embargo proceedings were initiated against me at various levels. The lawyers' fees alone were astronomical. It soon became very clear that I would have to quickly come up with a very large sum of money or we would go completely under.

My parents had been delayed in the U.S. all this time, but I finally received a telegram giving the date of their arrival. I decided to go into Bogota with Marina and meet them at the airport. This resulted in our first marriage fight. Marina was scared to death of going with me and facing her in-laws. I had to put a lot of pressure on her in order to get her to accompany me. We met my family at the airport and everything went well, just like I figured it would when I married Marina. Dad invited us to lunch at a fine restaurant as his way of showing us there were no hard feelings.

Several months later, Dad called me aside and told me that I had done the right thing in regard to my marriage. I was glad to hear this because throughout my life I have rarely done anything against his wishes. Dad told me he thought Marina was the right wife for me and said that he couldn't figure out how or where I had found her. He said he thought I had an ideal marriage and was glad that no one had had a chance to mess it up.

Marina and I had made it very clear to each other from the start that we wanted God to be at the center of our marriage. One night we discussed the growing, lucrative cocaine traffic. Several friends of ours were making a lot of money in the drug trade. Moral and social stigmas against the cultivation and trafficking of cocaine seemed to be breaking down in Colombia until it seemed like almost everyone was either in on the trafficking or else wanted to be. Marina and I decided to sever our ties with some of our friends in order to avoid being associated with the trade. Marina was fearful that I might get drawn into the drug business due to the enormous financial pressure I was under as I tried to save my business from bankruptcy.

The next morning another old friend of mine drove up to our house in an expensive new car. He had a wealthy "mafioso" with him from the city of Medellin, the capitol of the South American drug trade. They wanted to give me 6,000,000

Colombian Pesos (about $100,000,00 U.S.) to buy coca base for them. Coca base is unrefined cocaine. As a pilot I would be able to fly to the areas where the coca base could be cheaply obtained. It was an opportunity for me to make a lot of money. They wanted to do a deal of this size several times a month, and they had the money with them, ready to turn over to me with no strings attached. They said that they would return in a week for the coca base.

This time I did not even think twice about my reply. I told them in no uncertain terms that my relationship with God just wouldn't allow me to even consider their offer. I then proceeded to tell them in a diplomatic manner what I thought of the drug trafficking, I consider drug trafficking to really be trafficking with the souls of the human beings that are being destroyed by drugs. I knew that God's favor was much more important than my financial problems. I had a gut feeling that very soon the Mafioso drug traffickers and the corrupt, bribe receiving authorities who were catering to them, would reap what they had sown. They cautioned me to remain silent concerning their offer and drove away.

I began to pray that God would intervene in my financial situation. I admitted to God that most of my financial problems had been due to a lack of proper planning on my part. I told God that if He would help me out of debt, I would never borrow another cent without His approval.

The next time I went down to the bank that was embargoing me, I was in for a big surprise. The lawyer and bank manager who had been holding me over a barrel were in jail, charged with fraud and extortion. Six different people had filed charges against them. The bank was swarming with auditors from the main office. It turned out that my case had also been handled improperly. I met with the chief auditor and the regional manager of the bank. They apologized to me and refinanced my loan. On top of that they forgave me most of the previous interest charges and all of the lawyer's fees, saving me thousands of dollars. This good news was followed by a run of fish at Chaparral. For the very first time in the history of our fish business, we were able to not only catch a large quantity of fish, but we were able to sell for over twice the normal price due to poor catches in other areas of Colombia. In ten days we made almost $15,000.00 and were able to pay for the repairs of the 182. When I was able to make that payment, the Cessna aircraft dealer refinanced my overdue loan on the airplane. I began praising God for having mercy on me.

Now that I had the Cessna 182 back in service, I started working hard to pay all my obligations. I started to fly meat and food out to far away jungle towns that had no access by road. I saw the opportunity to make money flying gasoline out to the jungle for use in outboard motors and generators. It was dangerous to fly gasoline over the jungle and there were few pilots willing to take the risk. This drove the prices of the flights up dramatically so that I was able to meet all of my financial obligations.

I spent almost two years flying gasoline over the jungle. With over 150 gallons of car gas in the cabin, and 80 gallons of Av gas in the wing tanks, it was potentially a very explosive situation. Any type of accident would likely cause the airplane to burn. The airfields that I used were all short and narrow with trees surrounding them. They were wet and muddy during the rainy season and very treacherous. Sometimes a terrible fear would grip me of crashing and being incinerated. Any type of engine failure over the trackless jungle would spell the end for me. In addition, the area was noted for its bad weather. If I had not been under such terrible financial obligation, I would have never even dreamed of doing something this dangerous.

Fear is a terrible enemy. I learned to deal with it but I never could get rid of it completely. When I would feel that icy knot of fear building up in my stomach, I would commit myself to God and sing to myself as loud as I could over the noise of the engine.

Over the years I found I had built up a very high opinion of myself. I am a natural born optimist. I had considered myself to be a pretty decent Christian young man until I got married. Problems that I had been able to cover up as a bachelor could no longer be hidden under married circumstances. Even though I loved Marina with all my heart, I soon found that she seemed to have an uncanny ability to find and irritate all my inner problems. We started quarreling over many seemingly insignificant incidents. Sometimes our arguments would escalate into a full-fledged fight. Fortunately we both realized that it was important to reconcile our differences after an argument or fight, but our marriage conflicts became harder and harder to reconcile.

I began to notice a fundamental difference in the way men and women think. Sometimes we seemed to be on completely different wavelengths. I would be concerned about the immediate incident that had occurred and was disrupting our relationship. Most of the time I considered it to be relatively minor. Marina would add the present incident onto a long list of previous offenses that had occurred, starting with our fight at the folk festival in San Martin before we were even married. She would then negotiate from that position. Therefore every time we had a fight it kept getting harder and harder to reconcile our differences. Soon I became worried about the direction our marriage was heading. I was shocked to notice that the majority of our fights seemed to be mostly my fault. As the pressure in our marriage became more intense, I started to notice all kinds of dark, ugly traits deep inside my character that were threatening to destroy our relationship. Soon our "ideal marriage" was in serious trouble. I began to fear that someday one of our fights would go a little too far and I would lose Marina. I knew that I couldn't face life without her, yet when she was mad at me, she could insult me and rake me over the coals worse than any other person I knew.

I began to read books on psychology. They described our problems to a tee, using all kinds of fancy language, but didn't seem to help me out very much at all. Most of these books just made me feel more frustrated after I got done reading them. As I became more and more confused, our marriage continued to come apart at the seams.

Our fights would start out something like this: First I would have a bad day; something would go wrong in my work and upset me. I would come home and Marina would do or say something that would set me off. I would then insult her with a derogatory remark. She wouldn't always appreciate this, so sometimes she would react and insult me back. Then I would let loose some of my pent-up frustration and make a remark that would really hurt her feelings, such as, "If you talk and act like this, you must not love me anymore" or "What kind of a Christian are you if you treat me like this." I would almost immediately regret my words and try to patch things up but she would feel so hurt that sometimes it would be a while before she would even speak to me again. Sometimes it would take us several days to get things back on an even keel. I began to fear that sooner or later I would do or say something in a moment of anger that might permanently damage our relationship.

One day I ran into Ricardo Trillos. Ricardo was still studying the Sermon on the Mount. He now understood parts of it better. God had been dealing with his marriage and applying the Sermon on the Mount to Ricardo's own family life. I joined Ricardo in his Bible studies of Matthew, chapters 5, 6, and 7. Soon I too began to understand parts of it. Matthew 5:22 hit me right square between the eyes. Jesus said, "You have been taught up until now. 'Thou shalt not kill,' but I say, whoever even so much as harbors a grudge in his heart against his brother has killed him already and deserves to be brought to trial for murder. Whoever says to his brother, 'You fool' (the Greek word literally means 'empty-head'), should be brought before the Sanhedrin; and whoever calls his brother 'apostate' (the Greek word literally means 'empty-heart'), is in danger of hell's fire."

Jesus' teaching described my marriage fights to a tee. First I would build up anger inside, then I would release it by insulting my wife's intelligence, finally I would question the inner motives of her heart and devastate her feelings, putting our relationship into a tailspin.

I began to see that it takes two to make a fight and that even a very small initial incident can start off a downward spiral of cause and effect that has the potential to destroy a relationship. I remembered back to my childhood when I was going to boarding school. If another kid came over and stepped on my toe, I would step on his toe twice as hard to pay him back and to teach him a lesson. Unfortunately, the other boy would never learn the lesson. Nine times out of ten he would get mad and punch me in the nose. The original minor incident would escalate into a wild, free-for-all fist fight.

Jesus' words really hit me hard. It was obvious that He ran His kingdom on an entirely different basis from what I was used to. According to Jesus' words, I was in bigger trouble than I had even been able to imagine up until now. I studied further and discovered that Jesus' teachings seemed to center around the Golden Rule: "Do as you would be done to." He also said, "Don't judge and you won't be judged. Don't condemn and you won't be condemned." I began to see that Jesus' teaching centered on mercy and on giving other people the benefit of the doubt as to the inner motives of their hearts. I began to try out Jesus' teachings in my marriage.

As I began to understand Jesus' Sermon better and better, I would apply what I had learned to my own marriage situation. Soon Marina and I were in a positive, ever improving, upward bound relationship with God in the center. I had discovered the real meaning of the Sermon on the Mount in the very nick of time.

Now I could see that most of us human beings really want to do the right thing. None of us really enjoy problems, bitterness, strife, or violence. It is all too easy, however, for us to get trapped in a negative, vicious cycle. Jesus' description of the problem in Matthew 5:22 holds true for most broken marriages, broken friendships, split churches, and even severed international relationships! First anger and resentment are built up. Then the insults fly. Finally the other parties' inner motives and intentions are questioned and condemned. This sets the stage for the actual physical violence to begin. Many awful wars have begun with very minor incidents that simply escalated out of control.

Right as I'm writing this, here in this guerrilla camp, the news has just come over the radio of the downing of the South Korean airliner by the Russians. Even the guerrillas were shocked by the news. My guards tuned their short-wave radios to the Voice of America and we heard a press conference by President Reagan. Some of the guerrillas were impressed when the President said that the U.S. would not retaliate with violence, but that we would use every non-violent means to impress upon the Russians that this action on their part was unacceptable international behavior. Reagan said that he would like to be able to draw the Russians back into the camp of peaceful, law-abiding nations in the interests of world peace. The next day the guerrilla leaders issued orders prohibiting me from handling the radio. The guards were issued strict orders to only tune in Radio Moscow or Radio Havana Cuba.

It was interesting to note that the Soviet-controlled radio stations gave different accounts of the incident depending on the audience they were transmitting to. The broadcasts aimed at Central and South America flatly denied shooting down an airliner at all. They called it a spy plane. The broadcasts on the higher wavelengths aimed at Europe and Japan admitted shooting down an airliner, but they claimed that it had been done in the interests of national security.

In aviation there is a maneuver known as a tailspin. If the pilot attempts to climb too fast with the rudder off center, the airplane will pitch down and spin. The harder the pilot pulls back on the controls trying to go up, the worse the spin gets. Soon the airplane is out of control in a vicious downward spiral. Adding more power only causes the plane to spin faster. There is only one way to recover from the tailspin and avoid a fatal crash. The pilot must apply opposite rudder and then let go of the controls. Then the airplane will stop spinning all by itself.

Ricardo and I discovered that in His Sermon on the Mount, Jesus teaches us how to get our lives off on a positive, upward spiral that is the reverse of a tailspin. C. S. Lewis wrote in his book, *Mere Christianity,* "Good and evil are not static. They are dynamic. Each one is continually feeding on itself just like compound interest in the bank."[2] Thus good is continually getting better; while evil is always getting worse.

---

[2]   Lewis, C. S. Copyright 1952, Macmillan Publishing Co., Inc.

John the Baptist came to prepare the way for Jesus preaching, "Repent for the Kingdom of God is at hand." Then Jesus started His ministry and said, "The Kingdom of Heaven is among you." Later, to His disciples, Jesus said, "The Kingdom of Heaven is within you." The Sermon on the Mount explains how to enter the Kingdom of Heaven and how the Kingdom operates, contrasting it with the way things normally work in this world. Ricardo and I found that the order, or sequence in which Jesus teaches things, is just as important as the themes He is dealing with.

Jesus started His sermon by saying, "BLESSED ARE THE POOR IN SPIRIT FOR THEIRS IS THE KINGDOM OF HEAVEN." Maybe the people that were expecting Him to preach on fire and brimstone were a little disappointed, but Jesus taught a positive message right from the start. C. S. Lewis wrote, "Negatives are rarely useful in a debate, even when they are true."[3] Jesus pioneered this concept. The Greek word Jesus used, that has been translated "poor in spirit," literally means "beggarly." Jesus is describing a person who doesn't have a spiritual cent. Jesus says that the way into the Kingdom of Heaven is for us to declare spiritual bankruptcy. We can't make a deal with God, because we don't have anything to deal with. Everything we have originated from Him. The only way for us to enter God's Kingdom is for us to admit our faults, admit that we can't make it on our own apart from Him, and fall upon His mercy.

Next Jesus says, "Blessed are those who mourn for they shall be comforted." When we admit our mistakes and faults, and the full realization of how badly we have managed to mess things up sinks in, our natural reaction is to mourn. But cheer up! If we pay attention to Jesus' way of doing things, we will be comforted.

Jesus continues, "BLESSED ARE THE MEEK FOR THEY SHALL INHERIT THE EARTH." I used to have a hard time understanding the word meek and reconciling myself with it. It seemed to me that a meek person would be a milquetoast,

---

[3]   Ibid.

doormat, wishy-washy individual who lets everyone trample all over him. I didn't understand what Jesus meant until I studied His words in Spanish. Then I looked up the word in Greek and found out that the word Jesus used for "meek"[4] has no direct translation into the English language. The Greek word really means an attitude of heart and mind. The Spanish word *manso* comes close to portraying the complete meaning of what Jesus said. In Spanish, an example would be the way in which the word manso is applied to horses. The horse that is *manso,* is the perfectly trained horse that completely obeys the rider. It allows itself to be guided with just a very light pressure on the reins. It doesn't have to be a broken-spirited animal at all. It might be thoroughbred and high-strung, but it has given up its own plans and allows the rider to call the shots. This is a good example of what true faith in Jesus Christ is all about. Jesus wants us to quit trying to fit God into our plans and let Him fit us into His masterplan instead. He promises to completely fulfill and satisfy us if we allow Him to call the shots in our lives.

Jesus continues His sermon by saying, "Blessed are those who hunger and thirst after righteousness for they shall be satisfied." Righteousness can be defined as "doing what God wants or requires." When we enter into God's Kingdom by admitting our problems and giving up our own plans, a desire begins to well up inside of us to get our act together and do things right. Some of Jesus' thinking starts to spill off into our minds and we begin to do what God wants because that's what we want to do too. In the Bible God says that He wants to write His laws on the "tablets of our hearts." The apostle Paul said, "Let this same mind be in you that was in Christ Jesus." The Christian life isn't a legalistic list of do's and don'ts that we struggle to try to keep in our own strength. It is a dynamic, vibrant, delightful relationship with the Creator of the universe.

Here we have the basic Christian message of repentance and faith. We know that struggling through life's problems in our own strength is not the answer. On the other hand, if we

---

[4]   The Greek word is Praos (πραος)

just sit back and do nothing, expecting God to do everything for us, sometimes we are disappointed that nothing seems to get done. What are we to do? I struggled with this for several years. Deep inside, I knew that there was something missing from my Christian experience. The same thing seemed to be missing in many of the churches I had been attending, too. What was it?

Are you beginning to catch a glimpse of the incredible structure, and understanding of cause and effect that make Jesus' Sermon such a masterpiece? It isn't by chance that Jesus says next, "BLESSED ARE THE MERCIFUL FOR THEY SHALL OBTAIN MERCY." I didn't understand this until one evening when I started thinking back over my flying career. I had flown over 4000 hours, with almost half of it over the jungle. In eight years of flying treacherous terrain I had never had so much as a minor accident. Many other pilots had been killed or maimed flying in the jungle. Others had demolished their airplanes. Even the missionary pilots, who had one of the best safety records in South America, were averaging a major accident every 1200 hours of flying time. I prayed and asked God what was going on. Why was I being singled out for special treatment. Better pilots than me had had terrible accidents flying in the jungle or in the mountains of Colombia. I knew that I wasn't any better than some of the pilots that were dead, killed in flying accidents. Some of the casualties had been better Christians than me, too. I pressed God for an answer. Why was I being treated so special? I had had more close calls than anybody, yet here I was unscathed while I had watched other pilots make one mistake and get nailed. All of a sudden my thinking flashed back to a scene years ago. I remembered working on that house in Mapiripan just before Dad and Ricardo had arrived in the 170 for the first time. I remembered my prayer to the Lord and my promise to never turn down a mercy flight if it was really necessary regardless of financial considerations. I had kept my promise to God over all those years. I felt a quiet voice deep inside me, that over the years I have learned to identify as the still small voice of my Lord, impress upon me, "You never turned anyone down who asked you for mercy, so I never turned you down when you were in need of my mercy. Even when you got out of line and tried to do that flight for Pedro, I still kept you safe and taught you a lesson that you needed to know." I was completely overwhelmed. For a few seconds I started to catch a glimpse of how important mercy is to God. Jesus' teachings center on mercy. That's what Jesus' rescue mission here to planet earth is all about. Jesus wants each one of us to put a merciful attitude to work in our lives. He wants us to each treat our fellow man in the same manner that we would like God to treat us.

Think about it. What a difference a merciful mentality could make on our actions and reactions every day. How many times a day do we pass up opportunities to have mercy on someone else? Jesus said later in his sermon, "DO UNTO OTHERS AS YOU WOULD HAVE OTHERS DO UNTO YOU." Over the centuries men have called this the "Golden Rule." Mercy is also the "Golden Key" to inner peace and happiness. These guerrillas have taken away my wallet, my watch, even my comb, and have me tied up with a rope. They have separated me from my family. They wrecked my airplane. They are asking ten times more money for my release than my family is able to pay. Yet through this whole experience, up until now I have found that if I put Jesus' merciful mentality to work and refuse to let my mind dwell on negative thoughts of hatred, bitterness, resentment or revenge, no one has been able to take away my inner peace and happiness, no matter what they do.

After "Blessed are the merciful," Jesus said, "Blessed are the pure in heart for they shall see God face to face." If the result of admitting our faults and acknowledging our need for God with the attitude of the "poor in spirit" causes us to mourn; and if the result of giving up our own plans and letting God direct our lives as we come to Him with the "meek" attitude leads to a strong inner longing to clean up our act and do things right, having a "hunger and thirst for righteousness," could the end result of putting a merciful attitude to work in our lives be a "pure heart"? I think so.

Jesus has a term that He uses to describe people who put a merciful attitude to work in their lives, giving other people's inner motives the benefit of the doubt. The next thing Jesus said was, "Blessed are the peacemakers for they shall be called the sons of God." There seems to be an acute shortage of peacemakers in our world today. As you learn to use mercy, the golden key, you can be a peacemaker in your own home with your family, or maybe at work on the job. If you put Jesus' teachings to work in your life, you can influence everyone that you come in contact with.

"Blessed are you when men persecute you for the cause of justice, for yours is the kingdom of heaven." Jesus' seventh beatitude ends the same as His first. Jesus wants to launch us off on a breathtaking, uplifting spiral of mercy and love that has no limits, much more exciting than "Space Mountain" at Disneyworld. He wants to help us stop the fatal tailspin that most of us have gotten into. Jesus' beatitudes describe a wonderful, positive upward spiral of cause and effect that can transform us right into "sons of God." We can witness creation as God takes selfish, proud, rebellious humans doomed to death and failure, and makes sons of God out of us; magnificent, glorious creatures that He can eventually lift right out of nature so that we can spend all eternity with Him. Jesus says that we will be persecuted if we stick our necks out for what we know is right. He doesn't promise us a bed of roses in this life. He does promise us that during our stay on planet earth he will eradicate our selfishness, pride, and rebellion *if* we authorize Him to. Sometimes the treatment is painful, but He must dig deep enough in our lives to get at the roots of our problems. There is no place in heaven for yet another human ego trip. Justice and mercy must go hand in hand. In order to avail ourselves of God's mercy we must first recognize that He is just. As Christians we must be willing to give individuals the benefit of the doubt with a merciful attitude, while at the same time be willing to stick our necks out for what we know is right. We must oppose evil with every *legitimate* means at our disposal. Can you understand now why Jesus can love the sinner, but hate the sin?

As I was finishing typing this last paragraph, one of the guerrillas asked me a question which I will include in the book. Mariano asked, "Why did Jesus die? If He was really

God like you say, wouldn't it have been enough for Him to have just left us His message on mercy and love? The fact that you claim He died gives you away and proves that you just made this all up. Why, if I were God, and came down to earth like you say Jesus did, why I wouldn't have let anyone nail me to a cross. I would have called down the angels and defended myself. All-powerful God would have never let himself be put to death."

I answered, "Jesus died, because in a spiritual sense we've all been kidnapped. We have been kidnapped by our own selfishness. Our pride doesn't let us admit when we are wrong. This has led to a rebellion on our part against God. Selfishness, pride, and rebellion have held the whole human race captive, just like these three loops of rope around my neck and arms are holding me captive here in the jungle. If we continue going our own way we will die and be lost. Jesus came to pay the ransom for all of us. He came and broke the power of sin and death. Yes, He died, but then He rose from the dead victorious. Now He is standing by to help us through life's problems. If we place our lives under His authority, within His Kingdom, He will pry our fingers loose from all the problems that we insist on clutching onto. We are like the student pilot who enters a fatal tailspin. The panic-stricken novice can't let go of the controls, even to save his own life. The harder he pulls back on the stick, trying to go up, the worse the spin gets, and the faster he loses altitude. Jesus is like the expert flight instructor who wrenches the controls away from the terrorized student pilot. Soon He has the airplane climbing nicely back to a safe altitude. Then He lets the student try it again. Now if the student pilot continues to fight the instructor on the controls, there are only two courses of action open to the instructor. Most instructors would just land the airplane and tell the student to find a new instructor. The only other alternative is for the instructor to let the student go ahead and make another mistake in the hopes that he will scare himself badly enough to pay attention to what the instructor is trying to teach him. Fortunately, Jesus seems to have a lot more patience than most flight instructors I have known.

I finished Chapter Ten of this book on my fortieth day in captivity. I sent the typewritten manuscript with Vicente to Manuel, who was in a different camp. Chapter Nine of this book has been rewritten and several other places have been edited or abridged, but up to here, this is essentially the same book that I sent to Manuel. I have made every effort to keep it the same as much as possible. If you don't see eye to eye with some of the things in this book, remember that this was written from inside a guerrilla camp. Sometimes I think that there are two worlds, a spiritual world, and a physical world. Every once in a while as we go about living in the physical world we get a glimpse of the world to come. Now, it seems to us that this physical world that we live in is the real world, but someday this world that we live in will fade away, and we will come face to face with reality Himself. We will all be required to render accounts to our Creator, the King of the universe. Are you prepared to meet Him face to face?

Chapter Eleven[1]

October 25, 1983

I am surprised to notice that my stay in this Marxist guerrilla camp is having a profound effect on my life. Ever since I started looking upon this experience as an opportunity instead of a disaster, many positive things have happened. A month ago I thought that I knew it all, that I was 100% right and that they were 100% wrong. Now I am able to look at my life more objectively and even from time to time learn things from the guerrillas. Jaime and Manuel are the ones who have taught me the most. It is through my experiences with them that I have witnessed the principles of Jesus' Sermon on the Mount in actual practice. In this most difficult situation I have experienced a fierce inner struggle as to how to react to my captors. As I learn to put aside my own plans and ideas, and to rely on Jesus' plans instead, many exciting things are happening.

Deep inside, from the start of my captivity, I have felt that God has a purpose in allowing me to be kidnapped. I felt that maybe God wanted me to be a witness for Him in the midst of this atheistic, Marxist society. This feeling was accompanied by a feeling of severe depression when I would think about the shoot-out in the banana patch and the lie that I told Jaime

---

[1]   Author's note: The following chapter consists of excerpts from my English notebook, written in captivity, but not included in the book for Manuel.

about my gun shortly after I was captured. Maybe I had blown things so badly that it would be impossible for me to influence my captors in a positive manner about God.

My initial, almost subconscious, reaction to the kidnapping had been to lie and then to try and shoot my way out of it. Here I have been telling God for years that He is the King of my life, and then when I got into a difficult spot, what did I do? I resorted to lies and violence without even consulting Him. What if God has allowed me to be kidnapped for a purpose? If God has sent me to this guerrilla camp as His messenger of truth and peace, then I couldn't have failed more miserably at the start.

As day after day of captivity goes by, I am learning another important lesson. I find that as I enter into the spirit of Jesus' Beatitudes with the attitude of the "poor in spirit" and admit my faults and mistakes, that God is able to use my worst failures for good. I am finding out that a person doesn't have to be perfect in order to be effective for God; but we do have to be honest. The fact that I admitted my mistake in telling Jaime a lie about my gun has had a profound effect on my captors. I haven't had much luck winning the guerrillas over to my point of view when I get into ideological debates with them. However, they are impressed when I tell them about my mistakes and problems and about how God has intervened and helped me time and time again in my life. I tell them with heartfelt conviction that I don't believe that God has done so many things in my life, watching over me and protecting me, patiently teaching me many important lessons, just to abandon me now. I feel confident that God will see me through this experience.

Some of my captors have been touched by the book. Jaime just told me that he regrets ever having kidnapped me. He is making every effort to be nice to me. Jaime has personally built me a desk to write at and fixed it up with his spare tarp over the top so that I can write even when it rains. He has given orders that I can ask for anything I want to eat, whenever I want to, even at night. I am still tied up with the nylon cord, but sometimes Jaime comes over and takes it off for the afternoon. He tells me that he is under strict orders from Vicente to keep me tied up, but as long as he is personally present he can allow me to be loose. Boy, does it ever feel good to be out from under that rope!

Arnuval seems sad and depressed. When he is on guard duty, he rarely speaks anymore. He just sits there with his head down. Yesterday I asked him if anything was bothering him. He thought for awhile and remarked that he wished he could be a Christian like me. He said, "I think you are right, but I made a very serious agreement with this guerrilla organization when I joined. If I go back on my oath of allegiance to them, they can kill me. I have been thinking it all over and it seems impossible for me to reconcile the teachings of Jesus Christ with our Marxist ideology. For the time being I will have to continue being a guerrilla. It's too bad that I didn't meet you before I joined the guerrillas."

Arnuval gave me a sad look and didn't speak to me again for the rest of his three-hour shift of guard duty.

I later learned that each new guerrilla member is sworn in on Simon Bolivar's[2] sword (which was stolen from a museum), in an oath of allegiance to the international Marxist ideology ending with the statement, "We will fight unto death against the Yankees, the enemies of all mankind." This statement has also been included in the Nicaraguan Sandinista national anthem. Any member of a Marxist guerrilla cell who wishes to leave the movement and no longer participate in violence as the solution to Third World problems is branded as an oath-breaking traitor. Many sincere, well-meaning individuals join the Marxist guerrilla ranks, only to find guerrilla leaders interested in personal power instead of the welfare of the common people. Unfortunately, by the time a new guerrilla discovers this, he is trapped, unable to leave the movement without being hunted down and killed afterwards.

I have been praying for my captors every evening. I started praying that one of them would enter the Kingdom of God. I feel that if even one of them comes to know Jesus Christ and starts to put Jesus' Beatitudes to work in his life, that this

---

[2] Simon Bolivar is Colombia's equivalent of our George Washington.

whole experience will have been worthwhile. I have also been praying that God would give me guidance as to what course to pursue in the future. Should I try to escape again, or should I just sit tight and let God worry about getting me home safely? I don't want to make any more mistakes, so I am asking God to give me some definite instruction as to what to do.

On my 36th day of captivity I woke up in the night with a bright light shining in my eyes. It was a sharp, piercing beam of light that I couldn't even stand to look at until my eyes adjusted. At first I thought it must be the guard shining his flashlight at me. Then I noticed that it was a brilliant star, shining through a hole in the trees. I asked the guard what time it was. He replied that it was four o'clock in the morning. I repeated my question, wanting to know the exact time, "Four zero zero a.m." replied the guard.

I looked at that star, and I couldn't believe it. Here it was shining through a tiny hole in the trees at the precise angle to shine under the tarp above my hammock and hit me square in the eyes at exactly 4:00 a.m. My hammock is pitched in such a way as to position my head in exactly the right spot to be able to see the star. In five minutes the star disappeared behind the trees. I decided that it must have been Venus, the morning star.

Today is my 38th day of captivity. Yesterday I received a Bible and a letter from home, among other things. Last night we had a thunderstorm. I took advantage of the noise of the wind and rain to sing at the top of my lungs inside my hammock without the guards being able to hear me. I decided to stay awake all night in hopes of seeing the morning star again at 4:00 a.m. It was a terrible storm. Lightning flashed very close to our campsite and many dead limbs came crashing down, making a fearful noise every now and then. The wind was whistling through the tops of the tall trees, and I could feel my hammock move as the two trees between which it was pitched swayed back and forth. I can't get that star out of my mind. It was beautiful. I can remember that in the book of Revelation, the morning star is promised to overcomers, so I have been praying and asking God to make me into an overcomer.

The sky cleared and the rain stopped in the early morning hours. Finally the star appeared. It came over the horizon with a bright glow and shined through a small hole in the trees, low down on the horizon. I asked the guard for the time. He replied that it was exactly 3:00 a.m. I just had to see it better, so I told the guard that I had to get up to answer the call of nature, and he handed me my shoes. With my gaze fixed on the star I stood up. In doing so, I unwittingly bumped my head on the tarp above me. A lot of water had collected in the lower corner of the tarp due to the rain, and now all this cold water doused me on top of my head. It turned out that Javier was the guard, and we both laughed about my "automatic shower." In a minute the star slipped behind the trees and I got back into the hammock.

An hour later, precisely at 4:00 a.m., it appeared in the larger hole in the trees where I first saw it yesterday. I told Javier that I had to get up again, and he gave me permission to do so. I put my shoes on and stood up, and wouldn't you know it, I hit my head on that tarp again and got another dose of cold water right down my neck. I started to laugh about it, but all of a sudden I stopped laughing. I had emptied the water from the tarp the first time I got up. It hadn't rained since. Where in the world did that second dose of water come from?

I looked at that great big beautiful star. It was several times brighter than I can ever remember seeing the morning star before. It's light wasn't soft and pale like the moonlight. This star gave off light that was sharp and focused; a light that seemed to penetrate right into my brain. Was this the famous "Star of David?" Could this be similar to the star that the Wise Men followed to the town of Bethlehem to witness the birth of Jesus Christ so many years ago?

As I stood there in amazement, awe, and appreciation, I noticed that another star had risen on the horizon, following the exact same path as the morning star. It was a faint little star, and it was now in the small hole in the trees, way down on the horizon where the morning star had been at 3:00 a.m. I was fascinated by all this. After a few more minutes the pale, red glow of morning dawned. As soon as it got light enough to read, I opened my Bible. Today is the very first morning I have had a Bible to read. My Bible fell open to Revelation, chapter 21. The words seemed to jump out of the page right at me. I AM THE SEED OF DAVID; I AM THE BRIGHT AND MORNING STAR. THE LAMB SAYS COME. THE BRIDE SAYS COME. DRINK OF THE WATER OF LIFE. IT'S FREE.

I was completely overwhelmed. Things started falling into place, and I was finally able to understand this morning's object lesson. The Morning Star is symbolic of Jesus Himself. Jesus wants to share Himself with the overcomers, not just give them Venus as a present. The object lesson was now very clear. If I were to follow Jesus, just like that faint little star followed the exact same path that the morning star took, I would receive the "water of life" free. In fact, I received a symbolic double dose right on top of my head this morning, just to make sure I got the picture.

I was staggered! Here I had prayed and asked God to direct me. I would have been content with a dream or any small sign. Here He responded to my prayer by arranging for huge heavenly bodies to shine through little holes in the thick canopy of leaves at precise angles with exact timing, so as to hit me square in the eyes with a penetrating beam of light at 4:00 a.m. as I lay in my hammock, and wake me up! The jungle is so dense that normally it is impossible to see a star from any angle, let alone to try to see one out from under the blue tarp that the guerrillas had hung over my hammock.

A great happiness and joy began to well up inside me. God is in control of this situation, and the whole universe for that matter. These guerrillas are nothing compared to Him. Nancy just came over and served me a cup of coffee. I started telling her about the star, when all of a sudden, I was amazed to notice a six-pointed Star of David hung on a gold chain around her neck. How come I haven't noticed that before?

As I sipped my coffee, I wondered about my prayer asking God to rescue one of my captors. What a stupid prayer! I should really be praying for total victory. I ought to be praying that God will see fit to rescue all of my captors from the vicious tail-spin that they find themselves trapped in. From now on that is what my prayer will be.

September 22, 1983

Today is my 40th day in captivity. This morning I also saw the star at 4:00 a.m. Last night the moon was full. It thrilled me to watch the full moon setting while the morning star rose. I have been thinking about this all day. When it is night, we can't see the sun, but the moon can still reflect the sun's light to us. I see a spiritual parallel. There are many people in this world today who are living in spiritual darkness. They haven't developed their spiritual senses, so it is impossible for them to perceive God. Jesus left his followers a new commandment just before he left. He said, "Love one another even as I have loved you, so that the world will know that you are my disciples." As Christians we can reflect some of God's love towards those living in spiritual darkness. Just as the moon is always either waxing or waning, we Christians are either becoming more effective for God, or less so. This morning as I was pacing back and forth as far as this nylon cord will allow, I decided that what God is really after in my life is my "free will." I struggled for awhile with this idea. It seemed to me that if I completely gave my decision-making apparatus over to God, I would cease to exist as an individual. I thought about how badly I wanted to run away from this guerrilla camp and see my wife and little baby daughter again. If I let God make all the decisions from now on, I might never see them again. I might never leave this guerrilla camp alive. I can think of many Christians who wound up being martyrs. My own desire is to break away from the guerrillas as soon as a decent opportunity presents itself. Still, I thought, anyone who can arrange for whole planets to shine through little holes in the trees just to teach me an object lesson has to know what He is doing. I prayed and told God that I was willing to do whatever He saw fit. I told Him that he could do anything He wanted with me and that I trust Him completely. A great sense of peace came over me. It is clear that my job from now on is to worry about doing and saying what God wants done and said in this camp. It is God's job to worry about my safety and about how to get me home from here when my mission to this guerrilla camp has been accomplished. If I get killed, that is for God to decide. Since I am working for God, I will trust Him to take care of my wife and baby and not worry about them.

At noon today I finished typing this book for Manuel. It is exactly 40 typewritten pages closely spaced on both sides. I am beginning to wonder about all these number 4's and 40's. I have been impressed with the numbers 4 and 40 ever since this kidnapping began. The morning star keeps waking me up at exactly 4:00 a.m. Today at 4:00 p.m. a bolt of lightning hit our camp right between Jaime and Elkin. Both of them were dazed, and Jaime even smelled a little bit burnt afterwards. The strong smell of ozone lingers in the air. With the lightning blast a dry limb came crashing down on top of my desk and tore down the tarp, so I have had to move over to the hammock to keep from getting wet.

Still thinking about the number four, I read in the book of Genesis in my Bible that on the fourth day of creation God created the sun, moon, and stars. In my Spanish translation it says that the stars were created to herald special dates and events. Can the number four be a heavenly number? These thoughts are rushing through my head. What about the number 40? I remember about Moses and the ten commandments. Can the number 10 be symbolic in the Bible of God's justice? Four times ten equals 40. Can the number 40 be symbolic of God's heavenly justice, like when it rained for 40 days and 40 nights, and only Noah was saved from the flood because he listened to God and built an ark? Is it God's heavenly justice that I have been out in this guerrilla camp, separated from my loved ones for 40 days? Wait a minute! Jesus said that we should "Do unto others as we would have others do unto us for this is the law of Moses and the prophets." Jesus equates his teachings on mercy with the "law of Moses." Could the number 40 also be symbolic of God's heavenly mercy? Like when King David reigned over Israel for 40 years and brought peace and prosperity to the land? Is this kidnapping really God's heavenly mercy on me in disguise? Has God decided to have mercy on me and teach me many things here that I couldn't have learned under normal circumstances?

As the rain pours down, and I continue thinking, it dawns on me that there is really no upper limit on what God can do through this experience. I start to chuckle to myself. It is starting to look like maybe the guerrillas have done me a favor in kidnapping me. This experience is a tremendous opportunity for me to learn important lessons that I would have never learned in a million years of normal living! To top it off, I have a golden opportunity to influence many of these young guerrillas for good.

Now I am thinking about the faint little star that appeared on the horizon, rising in the exact same path as Venus, the morning star. Every morning Venus, the planet of love, shines through that little hole in the trees close to the horizon at exactly 3:00 a.m. Then at 4:00 a.m. it shines through the larger, higher hole, and this little, faint star comes into view in the smaller hole. I was wondering if the number three is also significant, so I opened my Bible to Genesis chapter one and read that God created all the fruit-bearing trees and seed-bearing plants on the third day of creation. Is the number three symbolic in the Bible of fruitfulness? I remember that Jesus started his ministry when he was 30 years old. He died when he was 33. It amazes me to read the Bible and find that every little detail seems to be spiritually significant while at the same time the Bible is also historically accurate. I have the distinct impression that if I keep my eyes on Jesus and follow Him just like that little, faint star follows the exact path of the morning star, that my life will be fruitful also.

Several days later:

Last night Elkin let me use his little short-wave radio for a few minutes. I was able to tune in the American Armed Forces radio and actually listen to the news. The guards aren't supposed to let me use the radio, but Elkin made an exception last night. I think his conscience is bothering him for participating in this kidnapping, so he is trying to be nice to me.

I was able to tune in a White House press conference. I am very impressed with the way President Reagan handled himself, and with the way in which he fielded questions from some obviously very hostile reporters without losing his cool or getting ruffled. The President refused to get upset or uptight even when some reporters viciously insulted and attacked him and his policies. Listening to President Reagan makes me feel warm and proud inside. I feel glad that I am an American. I am going to try and follow President Reagan's example and not let these guerrillas get me uptight with all their nasty questions. I wonder if President Reagan has ever read Jesus' Sermon on the Mount. I bet he has. He seems to practice Jesus' Golden Rule almost perfectly.

I continued listening to various news items and all of a sudden I heard something that upset me. Commentator Dan Rather came on and announced that President Reagan was receiving criticism from the right-wingers for not taking any drastic action against the Soviets in retaliation for their downing of the South Korean airliner. Dan Rather continued and said that the President was being accused of blowing a unique opportunity. They were saying that this was one of the most blatant acts of Soviet aggression liable to occur in our lifetime, and here President Reagan only replied with words and rhetoric to the Soviet violence.

I have been thinking about Dan Rather's statement, and the more I think, the more upset I get. I am sitting in the middle of a guerrilla camp witnessing the tremendous buildup of the international communist forces firsthand. There are thousands of Marxist guerrillas in southeastern Colombia controlling almost every phase of the lucrative cocaine traffic. These guerrillas are making astronomic sums of money running the drug traffic. This money is being spent on weapons and terrorism. Right now these forces are not interested in publicity or confrontation. They are content to sit quietly and milk the drug trade for all it's worth. The KGB, utilizing its well-trained Cuban counterparts, has everything nicely under control. All over the globe Soviet-controlled forces are quietly building up and gathering strength in all kinds of obscure, unlikely areas. It is only in complacent America that Dan Rather's statement can be taken seriously and actually be believed by many.

It seems to me, from my present vantage point, that the Soviets are obviously trying to take over and control everything that they possibly can. It looks to me like the South Korean airliner incident is just the start. I hate to even think about the Soviet aggression that we are liable to see in our lifetime if America doesn't wake up and start seriously opposing this threat. Most Americans have been lulled to sleep on world issues. If anything goes wrong in the world, it is easy to just sit back and criticize, blaming our president, or our Congress, or maybe the Secretary of State for the problem. The roots to some of our problems may lie a little closer to home than many of us would like to imagine. Our American government reflects the will of the American people. If the American people have lost or are losing the will to oppose what is wrong and stand up for what is right, how can we expect any different from our leaders? There are many things all of us can do to help and support our country as it faces difficult, trying times. We need to lay petty differences and party politics aside and pull together as a nation. If we put our selfishness and pride to one side and honestly seek to do what is right, God can bless our nation today, just as he has done in the past. Whatever happened to our national motto, In God We Trust? The last time I saw it, it was printed on the side of a stack of crisp 100 dollar bills in the filthy hands of a narcotics smuggler deep in the jungles of Colombia, South America. It makes me feel sad to see American dollars financing terrorism. I believe that if Americans would just quit buying drugs, it would go a long way towards drying up some of the problems of Central and South America, and it would make it a lot easier for our government to be able to help our Latin American neighbors, not to mention the terrible damage drugs are doing to people right within America itself.

I have been thinking about J.R.R. Tolkien's trilogy, *The Lord of the Rings*. As I let my mind escape from reality and wander off into Tolkien's fantasy world of Middle Earth, I am shocked to notice some striking similarities with our present world situation. A dark shadow is gathering strength and power across the globe, menacing and sinister, just like in Tolkien's novel.

Evil forces are massing in shadowy, out-of-the-way places all over our planet; waiting, biding their time. The western world has complacently allowed itself to drift asleep and not seriously consider the threat that is facing us.

As I continue to muse, deep in thought, I try to transpose my situation into Tolkien's Middle Earth. If, I fantasize, I really lived in Middle Earth, then my captors would be called 'orcs' instead of guerrillas. They would work for the dark Lord of Mordor instead of for the KGB and the Soviet Union.

In Tolkien's fantasy the real King returns and leads the fight against evil. However the evil power is not destroyed by force. The good forces, led by the true king, are about to be defeated when all of a sudden the ring-bearer finishes his quest. The Dark Lord's own ring of power is thrown into his own mountain of doom, causing the complete and utter downfall of all his evil power.

In the Bible there are some clues that maybe our world might have a similar ending. The true and rightful king of this earth, Jesus Christ, has promised to return someday and set this world right. The Bible also implies that evil will somehow turn on itself and aid in its own destruction. I wonder what would happen if more people spent a day in prayer and fasting, asking Jesus Christ to please come back and be the King of this world. What if President Reagan were to declare a national day of prayer and fasting in which we would collectively admit our national mistakes and failures and ask Jesus Christ to reign in our country and straighten out our many problems? What if Pope John Paul II and other religious leaders were to call for a world-wide day of prayer and fasting in which we could all collectively, as members of the human race, admit our failures and ask God to make the plans for our world from now on?

Sometimes I get depressed about my situation and the way in which the world is heading. Everything looks so hopeless. The whole human race has entered a fatal tailspin and the awful ending may not be very far off. This world seems to be headed for either a horrible nuclear holocaust, or else be engulfed by atheistic, totalitarian communism. Every year there is less freedom and more nuclear weapons. Wouldn't it be terrible if the ultimate monument to the end results of human selfishness, pride, and rebellion against God is to be the charred remains of this planet floating around in space for the rest of eternity, simply because man has literally blown the human race completely off the face of the earth using nuclear weapons?

But wait a minute. What if a nuclear holocaust isn't the worst thing that could ever happen to the human race? What if the bottom of our human tailspin has already been reached many years ago when men actually tried, condemned, tortured, and killed God Himself? Jesus rose from the dead, and He broke death's power. Before His ascension, Jesus promised to send us power from on high. He promised to send us His Holy Spirit. He fulfilled that promise on the Day of Pentecost and literally shares His victory and power with everyone who joins His Kingdom and becomes a true Christian.

I am now thinking back to those verses in the book of Malachi that caught Ricardo's attention so many years ago. They seem to be in code, having a spiritual application as well as a literal one. All of a sudden I am able to break the spiritual code and the decoded message staggers me:

Malachi 4:4-6

Remember the "law of Moses" and before the end comes, I will send the "Spirit of Elijah" unto you, and he will cause the hearts of the fathers to return to their children, and the hearts of the children to return to their fathers, lest I come and destroy your land completely.

Jesus says, "Do unto others as you would have others do unto you for this is the 'law of Moses' and the prophets." Jesus equates His teachings on mercy with the "law of Moses," or God's justice. Malachi literally means "my angel" or "my messenger" in Hebrew. What God is really saying through Malachi, His messenger, is that if we put a merciful mentality to work in our lives and practice Jesus' Golden Rule, He will send us the "Spirit of Elijah." In Hebrew Elijah literally means "The Lord is my God." In other words, mercy is the key to receiving and allowing God's Holy Spirit to flow through us and reconcile our family problems. Jesus also said, "Blessed are the peacemakers for they shall be called the *Sons* of God.

I believe God actually intends to reconcile us right into His own family! Then it won't be necessary for Him to destroy our land! God is offering us a way out. Our world doesn't have to end in a fiasco.

Moses received the Ten Commandments, and in the Bible Moses is symbolic of God's justice. Moses was a great man, but he made one small mistake, and God refused to let him cross the Jordan River (symbolic of death) and enter the promised land. All of us fall short of perfection on our own. We are doomed to die. None of us can measure up to God's standards on our own.

Remember the prophet Elijah? He was the one who called down fire from heaven. He also parted the Jordan river with his mantle and walked across on dry ground. Elijah is symbolic of God's faithfulness. Elijah didn't even die. He climbed into a "fiery chariot" and was caught up to heaven in a whirlwind.

How can we bridge the gap between Moses and Elijah? How can we satisfy God's justice? How can we receive supernatural help and power from God? Jesus Christ is the answer. In the transfiguration, Jesus stood between Moses and Elijah. Jesus is symbolic of God's mercy. Jesus said, "He who refuses to forgive destroys the bridge over which he himself must pass."[3] Jesus came down and had mercy on us, bridging the gap between us and God. Jesus' death was very symbolic.

The triple theme of God's justice, mercy and faithfulness is woven through the Bible from beginning to end. It is summed up in the book of Revelation when the Trinity of God, the Father; God, the Son; and God, the Holy Spirit; who are the very personification of Justice, Mercy and Faithfulness, fight against the bad guys. The villains, or the Terrible Trio, as I call them, are selfishness, pride, and rebellion, as represented by Babylon (the harlot), the false prophet, and the beast. It says that the dragon (Satan) has given all his power over to them. In the end of the book, the false prophet and the beast do in the harlot. Then they are both thrown into the lake of fire and destroyed.

---

[3]   Matt. 6:15 (paraphrase)

I don't mean to detract from a literal interpretation of this book, but by identifying the characters properly in their symbolic spiritual sense, we get a description of the spiritual battle that is going on inside of each and every one of us. God's purpose in putting us through this physical life is to completely eradicate the selfishness, pride, and rebellion inside each one of us.

In the Old Testament of the Bible, the prophets were somewhat similar to our news commentators today. The prophet would blow a trumpet whenever he had some news or a message for the people to hear. In the book of Revelation, John tells of a last trumpet that is to be blown announcing the end of the world. After thousands of years, Jesus' words still haven't faded into oblivion. They are coming through stronger and clearer all the time. Think about them. There is still a little more time, as the notes of God's last trumpet call linger in the air, calling men to forgiveness and mercy instead of violence and terrorism; calling for us to wake up and oppose evil instead of being lulled to sleep by wishful thinking.

One of the most unnecessary points of contention within the Christian church is the matter of whether or not the Christians will go through the tribulation. From my present position it doesn't seem to be worth arguing about. Every true Christian from the beginning of time has come through tribulation. Sooner or later every true Christian will have his faith tried by fire just like is happening to me in this guerrilla camp. The Bible says that the wood, hay, and stubble in our lives are consumed by the fire, but that the gold, silver, and precious stones are purified. There isn't a lot of persecution going on in America like there is in many countries of the world today, but it is still possible for a Christian to go through the fire of tribulation. I know of many Christians who are having a bout with cancer, or who have financial difficulties, or some other problem that has tried their faith to its very roots.

Numbers are very symbolic in the Bible, especially in the book of Revelation. I was intrigued with the number 666, which is the "mark of the beast." Six, of course, is the number of man. Man was created on the sixth day of creation. In the Bible 100 is symbolic of God's plan. Noah spent 100 years building the ark to God's plans and specifications. Abraham had Isaac when he was 100 years old, and so on. $33\frac{1}{3} \times 3 = 100$. Remember that three is symbolic of fruitfulness. God's plans are fruitful no matter how you factor them. Therefore 600 would be symbolic of man's plans. Ten is symbolic of justice (the Ten Commandments) or mercy (Jesus says that the Golden Rule equals the Law of Moses). Therefore 60 would be Man's justice or Man's mercy. On the first day of creation God said, "Let there be light!" One is symbolic of light. Therefore 666 in the Bible's spiritual symbolism would be Man's plans according to Man's law, illuminated by Man's light. This is the "mark of the beast" or the mark of rebellion against God.

It is interesting to note that both the "secular humanism" so prevalent in Western democracies, and the Marxist atheism, found in communist countries include the fundamental belief that mankind is capable of solving his own problems without God's help or direction.

Señor familia sterndal.

E. S. M.

Respetado amigos puntanos que con el mayor.
Respto que se merecen llega o su destino un cordial
y amistoso saludo deseando y haciendo votos por que.
nuestros negocios sean un éxito para que no sea
ni de parte de uds. ni de nuestra parte mía traba.
Y no puente desagredoc en lo que nos propongamos.
un tan interesado negocio.
Es así Señor stendalque nuestro interés no ha sido
el de causaste perjuicios sino de que nuestros negocios
sean una realidad sin presidentes desorbitantes.
nosotros como interesados en tal negocio quieres una
vez mas serles sinseros. que cuando les dijimos que.
tal suma hera nuestra Exigencia lo dijimos porque.
lo conosemos. Tus capacidades económicos. para que.
uds. sean que si nuestro interés es el de negociar
nos pusiteus puentes el estimo plazo y la ultima
Exigencia que tal suma y tal fecha. corresponde a.
tal sinseridad. y seriedad que Tuemos. pero si no se.
cumple pasaremos por la pena de comunicarles que no.
Responderemos por la vida del señor. Martin.

La exigencia ultima es de 12 M. llones y el plazo es at
el día 25 de D. cembre

Cordialmente   Captores

Chapter Twelve

June 26, 1984 Ketchikan, Alaska

I was finally released by the guerrillas on January 2, 1984, after 142 days of captivity. My return home, unbelievably and very happily, coincided to the day and to the hour with the 20th anniversary of our family's arrival in Colombia on January 3, 1964.

As I write this, I am looking out over the Ketchikan harbor. Three large cruise ships have arrived and flooded this town with tourists today. Numerous fishing boats and pleasure craft are motoring around in all directions. Every now and then I can see a float plane take off or land. In the background I see snow-covered mountains. The rocky beaches are strewn with drift wood, blown in by the winter storms. Yesterday I returned from a three-day boat trip around the Ketchikan island. It was a great time of relaxation with my family. I enjoyed seeing grizzly bear, black bear, seals, and sea lions in the wild. It feels great to be free and to be able to enjoy such beautiful country. I find that now I am able to appreciate with *gusto* many things that I once took for granted. I hope that we, the American people, will have the courage, strength, and determination to preserve our freedom as our country faces difficult times.

After I finished the book for Manuel on my 40th day of captivity, I had a lot of time on my hands for the next 102 days. On my 67th day of captivity, I was transferred upriver to the main guerrilla headquarters and training camp. Hundreds of guerrillas were in this area, and I was both pleased and surprised to find Manuel among them. He came over with a smile on his face and thanked me for the book. His wound was now almost completely healed and he could even carry his backpack again! I was astonished to find out that I was already something of a celebrity in the guerrilla camp. Manuel had been proudly showing the book to all his buddies and many of them had read it. They were all intrigued with the story of my shooting Manuel and of our incredible friendship afterwards. Most of the men seemed to respect and admire me and many of them would come over in their spare time and talk with me, asking my opinion on many matters and sometimes even opening up to me and discussing deep personal problems.

I was in high spirits, and by my 75th day of captivity I had even managed to talk Jaime and Vicente into taking off the rope and letting me walk around loose within a certain perimeter of the camp. My ever present guards would just stroll around with me. Different guerrillas would stop in from time to time during the day to converse and even consult with me on topics ranging from medical problems to ballistics. They still tied me up at night, but they were beginning to treat me like an expensive pet instead of a prisoner.

All this seemed too good to be true. During this time my captors refused to comment on the negotiation for my release, which was underway with my family. From time to time I would receive a package of food or clothes from my family, but my captors withheld the letters that my wife and family were sending me. Vicente would write out letters from me to my family and come over and have me copy and sign them. I did this several times, but on November 3, my dad's birthday, he came over with a really nasty letter for me to copy. I left out the worst part and put in a birthday greeting to my dad instead. Vicente left without checking over what I had written. He didn't realize that I had made the switch until he was turning the letter over to my wife and brother during one of their contact meetings. It kind of ruined his day and he was so mad when he got back that he wouldn't let me send or receive anything else.

The next day we started hearing news of the American invasion of Grenada over the radio. Radio Havana, Cuba, made quite a production out of it. Many of the guerrillas didn't seem too interested in the news, but some of them, especially the leaders, got very uptight. Giovani and some of the others who I had been suspecting all along of being Cubans due to their Caribbean-sounding Spanish accents made some remarks that really let the cat out of the bag. Some of them were so inflamed over the fact that American troops were invading Grenada and killing their Cuban countrymen that they wanted to kill me in retaliation. Fortunately it was all over so fast that the guerrilla leadership didn't decide to go that route.

There was a general mood of depression among the guerrilla leadership after the Cuban defeat on Grenada. Some of them started asking me worried questions about whether or not America would intervene militarily in Colombia if the guerrillas seemed in danger of taking over the country. I replied that I didn't know, but that if they didn't want that to happen, they should quit kidnapping and killing American citizens. I told them that President Reagan was determined to stand up against terrorism, and that one of the reasons triggering the Grenada invasion had been the President's decision to protect American lives (I had heard this on the radio).

Another factor contributing to the guerrillas' mood of depression was the rumor circulating around camp that a large weapons shipment, destined for them, had been captured on Grenada by the Americans. This made even the rank and file guerrillas very mad at President Reagan because they all love weapons more than almost anything else. For months the guerrilla leaders had been telling their men during their morning indoctrination sessions that a significant percentage of the money that the guerrilla unit was making through drug trafficking, extortion of ranchers and businessmen, and kidnappings was being spent on modern weapons. The leader would put all the figures on a large blackboard made from a black piece of canvas stretched between two trees. The blackboard was about 80 yards from where I was kept and I could see them writing on it every morning, but I was too far away to see and hear everything that went on in the morning indoctrination sessions. I could hear bits and pieces and every three days when I was allowed to bathe in the stream, they would walk me right by the blackboard. Many times their accounts and figures would still be written on it. They appeared to be telling the men that a lot of the money they were taking in was being sent to help their comrades in El Salvador. They also claimed to be sending men over there. I could see how this was good for morale. If any of the guerrillas from this unit were killed, say by the Colombia army in local combat, the leaders could just tell the men that they had been transferred to El Salvador. It also gave the men something to look forward to every evening as they would tune their radios to Radio Venceremos from Nicaragua and listen to the latest inspiring news. Every once in a while one of their comrades would actually return from a tour of duty in Central America and give glowing accounts of how the "war of liberation" in El Salvador was progressing. The guerrilla recruits were optimistically taught that Colombia would probably be in Marxist hands within two years. They were to tighten their belts and endure discipline, hardship, and "necessary evil" for this short amount of time. After the guerrillas won and were in power, then everybody would have "true freedom," just like in Nicaragua, Cuba, and the Soviet Union.

During this period of time most of the men seemed to like and respect me. Jaime, the squad leader, and Nancy, the nurse, both seemed very sympathetic. The shootout in the banana patch with Manuel, followed by the book, coupled with my reconciliation and present friendship with Manuel was the talk of the guerrilla camp. Most of the guerrillas would have likely never believed the story, or accepted the book, if Manuel and I hadn't been right there in the camp as living proof of what had happened. Even so, some of the more inquisitive ones would ask Manuel to show them his scar and the gun and ankle holster I had used to shoot him with, both of which were in his possession.

Giovani, the squad disciplinarian and control officer was becoming more and more upset with me as he saw me becoming more and more popular with the men.

Mariano, the gunsmith, also had a very obvious chip on his shoulder against me. He felt that I was winning over the hearts of the guerrillas with very clever lies and propaganda about God and the Bible. Giovani and Mariano were encouraged and backed up in their hatred of me by a young guerrilla leader named Eliezar. Eliezar appeared to be the control officer for the guerrillas' training institute which was attached to this guerrilla unit. I strongly suspected him of being Cuban also.

The basic training of over one hundred recruits, some of them female, was in constant progress around the clock. I could hear the drill instructors shouting and chanting cadence all day long and sometimes well into the night. I could hear shooting for hours at a time, both day and night as the new recruits were trained in jungle warfare. At night, if the weather was good, they would all sit around a campfire and sing inspiring, revolutionary songs. I was normally excluded from these campfire meetings because most of the local peasants were rounded up to attend. The guerrilla leadership was ashamed to have the people know that they were involved in kidnapping, so I was carefully kept out of sight during these occasions. Sometimes I could hear the singing, hundreds of voices strong, ringing through the jungle in the moonlight as the guerrillas did their best to live up to their boast of being "freedom fighters." The singing would be followed by speeches from fiery orators, who would instruct the people in Marxist ideology. Sometimes there would be a video presentation utilizing a Sony Betamax with a large screen. They would sometimes show an American movie, such as *Apocalypse Now,* which would be introduced as a documentary film on the Vietnam War. They would proceed to take some of Hollywood's most atrocious productions (or best works of art, depending on your viewpoint), and present them as our normal American way of life. They also had a lot of Russian documentary films on various topics. Most of their film library had apparently been edited and translated into Spanish in Cuba prior to being distributed to the guerrillas. I never got to attend any of the presentations, but I was asked to work on the generator and Betamax when they went on the blink.

The guerrillas seemed to have no shortage of equipment or ammunition, although modern automatic assault rifles seemed to be in short supply. Only about one-third of the troops had G-3's, M-16's, or AR-15's. The rest of them were armed with M-1 rifles, M-1 carbines, and an assortment of old bolt action rifles. Hand grenades and anti-aircraft weapons were also in short supply, although they did have some very modern rockets and 50 caliber machine guns.

I was very surprised that the guerrilla leadership didn't ban my book and keep me in isolation from most of their men. I guess part of it must have been the fact that they (the leadership) are always trying to justify everything they do. They didn't want to appear totalitarian or arbitrary to their men. They take pride in the claim that they don't torture people like they say the government does. They just kill anyone who is causing them a problem. If they kill a government official, it is because he is rotten and corrupt, not doing his job. If they kill a poor campesino farmer, it is because he is a tattle-tale, or a government spy. If they kidnap an American citizen, it is because he is a corrupt capitalist, exploiting the common people. If they kill him, then it is because he must have been a CIA agent. If they kill one of their own men, it is because he was a traitor, and so on. They never make "mistakes," but they do try to justify their actions.

Apparently these guerrilla leaders allowed me to speak out and my book to circulate because they wanted to appear fair to their men. They expected their men to see through the "lies" and "propaganda" that I was talking about, thus strengthening the ideology that was being taught officially. Therefore my first one hundred days or so of captivity were under increasingly favorable conditions.

Starting with the Grenada invasion and my alteration of Vicente's letter however, my situation started becoming more and more tense. The guerrilla leaders were very subtly stepping up the psychological pressure on me. They would spend days at a time creating the right mood or environment in an attempt to break me down mentally and emotionally. I was told that my situation was hopeless and that I was being abandoned by my family. I was urged to write an emotional plea to my family ordering them to comply with my captor's ransom demands. I replied that I was sure that my family was doing everything they could to get me out. I told my captors that they were the ones who had made a mistake and captured a poor missionary's son instead of a rich capitalist like they had thought. I told them that they had two choices, either kill me, or let me go for whatever small amount my family could afford. Jaime turned and asked me if I was afraid to die. I replied that dying is obviously uncomfortable, but yes, I was prepared to die.

A few days later my captors tied me back up again and left the rope on day and night. This wasn't Jaime's decision. Apparently Giovani went over Jaime's head and the guerrilla leadership agreed with him. A serious campaign was started to completely break me psychologically and then brainwash me. Every day new things were done to alter me and work towards that goal. My captors started telling me scare stories. Some of these stories were about wild animals. They told me some of the wildest, hair-raising tales about lions (mountain lions or cougars) and tigers (jaguars) that I have ever heard. These stories were designed both to intimidate me, reducing my ability to sleep, and to cause me to think twice before I decided to try and escape into the jungle again.

The next day they decided to put some more pressure on me, so they went out and shot a monkey. They didn't kill the monkey, they just shot it in the stomach. It was a mother, and it had a tiny baby monkey clinging to it. They dragged it over close to where I was and left it there. All day long I had to witness this little drama of the mother monkey's agonizing death with it's whimpering baby clinging to it.

Several days before, Mariano had been talking to me about my wife. He told me enough about her so that by his description of her, I knew that he had really met her. He then insinuated that the guerrillas had her in their power also. He told me that they would probably decide to brainwash her and put her through guerrilla training. Then they would put her into combat. He said that they might decide to release me some day after they had gotten all the money that our family had, but that they would always keep custody of my wife to make sure that I would never badmouth them after my release.

At first my mind went wild with thoughts of revenge and violence. Then, after a while, I was able to see that this was part of their attempt to break me down and brainwash me. I started making a determined effort to throw all their stories and dramas out of my mind and not to let my thoughts dwell on them at all. I would trust God that He would take care of my wife and I would close my mind to my captors' input. I decided to think about positive values instead.

The night after the monkey incident, a cougar (the guerrillas call them lions) actually arrived in camp! I was almost asleep in my hammock and Mariano was on guard. The lion came and got between me and him. It sniffed around for awhile, and finally left after several minutes. After it left, I asked Mariano why he hadn't shot it. He was all shook up and he said his flashlight had malfunctioned. He had been scared to shoot and miss because I and the rest of the camp were on the other side of the lion from him, so he had just waited, petrified with fear, until it left. Also, a shot from the guard was a warning of attack and would have caused the whole camp of hundreds of men to mobilize themselves. He had shot at a jaguar and missed several months before on guard duty. He said he had been disciplined so severely that time that he didn't want to take any more chances. Mariano called some of the other men over and they looked at the lion's huge tracks. The guerrillas seemed puzzled over why the lion had come so boldly into camp. Normally they avoid humans. From then on the guards seemed very nervous at night. They would shine their flashlights all around until they ran down the batteries. They all seemed to get more and more uptight every night. I was wondering about this when I realized that they were all starting to believe their own tall tales that they had been trying to scare me with. I slept soundly because I was the only one who knew the real reason why that lion had wandered into camp. I knew that cougar hunters would kill monkeys for bait. They would drag the monkey through the jungle, and then leave it in a clearing. The cougar would follow that trail, if he ran across it, and walk into their ambush. This lion had merely run across the trail of the mother monkey that the guerrillas had shot and dragged over for me so I would watch it die!

During most of my captivity I would start out my day by reading a Psalm from my Bible. I started reading Psalm 40 on my 40th day of captivity and each day I would read the next one. It started out as a neat way to keep track of the days, but soon I began to see that most of those Psalms were very relevant to my situation. Most of them had been written under difficult circumstances and I could easily identify with the writer. I would let my daily Psalm be my prayer to God and say it with the same heartfelt conviction that the original writer must have felt thousands of years ago. Psalm 91 was very special to me, as were many others. It almost began to seem like the book of Psalms could have been written just for me. Each one came at exactly the right day to help me understand and make it through that day's difficulties.

I began to wonder if I should have tried to escape back when my captors had left me loose for many days. Now I was tied up again, and they were obviously cracking down on me. Maybe I had blown a good opportunity. I was now deep in the jungle and would have little chance to reach civilization alive, even if I managed to break out of camp. I decided to ask God for another clear sign to show me if He would continue to protect me if I stayed in the guerrilla camp. I asked God to give me an opportunity to escape with equipment and supplies if that was what He wanted me to do.

The next morning, approximately my 110th day, I got up, read my Psalm, and began to walk back and forth as far as the nylon rope would allow. I was deep in meditation while I got my morning exercise. I walked parallel with my hammock. The tarp above the hammock would be covered with dead leaves that had fallen down during the night. In pitching the hammock my captors had chopped through some thick vines that had dried out and were now shedding their leaves. Every morning as I walked back and forth, I would slap the bottom of the tarp from beneath causing all the dead leaves to collect in the lowest part of the tarp. Then on my next pass by

154

the tarp, I would reach my hand in and scoop out all the dead leaves. On my first pass by the tarp I reached out and slapped the bottom of it. On my second pass I started to scoop the dead leaves out with my hand but on impulse, thought better of it and continued on by.

As I passed the tarp, I detected some motion out of the corner of my eye coupled with a soft hiss. I turned, and there was a snake, its face just inches from mine. It had been coiled in the pile of leaves on top of the tarp. It had been disturbed when I had slapped the tarp from the bottom, and now it was mad. It had struck at me as I walked by, missing my neck by inches. Its forked tongue flickered in and out between the needle-like teeth in its closed mouth as it prepared to strike again. I continued walking past and turned around when I got to the end of my rope. Arnuval was the guard. He came over and swatted the snake with the broad side of his machete to avoid damaging the tarp. The snake fell to the ground and headed straight for me with Arnuval hot on its tail. I couldn't run because I was tied up, so I jumped up in the air at the last minute as the snake approached me. It went by and hit a big tree with wide, spreading roots. Somehow it got turned around and came right back at us. Arnuval got tangled up in my rope and fell down. I tripped over him and clutched out blindly to keep from falling on top of the snake. I got a hold of something solid. It turned out to be the hilt of Arnuval's bayonet which was slung on his wide cartridge belt, fastened firmly around his waist. For a split second I considered drawing it, knifing him, and pushing him over on top of the snake, but then I thought better of it. I steadied myself and then helped Arnuval up. Arnuval swatted the snake with his machete again, killing it, and we both started shaking. For an instant it had been within my grasp to have snatched Arnuval's G-3 rifle, but I would have had to kill or wound him in order to escape. Somehow I hadn't been able to go through with it. The effects of shooting Manuel, coupled with the fact that I knew Arnuval so well by now, had spoiled my appetite for any further violence. The snake could easily have bitten one or both of us. It was a poisonous snake of the *fer-de-lance* family, about three feet long.

155

Arnuval looked at me, and I looked at him. Neither one of us spoke for a long time. Finally he remarked that he wasn't in favor of keeping me tied up. He also apologized for shooting the monkey. He said that he wished that he didn't have to obey so many stupid orders and he obviously meant it from the heart.

(Apparently the Marxist leadership was briefing the guards before they came on duty and appeared to be giving them each specific orders to do or say something designed to affect me in some way. The guards were then debriefed as they came off duty. Arnuval was this squad's specialist in psychological warfare, and he was now very obviously fed-up with his job.)

I thought the whole incident over and recalled Psalm 91 where it says, "And you shall trample the young lion and the serpent underfoot." Then I thanked God for taking care of me. It was clear that taking care of me in the guerrilla camp was no problem for Him. I took the snake incident as an obvious sign that God still wanted me in that guerrilla camp working for Him. I felt confident that I had made the right decision in trying to help Arnuval instead of knifing him, snatching his gun, and trying to escape. If I were to resort to physical violence again, it would ruin the effects of everything I had done and said up until now. The book and my life were having a tremendous effect on some of the guerrillas. If I took the viewpoint that God had sent me on a rescue mission to the guerrillas, everything seemed exciting. It was really a spiritual warfare I was waging and I decided to launch out on the offensive and attack, instead of always being on the defensive. I decided that I would boldly say or do whatever I felt God would have me do in any given situation, regardless of the consequences. I would use all the spiritual weapons and armament at my command. Even though I was physically tied up, and my captors were the ones who had all the physical weapons (machine guns, etc.), I would attempt to rescue my captors from the spiritual bondage that they were in. Many of them appeared to be in physical bondage also. There was a chance that I would eventually be released, but most of them were stuck out there until they either died of disease or were killed in combat.

Nancy, who had been very aloof at the beginning of my captivity, became more and more interested in what I was saying after she read my book. She started taking her turn at guard duty, using the opportunity to ask me questions. One day she looked at me with a puzzled look on her face and asked me, "Are all Americans like you?"

"No," I replied, "I'm one of the worst ones. Most Americans are a lot nicer than me and would never have shot one of you."

For an instant she looked shocked, as the hint of a whole new positive outlook on America began to flash through her brain. Quickly she recovered and we both laughed at my little joke, but seeds for thought had been sown.

Two days later she asked me another question. "What is life really like in Russia?" she wanted to know.

I thought for a minute, started to answer, thought some more, and finally I said, "The best example that I can give you of life in Russia is this guerrilla camp. Here you are each given the things that your leaders think you need in order to carry out your job. You don't necessarily get what you want. You are each treated as a cog in a machine. It is the organization or system (the machine) that is important to your leaders, not the individuals that make up the organization. Individuals are expendable; there is no individual freedom within this guerrilla camp that I can see. Life in Russia is roughly the same, but on a larger, more polished scale.

A look of horror and unbelief flashed across Nancy's face. "No! It can't be!" she exclaimed emotionally. "They told us that we have to endure discipline, hardship, and undesirable circumstances for just two years, until we are in power. They promised us true freedom after that, just like in Russia and Cuba. If what you are saying is true, we will never attain individual freedom."

Nancy became very interested in the Bible and in the book of ideological cartoons by Phil Saint that I had with me. There were some beautiful cartoons on topics such as terrorism, nuclear war, and Christianity that really caught her eye. She enjoyed the book so much that I gave it to her along with a New

Testament I had. Under the flyleaf I wrote, "To Nancy, in the hopes that you will find the personal peace and freedom that you have been fighting for."

She thanked me, then looked at me for a while with a thoughtful look on her face. Finally she said, "I envy you. You have your own personal peace inside." Her eyes were misty as she turned and walked away.

Young Alfredo switched around and started trying to befriend me towards the end. He told me that his father had been a man of deep religious conviction and that he had respected him. Unfortunately his father was gone, and social conditions had split up the family. Alfredo had been taken in by the guerrillas several years before when he was just eleven years old. Alfredo started coming over and playing chess with me instead of trying to get me into trouble all the time like he had been doing before. I spent a lot of time talking with him and giving him good advice, which he took seriously.

On an impulse, one of the next times Arnuval was on guard duty, I gave him a present. It was a small snake-bite kit with suction cups, a lymph constrictor cord, a vial of iodine, and a scalpel. I had managed to keep it stuffed inside a roll of toilet paper, secret from my captors all this time. Arnuval was touched and pleased. He was also shocked that I had a razor-sharp, three-inch-long scalpel in my possession. The snake-bite kit had been stuffed in one of the packages of candy I had received over a month before from my family. Somehow it had slipped through my captors' strict inspection of everything sent to me. I also had a box of matches hidden away in a package of Kleenex.

From time to time I would try to read passages from the Bible to my captors, but they never got very interested. Nancy was the only one who seemed to listen. Finally I got some results reading from the book of Proverbs. I explained about King Solomon being one of the richest and wisest men who ever lived and I started reading short riddles out of Proverbs to my guards. Soon they were all interested. Even Giovani would come over and discuss Solomon's proverbs with interest. Arnuval was intrigued, given his background in psychology.

One day I read him Proverbs 24:3-6, "By wisdom the house is built; with intelligence the foundation is laid, and by knowledge the rooms of the house are furnished with articles of great value and good taste." Arnuval puzzled for awhile and finally asked me to explain it to him.

I told him there was only one source of true wisdom. God spoke the universe into being with wisdom. We can use our human intelligence to get an education. (The guerrillas believe that education is the answer to all man's problems. Each guerrilla is on a continual study program at whatever level he has attained.) I told Arnuval that when we die, material things will no longer be important to us. The true articles of great value and good taste with which we can furnish the "rooms of our lives" are the experiences we have had, and the lessons we have learned. Whether or not the education we have obtained with our intelligence is true wisdom or not will be born out in actual experience as we go through life.

All of a sudden Arnuval exclaimed, "I see it!" He got out a pen and paper and wrote it all down. He said, "What you have been saying all these days really makes sense, and experience has proved it. I am in charge of the morning indoctrination session tomorrow for the whole camp, and I want to teach them this lesson out of Proverbs."

The next afternoon Arnuval was gone. Jaime left with him. The official explanation was that they had both been transferred. Giovani had been warning the guerrilla leadership that I was having a dangerous influence on the men. Arnuval's lesson from the Bible must have been the last straw that broke the camel's back. Jaime was sacked, and the new squad commander was Eliezar.

The training course for the new recruits had ended a week before. Apparently Eliezar as control officer decided to personally take over our squad in an attempt to undo some of the ideological damage I had inflicted on the unit. Two new men, Luis and Miguel, who were both green recruits, joined the squad along with Eliezar, bringing it up to nine men.

Under Eliezar my situation went from bad to worse. As I write this account, six months after my release, most of the negative things done to me during my last month of captivity have faded in my memory. I have had no flashbacks or nightmares. I believe that my decision to pattern my thinking on Jesus' Sermon on the Mount has been the reason that I have suffered no permanent psychological damage.

I am not going to give a play by play account of that last month. I would rather forgive and forget. During my last 30 days of captivity, an all-out effort was made to completely break me down, using every available means. My typewriter was taken away and dismantled; the small pieces and springs were turned over to Mariano to repair weapons. I was prohibited from doing any further writing, but my notebooks and Bible were not taken away. It was very hot, and I was not allowed to drink water; instead, a bitter, strange-tasting lemonade was provided for me. I believe that chemicals and mind-altering drugs were put in my food and drink. I suffered from intense migraine headaches most of the time. An effort was made to keep me from sleeping by shining flashlights in my eyes throughout the night. Some of my captors would say things like, "We're humane; we would never shoot you down when you are awake. When we need to eliminate you, we will just put a bullet through your head while you are asleep." Soon I found it impossible to sleep, even when they weren't shining the flashlight in my eyes. If I ever did doze off, I would be jolted awake when the ever-present guard lifted the edge of my mosquito net with his gun barrel to check on me. Mariano was expert at harassing me.

Towards the end I felt my mental control slipping. I started feeling intense claustrophobia under the mosquito net. I had to consciously strain to hang on to my serenity and keep from ripping off the mosquito net and ropes. I felt an intense, almost overpowering desire to start screaming at the top of my lungs. I felt hemmed in from all sides. I longed to see clear blue sky and wide-open spaces instead of trees and leaves. On Christmas Eve my captors moved me to a denser thicket of second growth in the middle of a cocaine-growing and processing laboratory which was being run by them.

Eliezar seemed determined to either snap my mind and pass me off as a religious fanatic who had finally gone religious crazy, or else provoke me into doing something for which they could legitimately shoot me. My book was having such an effect on the guerrilla camp that the leaders were paranoid, trying frantically to discredit me in front of the men. Some of the men were questioning the policies of the Marxist leaders after reading my book. They were saying, "Why do we have to kill so many innocent people? We are doing things that are wrong. How are we going to have freedom if we fight evil with evil? Maybe the *gringo* (me) is right. Maybe God is real. If He is, what is He going to think about us and some of the things we are doing?" The guerrilla leaders were starting to lose control of their men. So many men were involved in the dissension that it was impossible to crack down on all of them.

I started speaking out strongly about my beliefs to each of the guards as he came on duty for his three-hour shift. I told each of them that God valued them as individuals and that He had a plan for each of them. Then I proceeded to apply Jesus' teachings to each one's own personal situation. Due to the extreme pressure I was under, my words came out with a lot of force and conviction. Even Giovani was impressed. After I had talked with him for two hours, he finally broke down and said that he would like to get right with God, but that his case was hopeless. He had done too many awful, evil things. I replied by asking him a question: "If your friend owed a man one peso, and you owed the same man a million pesos, if the man forgave both of you, which of you would be the most grateful to him?" Giovani replied that he would, of course. I told him that with God things work the same way. It is never too late to admit our mistakes and failures and to let God take charge of our lives. The bigger the mess we have made of things, the more grateful we will be when He straightens us out and saves us from our problems. Giovani was extremely thoughtful from then on and stopped being belligerent towards me. He told me that his conscience troubled him greatly because of all the bad things he had done. He also told me that his mother was deeply religious and that she was praying for him every day. She had given him a heavy, gold crucifix, which he wore around his neck on a chain.

As I opened up to my captors and began to express my inner convictions in a positive manner, challenging each one individually to consider God and to consider things of eternal spiritual value, my inner tension eased and completely went away. I began to take the offensive in my conversations with Eliezar and Vicente. I told them that when they kidnap a corrupt government official or a drug mafia figure and relieve them of some of their ill-gotten gains, in a sense they are just helping further God's justice. If they interfere with God's people, however, it is a completely different state of affairs. I told them that if they take some of God's money or kill one of His servants, that then they are in big trouble.

I reminded them of the case when the M-19 guerrilla movement kidnapped and killed Chet Bitterman, a Wycliffe missionary, several years ago.

Before the Bitterman kidnapping, the M-19 group had done one spectacular operation after another. Within a month after killing Chet, the fortunes of the M-19 were in sharp decline. Hundreds of them were killed or captured by the Colombian Army in unprecedented military operations. The grand finale came when Jaime Bateman, the leader, fled the country in an airplane with a large sum of money, the proceeds of terrorism, heading for Panama. The aircraft he was in crashed, killing everyone on board. The money was never recovered and probably burned. Some of their remaining cells have been integrated into the F.A.R.C, the group that kidnapped me, using either name interchangeably.

The guerrillas complained that all this was the result of bad luck, but I think God lowered the boom on them after they killed Chet Bitterman. I believe God respects the free will of atheists until they go too far and take something or kill someone belonging to God. If our human free will is used to attack God's Kingdom, then God is free to intervene in any way that He sees fit.

I kept telling the guerrilla leaders that they had made a mistake in kidnapping me. I told them that I had no personal desire for revenge, that I was content to leave the matter in God's hands. I kept inviting them to come with me on a trip to the United States where they could see for themselves what America is really like. I told them that it wasn't their fault if someone had told them a bunch of lies about America and it's citizens, but that they should be responsible enough to check things out for themselves and not just blindly believe everything that they heard, read, or saw on a video screen. America isn't perfect, not by a long shot; there are those who abuse their freedom, but that is one of the inherent risks of having a free system. A great majority of Americans cherish and love the freedom they have. They consider "life, liberty, and the pursuit of happiness" to be God-given "unalienable rights." Many Americans have found that a proper relationship with God is the key to achieving these goals.

On my 140th day of captivity, New Year's Eve, Mariano was on guard duty. He and Eliezar were the only ones in our squad who were still antagonistic towards me. Relations between Mariano and me were very cool. The night before, I had dozed off a little. Subconsciously I had pulled the mosquito net off and stuck my head out. I had been rudely awakened by the barrel of Mariano's assault rifle, inches from my nose, as he drew back the slide and threatened to kill me. The rest of the night he had spent periodically shining his flashlight in my eyes, keeping his gun barrel centered on me with the safety off. He had gone off duty at 6:00 a.m., but now he was back at 9:00 a.m. for another shift. He and Eliezar seemed very uneasy. I think that they were worried that one of the other guerrillas might decide to help me escape and then leave with me. (I had been inviting them all to come to America with me and see for themselves what it was like.) I racked my brain for a way to break through Mariano's rough, cold exterior. If I could convincingly demonstrate good will, maybe I could penetrate the barrier of distrust between us. I had already given him some American toothpaste in a fancy container that pumped the toothpaste out. As a gunsmith, he had been fascinated with it, but he still seemed to hate and distrust me. A complicating factor in our relationship was that Mariano had been Manuel's partner. All this time he had been blaming himself for not backing up his partner when I shot Manuel. He had been fooling around on the river bank instead of backing up Manuel like he was supposed to do. Even though Manuel had forgiven me, Mariano had been nursing a bitter grudge against me from the start.

All of a sudden I remembered the box of matches I had hidden away in my box of Kleenex. I got them out and gave them to Mariano as an act of good will. He was impressed, to realize that I would voluntarily hand over something that would have been useful to me in an escape attempt, and I was able to have an excellent heart to heart talk with him.

"You kidnapped me to raise money for your cause and as an act of terrorism," I told him, "But God allowed this to happen so that I can tell you all about Him." Then I explained that Christianity wasn't a system like capitalism or socialism, but a personal relationship with God. I was just telling Mariano that it would do him good to broaden his horizons and visit other countries where he could see for himself what was really going on in the world, instead of listening to and blindly believing biased reports. I offered to show him around myself if I ever got a chance.

Right in the middle of our discussion, Eliezar walked over. He asked me if I wasn't going to invite him too. I replied that sure, he could come along too. Then he blew up.

"You are not in charge here. I'm in charge here," he screamed at me. "You don't seem to want to get out of here alive, do you?"

The atmosphere was tense, and I got the distinct impression that I might get shot if I said another word. Eliezar seemed to be looking for an excuse to kill me. I kept silent, and after a minute or so of staring me in the eye, he broke off his gaze and left.

Mariano seemed unmoved by this scene. After Eliezar left, he said to me, "Now what were you saying before we were interrupted?" I wasn't sure if he was being satirical, or if he genuinely wanted to continue our conversation. Earlier Mariano had been trying to tell me that there was freedom of speech within the Marxist guerrilla organization. I now asked him if this incident was an example of what he had been talking about. He didn't reply.

I sat down and started thumbing through my Bible. I was wondering what I should say to Eliezar the next time I saw him. It must have seemed to him that most of his men were paying more attention to what I said than to what he said. A week before, I had played a game of chess with him, checkmating him in nine moves in front of his men. I had intended to let him win, so I sacrificed a castle and a knight to his queen, while I just pushed a pawn forward one step at a time. He was so intent on wiping out my pieces that he didn't notice that when I moved my pawn the last step forward, it was backed up by a bishop and resulted in a checkmate. It had been a terrible humiliation for him, an important instructor of military strategy, to get checkmated in nine moves by a pawn. The men thought I had planned the whole thing and marveled, because Eliezar had an awesome reputation as a chess player in camp. Rumor had it that he had learned to play chess from the Russians while receiving his military training. Actually that chess game gave me some insight into the guerrillas' training procedures. They are good at following set procedures and standard responses, but if you do something unpredictable, like I did to Eliezar when I started giving away my pieces, they aren't trained to respond with original thinking. Their system stifles that.

I had been reading one Psalm each day of my captivity and from them had been getting specific directions from the Lord. Because of the potential danger of the situation, I decided I'd better not wait until tomorrow to read the next Psalm. I might not be alive tomorrow.

I opened my Bible to Psalm 141, and in verse three I found the specific directions I needed: "Set a guard over my mouth, O Lord; keep watch over the door of my lips" (NIV) I knew it was indeed a time to keep silent.

As I read further verses, five and six caught my eye: "Yet my prayer is ever against the deeds of evildoers; their rulers will be thrown down from the cliffs, and the wicked will learn that my words were well spoken" (NIV). In my Spanish Bible, the last part of verse six translated: "They shall be brought to the realization that my words were the truth." I took that to be a promise that God would apply my words directly to the consciences of my captors, convincing them of the truth. I began to feel very elated. I happily began to praise God for all the many things He had done in my life. I also began to praise Him for all the great things I was sure He would do for me in the future.

I had been praying for total spiritual victory ever since my experience with the Morning Star more than 100 days before. As I thought, I ran my hand down the side of the hammock in which I was seated, fingering the beautiful design woven into the sides of it. It was a hand-woven, wool hammock with bright colors, featuring a row of six-inch stars, woven in a double pattern down both sides in yellow and blue. All of a sudden I was electrified, as it dawned on me for the first time that these were six-pointed stars. They were Stars of David, just like I had seen around Nancy's neck! With trembling fingers I counted them. There were twenty-six. There are also twenty-six men in a standard guerrilla platoon which consists of three eight-man squads plus the platoon commander and the platoon control officer.[1]

Vicente, the company commander of the unit that kidnapped me, had assigned a whole platoon to my case. One squad guarded me. Another squad handled the security of the negotiation with my family, while the third squad provided security, supplies, and communication to the squad guarding me. Here I had just spent one hundred and forty nights sleeping in this hammock an obligatory twelve hours out of every twenty four, sometimes spending up to five hours a night praying for my captors. All the time I had been surrounded by twenty-six symbolic Stars of David, one for each guerrilla directly involved in my kidnapping!

As I relaxed in my hammock that night, trying to unwind and perhaps get some sleep, my thoughts turned to Eliezar. He

---

[1] A guerrilla company consists of three 26-man squads, plus the company commander and the company control officer for a total of 80 men. Eight full companies make up a battalion. The battalion commander and his staff make up an additional platoon, bringing a standard guerrilla battalion, or *frente,* as they call it, up to a total of six hundred and sixty-six men. The F.A.R.C. claim that they have over twenty *frentes* operating in Colombia.

was now the only one in our immediate camp who was openly threatening me. I included him in my prayers, asking God to change his attitude also.

About midnight, I heard a commotion. It got louder and louder. Guerrillas with flaming torches in their hands were heading for my hammock shouting and banging on things. I thought, "Oh, no! They must have gotten drunk since this is New Year's Eve, and now they are probably going to lynch me. When they got up close, however, they all began to sing, serenading me with a Colombian *Ballenato*. I recognized Mariano playing a harmonica, Elkin had a pair of pan lids he was playing like cymbals, and each of the others had some sort of makeshift instrument, which accounted for all the noise.

After they finished singing three boisterous songs, making the jungle ring, I climbed out of the hammock and stood up to address them, as was expected in keeping with Colombian tradition. I thanked them for their thoughtfulness and told them that they had just provided me with the material for an epic story to tell to my grandchildren about how I was serenaded at quarter till midnight on New Year's Eve, by a guerrilla band in the middle of the jungle.

I made a positive comment to each one in turn. They were all there except for Eliezar. He was seated on a log 50 yards away in the center of camp. I asked Mariano to go get him and was both pleased and a little apprehensive as they came back together. I looked at Eliezar and announced that I felt that we should all herald this new year as a year of friendship and reconciliation. I told him that I was sorry if I had offended him in any way and I held out my hand to him.

Eliezar hesitated for a split second; then he reached out and took my hand. "You are different from what I thought you were," he said gruffly, "If you continue to behave yourself, I will not cause you any more trouble." Then, not to be outdone by my overtures for peace, he produced two glasses. Handing me one, he proposed a toast to friendship!

Elkin came forward and filled our glasses from a bottle of wine that Nancy had been saving for a special occasion. Normally I am not much of a drinker, but this didn't seem like the time to balk, so I raised my glass and said, "To the New Year. Let us burn the Old Year behind us (in Colombia the Old Year is burned symbolically in traditional New Year celebration), and may 1984 be a year of friendship and peace."

At exactly midnight, Mariano fired a burst from his machine gun up into the air. Then Elkin detonated some bombs he had prepared for the occasion. Following this, Mariano held a torch to a cloth dummy he had soaked in oily gasoline, symbolizing the Old Year. The flames lit up the jungle, shooting high into the air.

I was in high spirits as I climbed back into my hammock half an hour later. The flames had died down to a dull glow, and most of my captors had gone back to bed. Javier and Elkin were on guard duty. It was starting to look like Mariano might really be giving up his grudge against me. He had taken part whole-heartedly in the serenade. As I lay back and thought things over, going over every detail of the New Year's celebration in my mind, Elkin walked over close to my hammock and broke the silence. "We know that you don't belong to the CIA and that you aren't a (Colombian) government agent," he announced confidentially.

Caught off-guard by his statement, I asked him, "What led you to that conclusion?"

"Real easy," he replied, "You aren't afraid of us. Our organization has captured government agents from time to time and we have always been able to eventually break them down psychologically and find out what they are, but you are different. Everyone in this whole part of the country knows of your air ambulance flying and speaks highly of you."

The part about me not being afraid almost completely floored me. I had been scared to death lots of times, but amazingly they apparently hadn't noticed when I was afraid. The Bible says that perfect love casts out fear,[2] and I think that is probably the explanation of what happened. When I started treating the kidnapping as an opportunity to reflect God's love towards my captors in an attempt to rescue them from the

---

[2]   1 John 4:18

vicious circle of hatred and lies in which they were trapped, my concern for them as individuals got through to them.

On the evening of my 142nd day of captivity at 5:00 p.m., three of my captors—Javier, Elkin, and Giovani—came running in unison at full speed over to my part of the campsite. They started taking down my hammock at top speed, while they announced in loud, excited voices that I was to be released. The order had just come over the radio. They were obviously very happy for me.

In less than 15 minutes, we were off. We hiked for half an hour until we came to a stream. There I was blindfolded and put into a boat. We traveled for five hours, starting and stopping several times. Finally we pulled up against the riverbank. After about ten minutes, Elkin reached over and removed first the blindfold, and then the rope. He told me to step out on the bank. I did so, and there was my brother, Chaddy. I went over and shook his hand, wondering if maybe this might be a trap.

Chaddy introduced me to the top guerrilla commander. We shook hands, and then I was introduced to a second man, who it turned out was the guerrilla's contact man for the negotiation. He wasn't a guerrilla, but he was the intermediary that my captors had used for the negotiation with my family. Both men were middle-aged and it was difficult to see their features in the soft moonlight.

Prior to my arrival, Chaddy had paid a ransom of five and a half million pesos (about $55,000 U.S.) for my release. Chaddy and I were now told that we owed an additional one million pesos to the intermediary for his work. When Chaddy protested, saying that this hadn't been in the deal, the guerrilla leader snapped, "I think your two lives are worth another million pesos." Realizing that we were at their mercy, Chaddy agreed to pay as soon as we could.

"We are really letting you go for a bargain price," the commander told us. "The going price for a ransom is many times what you are paying. We won't even make expenses on this kidnapping. I have heard a lot about you and I intend to read your book. Your family may continue to operate in this area.

We will not cause you any more trouble if you pay the additional money within thirty days."

After cautioning us not to talk to the press, the guerrilla leader told us that we were free to go. I was surprised when Giovani walked up and handed me my wallet and my watch, which had been taken from me right after I shot Manuel. I remembered a bottle of mosquito repellent I had in my pocket. Good repellent is difficult to obtain in Colombia and the stuff I had was excellent. Many of my guards had asked me to leave it with them when I left, and I had remarked that I would give it to the one who had been the nicest to me. Now I took out the bottle of repellent and gave it to Mariano. I then went through my bag, giving something to each one. I went around and said good-bye to each one, shaking their hands.

I held out my hand to Eliezar and said, "It would be nice if someday we could play another game of chess under better conditions." He gave me a wry grin and some of the men smiled.

Nancy came over and gave me a big hug. She said, "When I think of you, I will always remember the time you gave me that red candy and then said it was poison. I have never been so scared in my life."

I shook Giovani's hand next. I reached out and hefted the gold crucifix he wore around his neck, telling him to remember the real meaning of that crucifix and not to just use it as a good luck charm. He gave me a crooked grin.

The last man to whom I said good-bye was Mariano. He was standing off by himself under the trees. I walked over and held out my hand. There seemed to be something the matter with him. His gun barrel, slung over his shoulder was bobbing up and down. Looking closer, I was shocked to see that Mariano was sobbing. He took my hand and an awkward silence developed as we both searched for the right words to say. Finally he broke the silence. "Forgive me for the way I have treated you," he said, "I'm sorry about that incident the other night." There were tears in his eyes.

With a lump in my throat I replied, "*Tranquilo,* don't worry about that, remember the things I was telling you the other day when we got interrupted." I gave his hand an extra squeeze and walked away.

As I climbed into the speedboat with my brother Chaddy, I knew that I would continue to pray for Mariano as well as for Manuel and the other men I had come to know during my captivity. Chaddy took me upriver to a small town where we spent the night.

The next day my dad picked us up at a nearby airstrip. He was overjoyed to see us both safe. Chaddy insisted that I fly the 170 home. I looked the old airplane over, noticing the patches over the bullet holes and the new windshield. Even though the repair work had been skillfully done, the old airplane would never be the same. My life would never be the same again either. I had learned many important things through this experience.

I climbed into the pilot's seat and fired up the old Continental engine. It sounded smooth and friendly. After we were in the air I turned around and buzzed the field at high speed. Then I pulled the old airplane straight up. It was good to be free.

Epilogue

By Pat Stendal, 2004

After the events recorded in this book, Russell, Marina, and Lisa traveled extensively in the United States and Canada. Russell's ministry was in demand as he told of his experience of being kidnapped and preached on the Sermon on the Mount. He and his father, Chad, formed a small publishing house, Ransom Press, International, to distribute this book. Russell never lost his concern for the guerrillas he left behind in the jungle. "They are more kidnapped than I was," he told me, "I knew someone would come for me, but no one will ever come for them." *Rescue the Captors* became the title for his book.

In late 1985, two major events in Colombia called Russell and his family back to Colombia. First in November, forty-one guerrillas of the urban M-19 group attacked the Supreme Court building in downtown Bogota. Their plan was to take hostage the twenty-four members of the nation's highest court. It was an attempt to humiliate President Betancur. They wanted to place the president on trial before a captive Supreme Court and exploit differences that already existed between it and him. They gained control of the building in about twenty minutes by streaming up from an underground garage. To their surprise, the president refused to negotiate the release of over three hundred hostages. He ordered the police and army to re-capture the building. In the ensuing battle, twelve Supreme Court justices were executed and all forty-one of the insurgents died, some by suicide. For millions of comfortable, middle class citizens

171

of Bogota, this tragic incident finally brought home the fact that their country was at war.

In the aftermath of the Supreme Court incident, violence was perpetrated all over the country. Terrorist bombs shook Bogota from dusk to dawn. Machine-gun fire could be heard throughout the nights. As if this were not enough, the following week brought an even greater test. About 130 miles from Bogota, a snow-covered, volcanic mountain in the Sierra Nevada del Ruiz had been accumulating ice within its 17,716 ft. crater. When its peak exploded, the town of Armero and twelve other smaller towns disappeared under a sea of mud. Over 40,000 people were listed as dead or missing. Tens of thousands instantly became homeless and destitute. In the wake of these disasters, even the poorest Colombians were moved to aid the pathetic survivors. (Those rescued out of the mud by helicopter were without even the proverbial "clothes on their backs" as the mud had sucked off every stitch of clothing.) Trucks roamed the streets of Bogota, picking up donations of clothing and blankets. We all gave all the clothing, blankets, and shoes that we possibly could to meet the urgent need. Many of those pulled from the mud were the only person to survive in an extended family. Their grief was heartrending. Sympathetic strangers held them in their arms as they wept and mourned their loved ones. This was found to be the most successful immediate therapy.

A dormant spirit of giving and caring was rekindled, injecting the country's fragile democracy with a much needed shot in the arm. After the tragedy, a number of interesting facts surfaced. A Catholic priest had been killed in 1948 by a drunken mob for attempting to break up the annual traditional witchcraft celebration. The next day, the Archbishop of the area cursed Armero and predicted its destruction. I personally remember testimonies of Christians who lived in Armero, who were led by the Lord to leave the area just before the disaster. In one notable case, after a prayer meeting the pastor felt that the Lord wanted the congregation to stay in the church and pray all night. Some stayed and some left. The little church was built on a high hill and the next morning, the building was on a small island in a sea of mud. The parishioners who had stayed to pray were rescued safely. One pastor testified that a year previously, he and fellow Christians had been led to visit every house in Armero with the gospel.

Amidst this atmosphere, Russell and Marina returned to Colombia. They became leaders in a ministry of family reconciliation, using the principles learned from the Sermon on the Mount to rescue families, who are the basic building blocks of society. The publishing of books continued. Chad and I wrote *The Guerrillas Have Taken Our Son,* the story of the kidnapping from the point of view of the family. Russell followed with *The Beatitudes* and *God's Plan for Battle.* Chad's spiritual autobiography, *High Adventure in Colombia,* which includes our early experiences in the Kogi tribe, was written by Chad and me in 1994. Other smaller books were written by Chad and Russell. Russell also published Spanish versions of books written by men of God who had impacted his life. The literature ministry grew. The books were offered for a free-will offering to cover costs. Eventually, Colombia para Cristo, a non-profit organization, was incorporated both in the U.S. and Colombia. Russell spent seven years editing the first manuscript of the Spanish Bible, produced in 1569 by Casiodoro de Reina, who learned Hebrew from native speakers before the Inquisition destroyed all Hebrew scholars. He spent another year producing an English Bible using the same manuscript and also William Tyndale's original translation. All this work was done at night after a full day's work.

Meanwhile Chaddy continued farming in the jungle. The day Russell was released, the guerrilla leadership had given Chaddy permission to stay, even when they took over the area. "You have never been a gringo (an obnoxious American)," one of the leaders told him. Occasionally Chaddy was able to distribute Bibles and New Testaments to guerrillas who passed by his farm. One day in April 1986, not too long after Russell and Marina had returned to Colombia, Chaddy brought word to Russell that some of the guerrilla leaders wanted to see him. "Don't be stupid! You got away from them once!" he was told by well-meaning advisors. However because of the concern in his heart for his former captors and remembering the promise of the six-sided stars, he kept the appointment. This initial contact led to future encounters over the next few years. They asked him crucial questions. "We remember that when you were with us, you always told us the truth," one commander told him. After a year, two high ranking commanders were sent to apologize to Russell for the kidnapping on behalf of the entire guerrilla organization, and the doors opened for the distribution of Bibles, New Testaments, and other literature, including *Rescue the Captors,* to many guerrillas.

In late 1998, Russell, together with some community leaders from the nearby town of Puerto Lleras, started an FM radio station at the site of Lomalinda, the deserted Wycliffe Translation Center. (The radio transmissions from stations in the high altitude of Bogota pass right over the plains country to the east where most of the guerrillas were located.) Russell had me send out a letter and a map of the llanos. Three consecutive circles showed the coverage Russell hoped to implement. This project seemed to me to be prohibitively ambitious at the time, however at the present (2004) five transmitters from not only FM, but also AM and short wave frequencies reach much farther than the largest circle. We have received letters from Europe, Africa, and Australia as well as North and South America as the result of the short wave broadcasting.

The radio broadcasts led to invitations from communities inside the guerrilla area to hold "events." Russell responded with his old red Suburban vehicle loaded with Christian literature and young people from the sound studio in Bogota. These young people formed a group called *Fuerza de Paz,* the Strength of Peace. Many thousands of Bibles, New Testaments, and other Christian literature, including *Rescue the Captors* have been distributed to the guerrillas, paramilitary, soldiers, and police along all the road systems of eastern Colombia. Everywhere the radio programs reach, Russell and his associates find a friendly welcome. A number of guerrillas have been converted and they have miraculously been allowed to join Russell in his ministry. They distribute literature and solar-powered radios preset to one of the stations and talk with guerrilla leaders and their former companions, trying to win some of them to Christ. They have spoken about their experience in churches, police stations, and military bases as well.

Recently a large river launch named *La Diabla* (The She-Devil) was captured by the Colombian army and turned over to Russell. It has been restored, painted and renamed, *La Luz de la Verdad* (The Light of the Truth). By means of this boat, the ministry can be extended to the interior parts of the country that are not reached by the road net. The first trip, back into the very area where Russell was held while kidnapped, was a great success in spite of a bad start. The second day out, a gasoline explosion and fire destroyed the food supply and personal belongings of the passengers, and blackened and charred the new paint job. Two people were burned—a converted guerrilla leader and his four-year-old grandson. Both have recovered without disfiguring scars. The child was saved out of the midst of intense flames by valiant action on the part of some of the *Fuerza de Paz* young people. The large amount of Bibles and literature was safe as everything was still on the dock. It had been trucked to this spot by Colombian Army trucks.

Volunteers in the town where the explosion took place sanded and repainted the boat. None of the lettering or art work had been damaged. The mayors from three municipalities donated food supplies and gasoline so that the trip could continue. Within 24 hours the launch was able to resume. The whereabouts of *La Luz de la Verdad* was announced over the radio and in populated areas listeners lined the shores as the boat passed, waving white flags to show their solidarity with the "Peace Campaign."

Several articles about Russell and this unique ministry have appeared in the media. One was in the Dec. 10, 2002 issue of *The Washington Times* with the headlines, "In Colombia, a mission for peace — American reaches out to rebels." Another was in the Feb. 2004 issue of Charisma magazine, "Missionary Takes Gospel to Colombian Guerrillas, Paramilitaries - Once abducted by communist fighters, Russell Stendal uses books and radio broadcasts to preach a message of peace."

This is an ongoing work and your participation is invited by prayer and financial gifts. The next trip planned is much longer and will require strengthening the radio outreach as well as much more literature, food supplies, and gasoline. As Russell and Marina say, "Our passport into these areas is that the people know who we are by hearing us on the radio." Several operations are underway to increase the area of FM and AM coverage in preparation for this much longer trip, all the way to the border of Venezuela. This next trip will go into areas of guerrilla control where Russell is not presently known. An exception to this is the area where Giovanni is the commander. Russell has had recent contact with several of the other guerrillas mentioned in the story.

Tax deductible gifts can be sent to these ministries:

In the USA:	In Canada:
Spirit of Martyrdom	Colombia Para Cristo
P.O. Box 101	Society
Clarkdale, AZ 86324	12629 – 248th St.
www.spiritofmartyrdom.com	Maple Ridge, BC
www.fuerzadepaz.com	V4R 1K4

Write the check to the mission and designate for the ministry of Russell Stendal in Colombia.

To order books:
Some books are available from www.lifesentencepublishing. com and all are available from www.dwightclough.com

Appendix

This Appendix was co-authored by my close friend and partner, Ricardo Trillos. An expanded version will soon be available as a separate volume, entitled *Rescue Your Family*.

I.
ANIMAL MENTALITY

In the early days of our ranch, Chaparral, in eastern Colombia, it was very difficult to make ends meet. One day I flew to the ranch in our recently acquired '54 Cessna 170 and learned that my brother and the crew of men working with him were in desperate need of provisions. They were so hungry that they wanted to make me turn around and fly back into town for a load of supplies. I argued that even if I made the trip, we were all still overlooking the fact that we had no money to pay for an airplane load of groceries.

My brother, Chaddy, told me not to worry. He would take care of everything. He ushered me out behind the thatch roofed, dirt floored shack that served as the ranch kitchen and proudly pointed to one of the largest, fattest pigs I had ever seen. "There you are," he said. "We'll tie the pig up, load it in the plane, and you can sell her in town. You ought to be able to buy supplies and have enough money left over to gas up the 170."

As I began to remove the passenger seats from the old Cessna, I voiced a few misgivings regarding the prospective passenger. "You worry too much," Chaddy scolded, "We can tie all four feet together in a knot that I guarantee you will never come undone. Besides, this is a tame pig. It knows us. It's lived all its life eating table scraps behind the kitchen." (Mistake number one—to think it was only of secondary consequence that the knot remained tied, whereas the primary concern should have been that the feet of the pig remain in the knot!)

It took all of us to lift the 250 lb. hog into the small Cessna. I closed the door, strapped myself in, and started the engine. The pig lay on the floor giving an occasional low grunt. "This might not be so bad after all," I thought soothingly to myself as I taxied over to the end of the short grass runway and prepared for takeoff. Everything went fine until we were about half way down the airstrip. Just as the airplane was lifting into the air, the pig did a flip back into the baggage compartment. (There, a metal partition gave way and the pig's superior weight caused it to slide all the way into the plane's tail cone!) Realizing that the tail heavy aircraft would never fly properly, I closed the throttle and prayed that we would be able to stop within the remaining runway. It was close.

I shut down the engine, undid my seat belt, and struggled to pull the squealing pig (who still had all four feet securely tied together) out of the tail. I had visions of extensive damage to the tail structure and control cables of the aircraft, but fortunately the damage was limited to a bent baggage compartment partition. It took my brother and several other men to get the pig back into the proper position. I determined that this time I would really see to it that the pig didn't move, so I looped the co-pilot seat belt (which was still anchored to the floor) in between the legs of the pig and cinched it down tight.

I proceeded to start the airplane up and got ready to try and take off again (my second mistake). The second try was perfect and soon I had the old 170 level at 6000 feet on course for San Martin. I leaned back to enjoy the 90-minute ride. The grunts and squeals of my passenger were beginning to seem almost normal when all-of-a-sudden KA-WHUMP, KA-WHUMP, KA-WHUMP. I noticed with horror that the pig had just pulled its back feet out of the knot and was banging the side of the airplane with its hind end. On the third bang, the door latch broke and the rear end of the animal went right out of the aircraft. The pig was now dangling by its front feet, which were still held in place by the seat belt. I wondered how long the "guaranteed" knot would hold.

The airplane began to slue sideways as the open door deflected the slipstream. The pig was straining to get completely out. Oblivious to the fact that we were at 6000 feet, I could see her stretching one hind foot as far down as she could in a supreme effort to reach the ground. I reached over and began to pull on the pig's rear end with one hand. It was impossible to get a good grip, so I undid my seat belt, got out of the pilot's seat, and began pulling as hard as I could with both hands. The Cessna, left on its own without a pilot, began a lazy turn to the right. I was still worried that I would lose the pig (which represented a whole month's supplies). The slipstream had hopelessly jammed the door against the pig's hinder. It was impossible for me to pull her back inside, no matter how hard I tried.

In desperation, I got what seemed like a brilliant idea (but it was really my third mistake). Since this was an airplane, why not bank the plane and lift the pig up to a more favorable angle. Feeling confident that I now knew how to control the situation, I reached over and racked the old 170 into a 45 degree bank to the right. I grinned with satisfaction as the rear end of the pig rose to a higher elevation than its front end and rolled in a little more aileron for good measure. Now the only thing holding the pig was the pressure of the slipstream on the door. I gave the door a mighty kick and the pig fell back into the airplane. She fell right on top of me, and we both continued on through the aircraft until we hit the opposite door with a resounding crash. The second door latch snapped. All of a sudden everything reversed and I was the one with my rear end in danger!

I was pinned under the tremendous weight of the pig. The squeals of the pig were now much louder than the noise of the engine. The right door was now open enough for me to see that we were flying at a very unusual altitude. I desperately tried to reach the controls. I was able to kick the yoke a little with my left foot while I beat on the pig with both hands trying to make her get off. The pig retaliated by urinating and defecating all over me. I groped blindly in the back of the plane for anything I could use as a weapon. The stench was unbearable. My hand closed on an iron bar (a broken piece of our saw mill I was taking to town to be repaired), I hit the pig with it. She went completely berserk.

She got up and began to thrash and squeal and gnash her teeth. Somehow, the rope and seat belt on her front feet held. I was able to get to my feet, and began hitting her over the head with the iron bar. The head was too fat. I didn't have enough room in the tight cabin to get a good swing. Instead of subduing her, the pig became even more enraged. Finally, I found a rope and, after getting kicked a few times, was able to get a loop around the hind feet. With the rope and a seat belt I was able to partially restrain my furious passenger.

Now I began to notice that the old 170 was also having trouble. We seemed to have lost a bit of altitude. I got back into the pilot's seat and began to sort things out. The old airplane was really complaining. It was shuddering and shaking in a very abnormal manner. With both doors flapping in the breeze, it just refused to fly properly. The doors began to vibrate with a harmonic rhythm that sent shivers up and down the airframe.

I had to get up again and somehow manage to secure the left door with the other end of the rope which was tied around the pig's hind feet. I returned to my seat and tried to hang on to the right door with my right hand. By now I was really looking forward to our destination.

Foaming at the mouth and trying to bite my right ankle, the pig seemed to be getting her second wind. I found that the best solution was to sit on my right foot and handle the rudders with my left foot only (which fortunately seemed to be beyond her reach). I had visions of the pig getting loose and crashing into the tail cone again or possibly chewing me up with her two inch teeth. I began to pray. My right foot went to sleep.

After what seemed like an eternity, San Martin slowly drifted into sight. I lined the 170 up on the short runway. Some doubt, however, was beginning to creep into my mind about the feasibility of landing a taildragger with only one hand and one foot on the controls. It wasn't until we were on short final that I noticed the donkeys in the middle of the runway. All this time the pig had been working up some slack in the rope around her hind feet. She got her rear feet under herself and began to bang against the left door again. I pulled on the door with all my might with one hand and began to initiate a clumsy go-around with the other hand. The airplane slued violently as I let go of the controls to dump the flaps and add power. The pig got her hinder three or four inches out of the door and I had to pull with all my might on the door handle.

Intentionally, I buzzed the donkeys as close as possible under the circumstances hoping they would get off the runway. They just stood there and didn't even look up. Donkeys on the runway are terrible. When the airplane is almost on top of them, they might raise up one ear. After the plane misses them by a few feet, they put their ear back down again. Whenever something strange happens to them, they plant their feet and refuse to budge. After several passes a kid came out on a bicycle and herded them off the runway.

The pig fought me all the way to the ground. It was trying so hard to back out the door that I was able to sneak my right foot down onto the rudder pedals for the landing. Due to my having to hold the door with one hand, the landing had to be perfect. I had to let go of the controls with my left hand at a safe altitude in order to apply flaps and cut the power with the same hand. There would be no margin for error. Once we were near the ground it would be impossible to go around or even smooth out a bad bounce with a burst of power. If I applied flaps and cut the power too soon, we would undershoot the runway. If my timing was too late we would run off the end of the short airstrip. I decided to plan my approach a little high and use a side slip to get rid of excess altitude.

It worked and I was overjoyed to finally get the wheels on solid ground. The pig made one last try for my ankle causing me to make a couple S-turns on the landing roll. I was sure glad to finally unload the pig and personally deliver it to the local butcher shop. The butcher paid me the equivalent of almost one hundred dollars in Colombian currency. The two new door latches for the 170 cost one hundred and twenty dollars. That pig still owes me twenty bucks!

Audiences all over the country have nearly split their sides laughing whenever I tell this story and it is by popular demand that I include it in this special appendix to the fourth printing of this book. I still grin ruefully whenever I think back on this event. In one sense these happenings are hilariously funny, yet in reality, this may have been the closest I have ever come to getting killed in an airplane. It was after this experience that I became aware of the absolute necessity of thinking ahead and paying attention to little details in aviation.

The field of aviation is notoriously unforgiving to those who continue to make unwise decisions. Many pilots have paid for seemingly minor mistakes with their lives (and the lives of innocent passengers). The same is true in the field of marriage and family life. Many personal relationships have crashed and burned due to lack of attention to seemingly insignificant details.

It is easy to rationalize away our unwise decisions and actions instead of facing them. It is all too easy to keep a "pet pig" and tell ourselves that it won't ever get loose. There are many small, apparently innocent "sins" that can go "hog wild" at a moment's notice and completely devastate an entire family.

II.
The New Birth

Upon conception, a human baby develops and grows within its mother's womb for nine months prior to birth. During this time, the baby probably feels very secure. It lives in total darkness and feels completely surrounded and protected by its mother. Then, one day, everything changes. The womb begins to contract and squeeze. The poor baby's world is turned inside out as it is forced under extreme pressure through a dark tunnel towards a brilliant light that pierces the darkness. The baby probably doesn't feel like leaving the warm, dark, comfortable womb, But it has no choice. It either must be born or die. The shock and trauma of being born is such an intense experience that some doctors believe it may affect our subconscious for the rest of our lives.

I was raised in a Christian home. My parents were missionaries, and I was brought up in a spiritual "hot house." Throughout my growing-up years, most decisions as to conduct and acceptable behavior were spelled out quite clearly to me, and I was expected to conform unquestioningly to the status quo of the missionary organization that my parents belonged to. It wasn't until I got out on my own as the leader of a Christian farm project in rural Colombia, isolated from the outside world and all of a sudden responsible not only for my own spiritual well-being but for many other Christian workers as well, that I began to feel squeezed and under pressure. All the neat little rules, regulations, and spiritual principles that I had learned by rote began to come apart at the seams, as suddenly I found myself on the front lines, receiving broadside after broadside from the enemy. When I got into real, no-holds-barred spiritual warfare, I found to my utter shame and despair that I was really no more than just a spiritual wimp. After years of being pummeled and battered, forced time and time again by the enemy to give up ground, I began to wonder if under certain conditions it would ever be possible to have complete spiritual victory.

One day I was studying the Sermon on the Mount with my friend and partner, Ricardo Trillos. I had just finished reading an article in the Readers' Digest about the trauma of human birth from the baby's point of view.[1] Because a paragraph in the seventh chapter of Matthew[2] stood out for me, I looked up a parallel passage in Luke 13:24 which says: "Strive to enter the narrow gate because many, I tell you, will try to enter and will not be able to." All of a sudden I caught a glimpse of light and I saw a comparison. Entering the Kingdom of God through the narrow gate is similar in many ways to childbirth. In fact it is called being born again. Entering the Kingdom of God can also be a terrifying and traumatic experience as we are pushed, squeezed, and molded into the kind of people that can be used of God in the Kingdom.

I decided that I had been guilty of resisting God's hand on my life and had therefore been unwittingly spending an unnecessary amount of time in that spiritual birth canal being squeezed all out of shape instead of coming out into the light and being born. I decided that I was going to forget my big missionary plans and projects, and instead I would concentrate on discerning where God was moving and then try to jump on His bandwagon. I began to react towards problems and adversity as opportunities to learn important things and as opportunities for God to use me to bring glory to Himself. My life changed to one of victory in Jesus Christ. I still have problems, difficulties, and even an occasional defeat; but now I can clearly see the design and purpose that God has for my life. If I have the

---

[1] *Reader's Digest* Mar. 1983
[2] Matthew 7:12-14

right attitude, God can reign over everything that happens in my life and teach me something useful from even the most difficult experiences.

What follows is a message on family reconciliation that God taught my partner, Ricardo Trillos, over a period of more than seven years. Even though Ricardo did not do any actual writing in this book, his name is included because he was a great source of inspiration to me and provided much of the motivation and many of the ideas set forth in this book. Ricardo began giving seminars on marriage and family reconciliation many years ago and used bits and pieces of Jesus' Sermon on the Mount mixed with the psychology of dynamics of communication and other modern concepts. Five years ago Ricardo spent several hours explaining God's message of family reconciliation to me in a hotel room in Bogota, Colombia. I was so intrigued that I began to study Matthew chapters 5, 6, and 7 with him. As we began to study Jesus' sermon, we were both impressed with its structure. The order and continuity of Jesus' teaching seemed to be just as important as the actual words. As we received light on the Sermon on the Mount, we began using more and more of it in our seminars. Finally we came to the point where we dropped the other material we were using and began teaching Jesus' sermon in complete form from beginning to end.

We were totally unprepared for the results. Hundreds of couples signed up for our seminar. We began to see marriage after marriage and family after family be completely transformed. Marriages that had been classed as hopeless basket cases by other counseling agencies descended on us in droves. In many cases one or both spouses were not Christians. In other cases the families were split and only one spouse would agree to attend the seminar. Ricardo and I watched with wonder and awe as God began to work miracles right in front of our eyes. We watched as even the most hardened and resistant individuals were restored and reconciled with God and their families.

We learned many lessons the hard way. The greatest lessons that Ricardo and I learned were from mistakes and trials that were perceived within our own families. We found in over seven years of ministry in family reconciliation that no amount of brilliant counseling or personal effort will guarantee the reconciliation of a broken home or marriage. The only one who can do it is God's Holy Spirit. Whether or not the Holy Spirit is at liberty to reconcile a home or marriage depends on the attitudes of each of the persons involved. If even one person in any given home is willing to put into effect in his or her life the attitudes that Jesus describes in his Sermon on the Mount, then there is hope, and reconciliation can begin. The five poems by Mrs. Doris McLaughlin are a fruit of this message of family reconciliation. Doris decided to unilaterally put Jesus' message into effect in her troubled family several years ago after talking with Ricardo and myself. As God began to put the pieces of her marriage back together, He gave her these beautiful poems.

I am astounded at all the trouble God went through in order to teach Ricardo and me about family reconciliation. Even though we were very slow learners, He never gave up on us. This message is not the result of our own intelligence. We were taught painstakingly, step by step. By allowing us to face difficult situations, God taught us to rely on His wisdom instead of our own. In the words of the Apostle Paul:

"All this from God, who reconciled us to himself through Christ and gave us the ministry of reconciliation:" II Corinthians 5:18 (NIV)[3]

---

[3] Scripture quotations marked (NIV) in this appendix are from the Holy Bible, New International Version. Copyright © 1973, 1978, International Bible Society. Used by permission of Zondervan Bible Publishers.

LINE UPON LINE

Line upon line,
    precept on precept,
  higher than high,
      live unto me.
  Fellowship sweet,
     higher than high,
    live unto me.
       Lift up your hands,
     and lift up your voice.
      Higher than high,
     live unto me.
       Lift up your voice
     and lift up your hands.
     Line upon line,
      precept on precept,
        higher than High
       Live unto Me.
         Higher than high,
        live unto Me.

I am your Lord.
  I am your Savior.
Higher than high,
    live unto Me.
  Fellowship sweet,
     higher than high,
    live unto Me.
      Lift up your hands
     and lift up your voice.
      Higher than high,
     live unto Me.
       I am your Lord.
      I am your Savior.
       Line upon line.
      precept on precept,
        higher than high,
       Live unto Me.
         Higher than high
       Live unto me.

Doris McLaughlin

III.
THE RIGHT ATTITUDE

Blessed are the poor in spirit,
for theirs is the kingdom of God.
(NIV)

With these words Jesus began his first complete, recorded sermon. John the Baptist had come to prepare the way for the Christ, preaching "Repent, for the Kingdom of God is at hand." The Jews had been looking forward to the coming of the Kingdom of God through the Messiah for thousands of years. They had been pushed and squeezed, taken advantage of, and oppressed by almost all of their surrounding neighboring countries for millenniums; yet through all their suffering and problems they had never completely given up hope that someday, if they could only keep God's law, King David's heir would appear and deliver them forever. Chapter 12 of the Book of Revelation fittingly describes the Jewish nation as a woman in travail giving birth to a man-child who was to rule the nations.

The Jewish religious system was extremely complex. To be a good Jew not only required a lot of education, it also required constant devotion to ritual and detail. Upon spending such a large percentage of their time, energy, and finances "appeasing God," many Jews considered themselves to be on such a higher spiritual plane than anyone else, they would not even eat at the same table with someone who was not a Jew.

Enter Jesus, preaching that the Kingdom of God belonged to the spiritual beggars (the Greek word translated "poor in spirit" literally means beggarly or destitute), and it made the Jewish religious leaders very angry and bitter. Not so, however, with the Poor in Spirit. They rejoiced and believed, and Jesus healed them of every known disease, cast out demons, fed them physically, and fed them spiritually. By the time Jesus preached the Sermon on the Mount, a great multitude of spiritual beggars were following him everywhere.

Jesus' words make sense in our present day and age, also. We cannot negotiate our way into God's Kingdom. To begin with, we have nothing with which to negotiate. Everything that we have originated from God. Our only hope is to admit our faults and failures. We don't have to be perfect to come to God, but we do have to be honest. We must be willing to lay our cards face up on the table, stop bluffing, and say: "Here I am. These are my problems. I need help." Honesty or repentance, as some call it, is the first step towards reconciliation with God. Honesty on the part of at least one family member is also the first step towards family reconciliation. I considered myself to be an outstanding, upright young Christian man until I got married. Then I was rudely awakened to the unpleasant realities of many areas of my life that I had been able to subconsciously sweep under the rug as a bachelor. Under the pressures of marriage I was unable to keep anything covered up. In fact, my undesirable traits seemed to reveal themselves at the worst possible and most inopportune times. I soon discovered that the quickest way to contain the damage after a fiasco was to honestly face my problem both before God and my wife.

> *Blessed are those who mourn,*
> *for they shall he comforted*
> *(NIV)*

When we honestly admit our mistakes and our failures, and the full realization of how badly we have managed to mess things up sinks in, our natural reaction is to mourn. Honesty and repentance can bring into sharp focus the extent to which we are victimizing other people and the extent to which other people are victimizing us in an endless vicious cycle. When God's Holy Spirit begins to shine the spotlight of His truth and illuminate with conviction the results of all our selfish actions and reactions, it can be a very sobering experience.

Blessed are the meek,
for they shall inherit the earth
(NIV)

I used to have a hard time understanding the word "meek", and reconciling myself with it. It seemed to me that a meek person would be a milquetoast, doormat, wishy-washy individual with no backbone, allowing everyone to trample all over him. I looked up the word in Greek and found out that the word Jesus used for "meek" has no direct translation in the English language. The Greek word really means an attitude of heart and mind that is in submission to God and to God's plans exclusively. The Spanish word, *manso*, comes close to portraying the complete meaning of what Jesus said. In Spanish, an example would be the way in which the word, *manso*, is applied to horses. The horse that is *manso* is the perfectly trained horse that completely obeys the rider. It allows itself to be guided with just a very light pressure on the reins. It doesn't have to be a broken-spirited animal at all. It might be thoroughbred and high-strung, but it has given up its own plans and allows the rider to call the shots. This is a good example of what true faith in Jesus Christ is all about. Jesus wants us to quit trying to fit God into our plans and let Him fit us into His masterplan, instead. He promises to completely fulfill and satisfy us, if we allow Him to be in charge of our lives. The same holds true for our families.

Blessed are those who hunger and thirst for being and
doing right, for they shall be completely satisfied
(Williams)[1]

When we enter into God's Kingdom by admitting our problems and giving up our own plans, a desire begins to well up

---

[1]   From the Williams New Testament in the language of the people, by Charles B. Williams. Copyright 1937, 1966, 1986 Holman Bible Publishers. Used by permission.

inside of us to get our act together and do things right. Some of Jesus' thinking starts to spill into our minds, and we begin to do what God wants because that's what we want to do, too. In the Bible God says that He wants to write His laws on the "tablets of our hearts." The apostle Paul said, "Let this same mind be in you that was in Christ Jesus." The Christian life isn't a legalistic list of do's and don'ts that we struggle to try to keep in our own strength. It is a dynamic, vibrant, delightful relationship with the Creator of the Universe.

Here we have the basic Christian message of repentance and faith. We know that struggling through life's problems in our own strength is not the answer. On the other hand, if we just sit back and do nothing, expecting God to do everything for us, sometimes we are disappointed that nothing seems to get done. What are we to do? I struggled with this for several years. Deep inside, I knew that there was something missing from my Christian experience. The same thing seemed to be missing in many of the members of the churches I had been attending, too. What was it?

Are you beginning to catch a glimpse of the incredible structure and understanding of cause and effect that make Jesus' sermon such a masterpiece? It isn't by chance that Jesus next beatitude is:

Blessed are those who show mercy,
for they shall have mercy shown to them
(Williams)

I hadn't understood this one until one evening when I started thinking back over my flying career. I had flown over 4000 hours with almost half of it over the jungle in Colombia, South America. In eight years of flying treacherous terrain in single-engine aircraft, I had never had so much as a minor accident. Many other pilots had been killed or maimed flying in the jungle. Others had demolished their airplanes. Even the missionary pilots, who had one of the best safety records in South America, were averaging a major accident every 1200 hours of flying time. I prayed and asked God what was going on. Why was I being singled out for special treatment. Better pilots than I had had terrible flying accidents in the jungle or in the mountains of Colombia. I knew that I wasn't any better than some of the pilots that had even been killed in flying accidents. Some of the casualties had been better Christians than me, too. I pressed God for an answer. Why was I being treated so special? I had had more close calls than anybody, yet, here I was unscathed while I had watched other pilots make one mistake and get nailed. All of a sudden my thinking flashed back to a scene eight years before.

I had been working as the leader of a Christian farm project in a remote rural area of Colombia. One of my friends and co-workers had become injured and there was a need to remove him to the hospital. My friend almost died because the airplane operator required payment in advance, causing a day's delay. I remembered praying and telling God that if he would provide me with an airplane, I would never turn down someone in genuine need, regardless of financial considerations.

I kept my promise to God all those years. I felt a quiet voice deep inside me, that over the years I have learned to identify as the still, small voice of my Lord, impress upon me, "You never turned anyone down who asked you for mercy, so I never turned you down when you were in need of My mercy." I was completely overwhelmed. For just a few seconds I started to catch a glimpse of how important mercy is to God. Jesus life and teachings center on mercy. Jesus even gave his life for us in a supreme act of mercy, when we were still in rebellion against God. Jesus is the very personification of mercy. I use the term mercy because we did not deserve to have Jesus die for us and provide a way for us to be reconciled to God and to one another.

In several years of marriage counseling, a common complaint that we have heard from troubled couples is: "We have to get a divorce because we don't love each other anymore. Our marriage is hopeless."

Love is a very delicate plant. If not constantly nurtured and watered, love will wither and die. In many homes it is dead. Love is an emotion that is very difficult to call up and feel towards someone who is acting in an unlovable manner. Mercy, on the other hand, is a decision. Mercy starts in our mind with merciful thoughts that give the other person the benefit of the doubt. This paves the way for merciful words and deeds. When we treat other people in a merciful manner, it affects the way they treat us, which affects the way we treat them, which affects the way they treat us, and so on. Mercy is the seed of love. When we reach out to someone in mercy, we are planting seeds that bear fruit and allow God to have mercy on us. It is possible for love to blossom and bloom, seemingly out of nowhere, in homes that were once as barren as a desert.

> *Blessed are the pure in heart,*
> *for they shall see God face to face*
> *(NIV)*

My own first year of marriage was a rocky one. It utterly astounded me to see how so many seemingly insignificant little details could disrupt my marriage and snowball into fights with my wife; fights that could last for days. When things were going wrong, and I was upset or angry, my wife would unwittingly do something else wrong that would cause my anger to erupt into words. The insults would fly back and forth between us. We began to question each other's real motives for getting married in the first place, even though we had both clearly been able to see God's hand in our courtship and marriage as our relationship had developed.

I began to notice that men and women seem to think in different ways. After a squabble with my wife, I would immediately try to resolve the problem. Since the problem that had disrupted our relationship had probably been a very small one, I could never understand why she would make such a big deal about making it up afterwards. Sometimes she wouldn't speak to me for days. I finally realized that in her mind, she wasn't just dealing with the immediate problem. She was adding the present problem to a long list of previous problems, and then negotiating from there with phrases like, "you always do this" or "you never do that."

FRIENDS & LOVED ONES REDEEMED

VICTORY

9. **Reward in Heaven**

   Gold, Silver & Precious Stones

8. **The Persecuted**

   Satisfaction, Fulfillment

7. **The Peacemakers**

   Fruits of the Spirit, Integrity

6. **The Pure in Heart**

   Healing, Miracles & Spiritual Gifts

5. **The Merciful**

   For Righteousness (Justice)

4. **Those Who Hunger & Thirst**

   Submission to God's Authority

   Faith in Jesus Christ as

   Lord and King

3. **The Meek**

   Awareness of God's Law

2. **Those Who Mourn**

   Openness, Honesty,
   Repentence

1. **The Poor in Spirit**

THE HOUSE ON THE ROCK

Appendix

When things were going downhill and I was under pressure, I found that I could handle negative circumstances in a loving Christian manner if I could just have a little time to pull myself together. If I had time to pray and meditate for a while about how to respond to a given situation, I could come up with a Christian response most of the time. It was when I was caught off guard that I would mess up and fly off the handle. It was my subconscious reactions that were getting me into serious trouble. I started to get very worried about the direction my relationship with my wife was heading. Each fight was getting harder and harder to resolve and sooner or later I was bound to say or do something which would permanently scar our marriage. In fact, I was worried that I might have already done irreparable damage on several occasions. My marriage seemed to be heading straight for disaster and I was powerless to do anything about it.

I learned about mercy in the very nick of time. As I started to apply Jesus' teachings to my own family situation, I was astounded by the results. When I began to mercifully give my wife the benefit of the doubt regarding any of her words or actions that troubled me, she sensed that my attitude was less critical towards her. This helped her to have a better attitude towards me. Soon our relationship was getting better and better instead of worse and worse.

As the months passed and I concentrated on saturating myself with a merciful attitude backed up with merciful actions towards my wife, I could hardly believe the progress in our relationship. We began communicating again in the same deep, intimate, heart to heart manner of our initial courtship and romance. What really floored me was that I began noticing that even my subconscious reactions under pressure were improving. It seemed like God was somehow able to use my own merciful attitude to reach deep inside me and begin a healing, purifying process in areas of my life that were even beyond my voluntary control.

God designed our complete human make-up—physically, mentally, and spiritually. If anyone knows what makes a human being tick, it is Him. In His Beatitudes, Jesus describes the dynamics of the Kingdom of God. First we must enter the Kingdom with an attitude of true repentance as spiritual beggars (poor in spirit). This will cause us to mourn, as the full extent of our problems sink in. But cheer up, He will comfort us if we place our faith in Him as King of our lives with a "meek" attitude, and then we will inherit the earth. When we put Jesus in charge of our lives, we will feel a desire to get our act together and please Him. We will begin to hunger and thirst for righteousness (doing what God wants or requires) until we are satisfied. Then if we reach out to others in mercy and forgiveness, God will show mercy on us and forgive us. God will also begin to heal and purify us in our hearts. When Jesus says, "Blessed are the pure in heart for they shall see God face to face," he really means it. At this point God can reestablish two way communication with us just like he enjoyed with Adam before the fall.

In order to have a "pure heart" our conscience must be void of offense. God has given us a conscience to tell us when we have done something wrong that might damage our communication with Him. Being "pure in heart" does not necessarily mean that we have attained sinless perfection. It means that we have confessed and forsaken, by His help, all known sin and that we are yielded to His will. It means that we are at peace with God. It is also necessary to have a "pure heart" in regards to our spouse, if we hope to retain intimate communication in our home. A merciful, forgiving, attitude that gives the other person the benefit of the doubt will go a long way towards keeping the lines of communication open in our families.

Make no mistake. If we enter into the attitudes that Jesus describes, God will do what He promises. If we come to him as "Poor in Spirit," God really will let us into His Kingdom. If obedience to Him causes us to mourn, He really will comfort us. If we obey King Jesus meekly, we really will inherit the earth. If we mercifully forgive those around us, God really will sanctify us. If we allow Him to, He really will restore and purify our hearts and open up "face to face" communication with us through his Holy Spirit. These promises are for now. Jesus isn't just promising "pie in the sky" at some future date. He is promising us dynamic power now to change us within and without.

Blessed are the peacemakers for they shall be called the sons of God (NIV)

Jesus would like to use each and every one of us to bring His peace to those around us. As we enter into the spirit of Jesus' teaching, His Holy Spirit will begin working in our lives and begin to heal broken relationships with those around us, starting in our own family. As we co-operate with King Jesus, we will begin to find that even our worst mistakes and failures can be changed into something positive if we will honestly admit them, meekly submit our problem areas to His control, and mercifully forgive others who have similar shortcomings. If we allow the Holy Spirit to train us to be peacemakers, we will be amazed to notice that our mistakes and failures are becoming fewer and farther between. God would like to adopt us right into His own family and call us His sons. Our ultimate role as peacemakers is to help those around us make peace with one another and with God.

Blessed are those who suffer persecution for the cause of justice, for theirs is the kingdom of God (Williams)

Jesus says that we might be persecuted if we stick our necks out for what we know is right. He doesn't promise us a bed of roses in this life. He does promise us that He will work all things out for our overall good. The Bible says that every Christian will have his faith tried as with fire. God talks about refining us like gold and silver. The fire burns away the wood, hay, and stubble, leaving the gold, silver, and precious stones. Sometimes the treatment is painful, but God must dig deep enough in our lives to get at the roots of our problems. If we are willing to stick our necks out for justice (being and doing right), God will use any persecution that develops to rub off any rough edges we might have. Justice and mercy must go hand in hand. In order to avail ourselves of God's mercy, we must first recognize that he is just. As Christians we must be willing to give individuals the benefit of the doubt with a merciful attitude, while at the same time be willing to stick our necks out for what we know is right. We must oppose evil with every "legitimate" means at our disposal. Can you understand now why Jesus can love the sinner but hate the sin?

"Blessed are you when people abuse you
and persecute you,
and keep on falsely telling all sorts of evil
against you for my sake.
Keep on rejoicing and leaping for ecstasy,
for your reward will be rich in heaven;
for this is the way they persecuted
the prophets who lived before you"
(Williams)

This sums up the change in attitude that Jesus wishes to impart in us. Instead of feeling sorry for ourselves and having a pity party every time someone gives us a rough time, we can learn to turn difficulties into opportunities. If we react to insult and injury (especially in a family environment) with mercy, forgiveness, love, and justice, it is actually possible for Jesus to reach out and touch other people through us. Jesus tells us about receiving a great reward in heaven. For example, if your spouse weren't a Christian and if through enduring some insults, persecution, and false accusations, you were able to conquer your spouse with Jesus' mercy and love, wouldn't your loved one be a great reward to enjoy in heaven for all eternity? How would you feel if you made it to heaven by the skin of your teeth, then discovered that some of your family didn't make it?

You are the salt of the earth. But if the salt loses its
saltiness, how can it be made salty again? It is no
longer good for anything, except to be thrown out and
trampled by men. You are the light of the world. A city
on a hill cannot be hidden. Neither do people light a
lamp and put it under a bowl. They put it on its stand,
and it gives light to everyone in the house. In the same
way, let your light shine before men, that they may see

your good deeds and praise your Father in heaven.
(NIV)

If we put Jesus Beatitudes to work in our lives, we will become the salt of the earth and the light of the world. The object in being salt and light is so that other people can see our good deeds (acts of mercy and justice) and praise our Father in heaven (reconciling themselves to God). We must be careful to let people know that it is Christ in us who is doing the good deeds and that we would not be doing them without His direction and power.

> *Do not think that I have come to abolish the law or the prophets; I have not come to abolish them but to fulfill them, I tell you the truth, until heaven and earth disappear, not the smallest letter, not the least stroke of a pen, will by any means disappear from the law until everything is accomplished. Anyone who breaks one of the least of these commandments and teaches others to do the same will be called least in the kingdom of heaven. But whoever practices and teaches these commands will be called great in the kingdom of heaven. For I tell you that unless your righteousness surpasses that of the Pharisees and the teachers of the law, you will certainly not enter the kingdom of heaven. (NIV)*

Prior to Jesus in Old Testament times, men knew what God wanted of them. The problem was that they couldn't live up to God's standards no matter how hard they tried.

> *"He has showed you, O man, what is good. And what does the Lord require of you? To act JUSTLY and to love MERCY and to walk HUMBLY with your God."*
> Micah 6:8 (NIV)

Justice, mercy, and reverence of God are woven throughout the Old Testament. Jesus came to fulfill and culminate everything that God had been doing up until then. By making his Holy Spirit available to each and every one of us, Jesus was able to bridge the gap, and make it possible for us to actually be able to practice God's commandments in a way that was impossible under the Old Covenant. Jesus wants to make us all into one body or family of which he is the head. If we submit to his authority with the meek attitude, and if we reach out in mercy and allow his Holy Spirit to flow through us, Jesus will actually begin to become our righteousness right now.

At first we can only live the Christian life for short periods of time without falling flat on our faces. As time goes on and we grow in faith and grace and our mistakes start getting fewer and farther between. We can witness creation as God takes self-ish, proud, and rebellious humans, doomed to death and failure, and makes sons of God out of us, turning us into magnificent, glorious creatures that He can eventually lift right out of this physical world so that we can spend all eternity with Him.

TRUE LOVE

True love is such a rarity.
   There is so much disparity,
between what is good and kind and pure,
   and what is really used as a hook and lure
to hunt men's souls and destroy their hearts
   to keep them from loving and doing their part
to alleviate suffering, pain, and disgrace to
   demonstrate true love to the whole human race.
There are those whose affections
   are based on sex, and pride, and selfishness
whose motive is that their own self be blessed.
   And when the one they love doesn't do
what they said or wanted them to,
   they say, "That's fine! OK! We're through.
Get out! I've had enough of you."

Now, I ask you. Is that true love or is it just lust?
   Do they devour one another and eat up their trust
to take what's given and reject you when through?
   So when you've been hurt and played for a fool,
do you clam up and become very cool
   towards the one who has done this to you?
Do you walk through life burned and spent?
   Do you allow bitterness, anger, hurt, and pain
to cause you to stumble and rob you again
   of life in Jesus and the peace that he gives you?
And when you're in this spot what do you do?
   Who is there to comfort you?
Well, you call upon God when you've walked away
   from the one who has hurt you and done you this way.
"But," you say, "They have done it before and they will do it
   again.
How can I continue being hurt by them."

You must give it to God and forgive that sin.
   Confess your faults. Ask God to forgive them.

Ask God to forgive you for rejecting them.
    If you choose to love, the healing will begin.
Cleanse yourself of all bitterness and strife.
    Cleanse yourself and begin a new life.

Love is not bitter, is not unkind,
    so put on her heart and renew your mind.
Her thoughts are tender, gentle, and good.
    You can't give love and carry dead wood.
Let go of the old and begin anew.
    Today is a new day made just for you.
Put their needs first, pay no attention to wrongs,
    just go on loving all day long.
If not, you'll suffer for what you do.
    You will suffer and they will, too.

Give up envy, jealousy, and spite—
    just love your spouse with all your might.
Don't seek a reward for the things that you do,
    and keep no record of the wrongs suffered you.
Don't be proud or seek your own glory—
    just let love tell her own story.
Don't be boastful, haughty, or loud
    and don't show off in front of a crowd.
Promote the others, be gentle and meek.
    and tell your old self to take a back seat.
To be lowly and humble is not being weak.
    Praise and appreciate others, and speak
of the good, kind things that they do.
    Think of the others and take no thought for you.
This is His love which will flow through you.

Give up all rights which you have for yourself—
    set them aside. Put them on the shelf
Resist the temptation to think evil in your heart,
    for this day, God has given you a new start.
True love endures and bears all things,
    so let love develop and let your heart sprout wings,

as joy overflows from God's heavenly springs.
    Let God's peace umpire you,
as you go on loving in the things that you do.
    Tear down those walls that were built like Jericho.
Look to Him and expect your miracle.

Doris McLaughlin

IV.
THE FATAL TAILSPIN

*"You have heard that it was said to the people in the old days,
'Thou shalt not murder,' and anyone who does so must stand
his trial. But I say to you that anyone who is angry with his
brother must stand his trial; anyone who contemptuously calls
his brother a fool must face the supreme court; and anyone
who looks down on his brother as a lost soul is himself heading
straight for the fire of destruction."*
(Phillips)[1]

How can such "beautiful people" have such horrible divorces? How do personal relationships fall apart? Jesus
says it all starts the minute we begin to harbor a grudge against
someone else in our family (the Greek word translated "brother" is genderless). Jesus equates this with physical murder. In
Jesus' day, if the judge found a person guilty as charged (in this
case of murder), the prisoner was then taken before the Sanhedrin (supreme court of the Jews) where his punishment was
determined. If our anger builds to the point that it overflows
out of our mouth in words of contempt or insult to our brother
(or wife), there is no question that we are guilty as charged—of
murder. The only question is what punishment we deserve. If

---

[1]   Reprinted with permission of Macmillan Publishing Co. From the New
      Testament in Modern English, Revised Edition. Copyright J. B. Phillips
      1958, 1960, 1972.

things deteriorate further to the point that we are cursing (condemning) our brother, Jesus says that we are in grave danger of facing God's punishment as well as man's.

Jesus describes three steps to the break-up of a personal relationship. Firstly, anger is allowed to build in our mind against our brother (or wife). Secondly, our bottled up angry thoughts spill out as words of insult to the other person's intelligence (the Greek word translated "fool" in Matt 5:22 literally means empty-headed). Finally, the inner motives of the other person are questioned and condemned. This causes heart to heart communication with the other person to abruptly cease.

I used to think that the answer to marital conflict was to teach "dynamics of communication" according to modern psychology. It always amazed me that the same people who had seemed to communicate so intimately and thoroughly in courtship as lovers could suffer complete communication breakdown a few years later in marriage. I found out through bitter experience in my own marriage; if my wife and I were to the point of questioning each other's inner motives of the heart, it didn't matter how many brilliant communication techniques I employed. We were never able to reestablish heart to heart communication until the root causes of anger, bitterness, and unforgiveness were dealt with.

When I was a boy in boarding school, every time another kid gave me a shove or stepped on my toe, I would shove him back or step on his toe twice as hard in order to pay him back and teach him a lesson. Unfortunately, the other boy would never learn the lesson. Nine times out of ten he would get mad and punch me in the nose. Then I would have to punch him back twice as hard in order to teach him not to punch people in the nose. The original minor incident would escalate into a wild free-for-all fist fight.

After I was grown up and married, sometimes I would come home after a tense day at work intending to relax, only to have my wife upset me with some minor irritation or misunderstanding which, after a number of repetitions, would gradually build an unbearable amount of stress and anger inside me. Determined to be the Lord of my own castle (home), I would proceed to straighten her out by telling her what I would and would not put up with. Instead of obtaining peace and quiet, soon the insults would be flying between us. The insults would rapidly get nastier and more judgmental, ending with remarks such as: "What kind of a Christian are you if you are going to treat me like this," or "If you are going to say that to me, then obviously you don't love me anymore." The other person would reply: "Well, you probably never really loved me in the beginning after all. You were just after sex, or money, or social status, or ?? (take your pick)."

C.S. Lewis once wrote: "Good and evil are not static; they are dynamic. Each one continually feeds on itself just like compound interest in the bank. Good is always getting better, and evil is always getting worse."[2] It is all too easy for a personal relationship to enter a vicious cycle which, if allowed to progress, will turn into a fatal tailspin and completely devastate what was once an intimate relationship. Friendship and trust that have taken years to develop can be destroyed in five minutes of carelessness.

Jesus' formula holds true even for international incidents. First, minor disputes and misunderstandings arise, producing tension and anger. Then the insults fly. Finally, the motives of the other side are questioned and trust is broken. This sets the stage for the actual physical violence to begin. Many horrible wars have occurred simply because minor incidents were allowed to escalate out of control.

*"Therefore, if you are offering your gift at the altar
and there remember that your brother has something
against you, leave your gift there in front of the altar.
First go and be reconciled to your brother; then come
and offer your gift." (NIV)*

When our conscience begins to make us feel uneasy and insecure, due to a damaged personal relationship in our life,

---

[2]   *Mere Christianity,* Lewis, C. S. Copyright 1952, Macmillan Publishing Co., Inc.

how easy it is to head for church to salve our conscience instead of swallowing our pride and going to see the person we have wronged. Jesus says that he doesn't want to see us in church, or even receive an offering from us, until we have tried our best to reconcile any broken relationships with those around us. Even if the problem seems to be only 1% our fault and 99% the fault of the other party, we are still required to seek the other person out. One time the Lord led me to seek out another fellow worker who seemed to have a grudge against me and who was apparently spreading vicious rumors about me. After many days of resisting the Lord and feeling certain that the problem was 100% the other person's fault, I finally went. The only thing that I could think of to say was that I was sorry that our relationship was not what it should be. One thing led to another, and by the time we really got down to brass tacks, it was apparent that I really had been the cause of a problem that had been festering for months. My obedience to the Lord led to the reconciliation of the problem and the forming of a strong friendship that has endured to the present.

> *"Settle matters quickly with your adversary who is taking you to court. Do it while you are still with him on the way, or he may hand you over to the judge, and the judge may hand you over to the officer, and you may he thrown into prison. I tell you the truth, you will not get out until you have paid the last penny."*
> *(NIV)*

In this present life, we are all, in a figure of speech "on our way to court." Any adversary or plaintiff who claims to have been injured by us, who is not settled within the time allotted us to live here on earth, will have the opportunity to present his case and accuse us before God. Jesus says that we will be required to pay dearly for any past due debts. Broken relationships extract a terrible toll even in this present life. Broken family relationships that are not reconciled can cause unending grief for all parties concerned. Most patients requiring

THE HOUSE ON THE SAND

1. **Human Motives**

   Lofty Ideals, Selfishness

2. **Insensitivity to God's Law**

   Anger, Frustration

3. **Self-Righteous Pride**

   Blindness to Truth

4. **End Justifies Means**

   Lawless Violence

5. **Revenge**

   Unforgiveness, Guilt

6. **Hypocrisy**

   Living a Lie, Rationalization

7. **Rebellion Against God**

   Confusion, Uncertainty

8. **Hatred Kills Love**

   No Hope, Lack of Conscience

9. **Spiritual Death**

   Divorce, Murder, Suicide

TOTAL DESTRUCTION OF THE FAMILY AND SOCIETY; CHAOS

psychiatric treatment have, at the root of their problem, an unreconciled hatred for someone, coupled with bitterness and unforgiveness. Tragically, this can easily develop in the case of an innocent victim of a crime who harbors a bitter grudge against the party responsible, instead of deciding to mercifully forgive and put the matter to rest.

> *"You have heard that it was said, do not commit adultery. But I tell you that anyone who looks at a woman lustfully has already committed adultery with her in his heart. If your right eye causes you to sin, gouge it out and throw it away. It is better for you to lose one part of your body than for your whole body to be thrown into hell. And if your right hand causes you to sin, cut it off and throw it away. It is better for you to lose one part of your body than for your whole body to go into hell (NIV)*

If there is an unresolved, unreconciled problem in a home, similar to the one that Jesus has been describing here in Matt. 5: 27–30 and if we are on the outs with our spouse even temporarily, it opens us up to a very dangerous temptation. As we walk down the street, all the other members of the opposite sex that we see take on added attraction. The thought occurs to us: "Hey, why didn't I marry one of these beautiful people instead of the 'old grouch' that I left back at home." As the mental fantasies build in our mind, our eyes start roaming onto any opportune target that presents itself. Sooner or later chance presents us with the possibility of actually living out one of our fantasies. The transition from mental adultery to physical adultery is surprisingly smooth provided that the relationship with the original spouse remains interrupted.

But, you say, Jesus couldn't possibly have intended us to take this passage literally. Well, whatever you think, Jesus words are literally true; it really would be better to wind up in heaven with one eye than in hell with two. In Jesus' day a person could actually get his eye plucked out for being a "peeping Tom." An adulterer would have been lucky to have had just his hand amputated for taking a hold of someone else's wife. Death was the normal penalty for adultery.

The point that I believe Jesus wants to make is that seemingly innocent little impure thoughts wreak tremendous havoc on our lives and cause us permanent loss. If we allow impure thoughts such as anger, malice, unforgiveness, or impure sexual fantasies a place in our minds, they are seeds that we will be unable to prevent from germinating and translating themselves into actions. If this happens we might bear the scars of our folly for all eternity.

> *"It has been said, 'Anyone who divorces his wife must give her a certificate of divorce.' But I tell you that anyone who divorces his wife, except for marital unfaithfulness, causes her to commit adultery, and anyone who marries a woman so divorced commits adultery." (NIV)*

Divorces start out with little, seemingly insignificant details and fester until they are out of control. Even a minor little grudge, if nursed long enough, can develop into a full-fledged divorce. Once adultery has taken place, all it takes is one more minor spat with the spouse, and bags are packed, bridges are burned, and the family destroyed in favor of beginning marriage anew with the "someone else" who is available and waiting.

Jesus is not setting forth a new or abstract policy on divorce here. Listen to what God has to say in the Old Testament about divorce.

> *"Another thing you do: You flood the Lord's altar with tears. You weep and wail because He no longer pays attention to your offerings, neither accepts them with pleasure from your hands. You ask, 'Why?' It is because the Lord is acting as the witness between you and the wife of your youth, because you have broken faith with her, though she is your partner, the wife of your marriage covenant. Has not the Lord made them one? In flesh and spirit they are His. And why one?*

> *Because he was seeking godly offspring. So guard yourself in your spirit, and do not break faith with the wife of your youth. 'I hate divorce,' says the Lord God of Israel, 'and I hate a man's covering himself with violence as well as with his garment,' says the Lord Almighty. So guard yourself in your spirit, and do not break faith." Malachi 2:13–16 (NIV)*

God can forgive and restore us after a divorce, but something is irrevocably lost whenever a marriage is broken. Jesus' words seem to leave open the possibility for divorce by an innocent party whose spouse has broken faith with them. When faith is broken in a home by one or both persons, physical violence almost inevitably follows. Most counselors will recommend at least temporary separation of spouses if acts of violence become increasingly common in the home. Alcoholism and/or drug use will further complicate the vicious circle and lead to still more irrational acts of violence within a home.

> *"Again you have heard that it was said to the people long ago, 'Do not break your oath, but keep the oaths you have made to the Lord.' But I tell you, do not swear at all: either by heaven, for it is God's throne; or by the earth, for it is his footstool; or by Jerusalem, for it is the city of the great king. And do not swear by your head, for you cannot make even one hair white or black. Simply let your 'yes' be 'yes,' and your 'no,' 'no'; anything beyond this comes from the evil one."*
> *(NIV)*

Most marriages begin with vows made to God in a church. Divorces end in criminal court with at least one of the parties attempting to convince the judge that they have been injured by the other party sufficiently enough to require a divorce. When credibility is lacking, it is easy to say things like: "Why, the earth can open up and swallow me if I'm not telling the truth" or "Why, lightning can strike me down from heaven if such and such isn't right." When really backed against a wall, the Jews swore by the Holy city, Jerusalem, as a most sacred oath. In our present courts of law we swear on the Bible. Jesus says that if we can't just say "yes" or "no" and be believed, maybe we should examine our lives. The enemy, Satan, might be feeding us a lie enabling us to rationalize our actions.

Notice that Jesus doesn't mention the devil until here, well into his sermon. In Jesus' description of the vicious cycle of how personal relationships can be destroyed, starting with a buildup of anger and ending in a divorce, the place that he tells us to watch out for the Evil One is at the very end, when the Enemy would like to help us rationalize our problem and pretend that it really wasn't our fault.

If at any stage during the breakup of a personal relationship, we are able to honestly face our share of the blame and come to God with the broken attitude of the "poor in spirit," throwing ourselves upon his mercy, it is possible to break the vicious circle of evil feeding on itself and replace it with the positive, opposite, upward spiral of mercy and love described by Jesus in his beatitudes. Remember: Good can also feed on itself and get better and better the longer we spend planting seeds of mercy, forgiveness, love, and justice. In the Kingdom of God the sky is, literally, the limit. Unlike evil, which can only corrupt and destroy that which was once wholesome and pure, good is creative and knows no upper bounds. There is no upper limit to what God can do with a human life if we are willing to co-operate with him.

GOD'S WAY

I see it Lord. Because my allegiance is to you,
 and no other's love will do,
I'm free, you've satisfied me,
 because in your faithfulness you purified me
and you love me unconditionally.

My husband's love could not satisfy me.
 He was not the way I wanted him to be.
Yet I thought I loved him totally.
 So often in anger he rejected me,
and his anger affected me.

I sat alone to brood and stew
 over all the things he would say and do.
How could I win him back to me?
 What could I do to appease his wrath?
How could I get him to come back?

I found his love was not for me
 but for what he wanted me to be,
because he loved me so selfishly.
 It seemed to me he was contrary
to the man I knew and decided to marry.

Soon it became apparent to me
 that I, too, was as selfish as he.
Our lives were spent in discontent
 until we built up great walls of resentment.
So in my heart I turned and left.

I left him and he left me,
 although neither wanted to be free.
So we remained there physically—
 we both remained there in our home,
but we remained there both alone.

So I prayed and asked of You,
   "Heavenly Father, what shall I do?"
You looked upon my affliction,
   the bitterness, and care.
You said, "My little one. Don't live there.

Your life in me does not exist
   in matters so dark and gloomy as this.
Come to me. Give it to me and walk in my ways.
   I will give you grace
and empower you as in this hour you seek my face.

The death of a marriage had surely come,
   and you felt so completely undone.
Your grief was real and very great.
   It was for this I had to wait
that selfish love would dissipate.

Now, I have made my right arm bare—
   I will come and repair
all the ruins of despair.
   I will come and fight for you.
I love you and your husband too.

I will make you love anew.
   If you will love him as I love you,
let go of the heartache, bitterness, and pain.
   Forgive him and start to love again.
Are you willing to open your heart?

If you are, I'll do my part.
   Will you be careful to understand
and not resent his reprimand?
   And when you think bad thoughts of him,
be very careful to reject this sin.

You cannot judge his heart's intent.
   How can you know its content?

You cannot afford to resent it.
 Sow seeds of mercy
and not resentment.

You cannot love me and not love him.
 Let your thoughts be kind towards him.
Repent and let my love shine in—
 Give him the benefit of the doubt.
Keep that strife and trouble out.

Do for him what I've done for you.
 Act out my love that I've given to you,
as you do the things I tell you to.
 Don't respond to his anger or bad deeds.
See that you respond only to his needs.

Remember how I stood the test,
 when in unselfish love I gave my best.
They plucked my beard from off my face,
 while I endured their spitting, shame, and disgrace.
I offered absolutely no resistance.

It was my mercy that crucified me.
 Soon mankind would be free.
My compassion endured their cruelty.
 It is my will that you be in every way conformed to me.
I have given you victory.

I'm determined that you will win.
 over pride, selfishness, and sin.
Let my peace garrison thee.
 I will smite the enemy.
Your household will be won to me."

Doris McLaughlin

V.

FORGIVENESS

*"You have heard that it was said, 'An eye for an eye
and a tooth for a tooth.' But I tell you not to resist the
one who injures you; but if anyone slaps you on one
cheek, turn him the other, too; and if anyone wants to
sue you for your shirt, let him have your coat, too. And
if anyone forces you to go one mile, go with him two.
If anyone, whoever he may be, keeps on begging you,
give to him; if anyone wants to borrow from you, do
not turn him away.' (Williams)*

This is one of the most difficult passages in the Bible. There
are those who say that it is so impossible and Utopian that
the Sermon on the Mount can't possibly be intended for our present day and age. Others use this section to support pacifism. I do
not claim to fully understand all the ramifications of this passage,
but the most logical place to begin "turning the other cheek" and
"going the extra mile" is obviously within our own homes.

If someone is angry with us, we are not to stand up for our
rights and start an argument. Jesus is asking us to bear with
the other person and help them in any way that we can. I understand that the part about "turning the other cheek" is really
an idiom in the Greek that means: don't insist on arguing for
your rights. If our response to insults or injury is "an eye for
an eye and a tooth for a tooth," it will most likely escalate the
problem and a vicious circle will develop. It is only when we

are willing to give up some of our "rights" that progress can be made towards peace.

It is possible for any of us to have a bad day. There are days when my wife wakes up feeling sick and grouchy. If she snaps at me or does something to offend me, I have learned that this is not the time to "straighten her out." If I bear with her and help her, she quickly returns to her normal self. The same is true in reverse when I come home from work with a headache or when I'm a little uptight about something. We have learned through experience that it is best to defuse potential explosions before they can go off.

> *"You have heard that it was said, 'You must love your neighbor and hate your enemy,' But I tell you, practice loving your enemies and praying for your persecutors, to prove that you are sons of your Father in heaven, for he makes his sun rise on bad as well as good people, and makes the rain come down on doers of right and of wrong alike. For if you practice loving only those who love you, what reward will you get? Do not even the tax-collectors practice that? And if you say 'good morning' to your brothers only, what more than others are you doing? So you, my followers, ought to be perfect, as your heavenly Father is." (Williams)*

The previous chapter described the destruction of personal relationships in the first person when we are responsible for causing the problem and the other person is merely reacting to our inputs. What happens if we are the "innocent victim"? How are we to respond when someone else is hurting us? What if the one who is injuring and persecuting us is a member of our own family?

A man's worst potential adversaries are in his own home. When my wife gets angry with me and becomes my adversary, she can rake me over the coals worse than anyone else that I know. My wife knows exactly where I keep all my "dirty laundry." If she ever decides to insult me, she can do an expert job because she is intimately familiar with all my shortcomings.

Jesus says we are to "practice" loving our enemies and praying for our persecutors. What better place to start practicing than in our immediate family situation. This is the way to convince other people that we really are sons of God.

The physical laws of the universe, such as the Law of Gravity, affect all men. For example, a 150 pound evil man weighs just as much as a 150 pound good man. The Spiritual laws of the Kingdom of God also affect all men. If we learn to love our enemies and to overcome evil with good, we are setting in motion right actions that will reap rewards according to Spiritual laws and produce a reward in heaven. What greater reward could we ask or hope for than that our lost, spiritually dead, unsaved, loved ones be reconciled to God and spend all eternity in heaven with us.

My partner, Ricardo Trillos, and I were very concerned for a friend of ours who had been separated from his family and six children for over five years. Ricardo was very persistent in explaining Jesus' plan for family reconciliation to our friend, but to no avail. Ricardo even sought out this man's ex-spouse, but she wanted nothing to do with him after being left alone to fend for the children for so many years. One of the children, however, decided to put Jesus' message to work in her life. Through the love of one of the daughters, God began to work a miracle in the lives of our friend and his spouse. Within a year they were back together again. Now, three years later, every time that I see this particular couple, they remind me of newlyweds except that they are middle aged.

I have witnessed families that were literal basket cases. I have seen them turned into showcase examples of loving Christian homes through the decision of just one member of the family to put Jesus' spiritual principles to work in their lives. When God's Holy Spirit is allowed to shine through at least one member of a family, a process is set in motion that will ultimately envelop everyone else in the house. The Apostle Paul said to the Philippian jailer in

Acts 16:31, *"Believe on the Lord Jesus Christ and you shall he saved—You and your house (household)."*

Appendix

Everyone says, "I would change if she would change," or, "I would change if he would change." If we sit around waiting for the other person to take the lead, we may be in for a long wait. According to some psychologists it takes 100% effort on the part of both husband and wife to put a troubled marriage back together and even then, a successful outcome may be in doubt. I have run into many troubled marriages in which it seemed like only one party really wanted help. Jesus offers hope to cases like these. One person is all that is needed to provide God with a point of contact and to enable Him to get ahold of an entire family. God treats a marriage as one whole, not as two halves like we do. If God can get one person to have the right attitude, it is possible for the entire family to be reconciled—both to God and to one another.

> *"Take care not to do your good deeds in public, to attract the attention of people; if you do, you will get no reward from your father in heaven. So whenever you do your deeds of charity, never blow your own horn in public, as the hypocrites are in the habit of doing in the synagogues and on the street corners, to be praised by the people. I solemnly say to you, they already have their reward. But whenever you, a follower of mine, do a deed of charity, never let your own left hand know what your right hand is doing, so that your deed of charity may be secret, and your father who sees what is secret will reward you. Also, whenever you pray, you must not be like the hypocrites, for they love to pray standing in the synagogues and on the street corners, to attract the attention of people. I solemnly say to you, they already have their reward."*
> *(WILLIAMS)*

When we become followers of Jesus, and when the Holy Spirit begins to do good works both in and through us, we become highly susceptible to an extremely dangerous problem—namely *pride*. By this I do not mean the wholesome sense of pleasure and accomplishment that we often feel in a job well done. I mean the type of pride that lifts itself up at someone else's expense. Pride is a unique sin. By its very nature it isolates people from one another. There is such a thing as the so called "code of honor" among thieves. Unchaste or adulterous people can have a certain amount of fellowship. On the other hand, two proud people are mutually exclusive. The audience will only pay attention to one grandstander at a time. Proud people are in constant competition with one another like the hypocrites that Jesus talks about who blew their own horn in public and prayed standing on the street corners. Pride was Satan's sin. Pride works in direct opposition to the Holy Spirit, and if allowed to flourish, it will destroy mercy, forgiveness, and reconciliation. When we begin to put Jesus' merciful mentality to work in our lives, it is easy to get caught up in self-righteous pride. As we begin to actually respond to insults and injury with mercy, forgiveness, kind words, and good deeds, it is easy to start to look down on others or to demand recognition for the good deeds that we are now doing. After the first few times of "going the extra mile" or "turning the other cheek," the next time a similar situation presents itself there is a strong temptation to demand compensation or recognition by telling the other person that it is now their turn to make concessions. If the other person refuses, a strong sense of self-righteousness can set in. If pride is allowed to develop, it will leave a very foul taste in the mouths of those we are trying to reach. On the other hand, if we do our good deeds in secret without letting our right hand know what our left hand is doing, God can bless and reward us.

> *"But whenever you, follower of mine, pray, you must*
> *go to your most private place, shut the door, and pray*
> *to your Father in secret, and your Father who sees*
> *what is secret will reward you. And whenever you pray,*
> *you must not keep on repeating set phrases, as the*
> *heathen do, for they suppose that they will be heard in*
> *accordance with the length of their prayers. So then*
> *you must not be like them, for your Father knows what*
> *you need before you ask him. So this is the way you*
> *must pray: (Williams)*

> *Our Father in heaven, hallowed be your name, your kingdom come, your will be done on earth as it is in heaven. Give us this day our daily bread. And forgive us our debts, as we have forgiven our debtors. And lead us not into temptation. But deliver us from the evil one." (NIV)*

Our Father in heaven,

When was the last time that you went into your room alone, shut the door, and began your prayer to God with the phrase: "Our Father"? I normally begin my prayers with: "Dear God," "Dear Lord," "My God," or "Dear Father in Heaven." It would never occur to me to open a prayer with "Our Father" if I were alone by myself in a closed room. Why then does Jesus instruct us to go to our most secret place, shut the door, and then begin our prayer with "Our Father"? I believe that Jesus wants us to develop such an attitude of concern for those around us (such as our family) that our prayers will automatically be "Our Father." Jesus wants us to identify with and intercede for those around us just like he does for us. Instead of asking God for long lists of things for ourselves and commiserating over all the petty little things that people have done to offend us, I believe that God likes to hear us ask for our collective needs and demonstrate that we are at least as concerned for others as for ourselves. When Jesus' message begins to bear fruit in our lives, more and more of our prayers to God begin to subconsciously start out "Our Father." As we are reconciled to those around us, our prayers become much more powerful and effective.

Hallowed be Your Name,

God is way up in heaven; we are down here on the earth. How do we make contact with him? How can we possibly bridge the tremendous gap between us and Him? We can begin by saying to God: Hallowed (reverenced) be Your Name. The first step in making real contact with God is to respect Him and tell Him that He is a just God and that we need Him. This is the same attitude that is reflected in Jesus' first beatitude:

"Blessed are the poor in spirit for theirs is the kingdom of heaven"

Thy kingdom come,

It takes a lot of nerve to say to God: "Thy kingdom come." God's kingdom always seems to interfere with what we think is fun. When we ask God's kingdom to engulf our lives, it seems like we will lose all of our security and possibly even our individuality. Who wants to jump off the cliff with the flag flying. Remember Shadrach, Meshach, and Abednego in the book of Daniel. They were required to kneel down and worship a statue of the king of Babylon. If they refused, they were threatened with being bound and thrown alive into a fiery furnace. Their reply was that they would worship God alone and that God could deliver them from the fiery furnace. If God didn't deliver them, they still wouldn't kneel before the statue. As you remember, when they wound up being thrown into the fire, a strange thing happened. The king was amazed to see them walking around unharmed in the midst of the fire. The only things consumed by the fire were the cords that bound them and the men who threw them into the furnace!

Jesus said:

"Blessed are those who mourn, for they shall be comforted."

The decision to say "Thy Kingdom come," may cause us to mournfully relinquish all the "fun," "pleasure," and "security" in our lives, but it turns out that the only things God takes from us are those things which were harming and enslaving us. It isn't even possible to know the true meaning of the words "fun," "pleasure," and "security," until we are reconciled with God and living in His Kingdom.

Your will be done on earth as it is in heaven

Appendix

Right now God's will is being done 100% of the time in heaven. Unfortunately, that is not the case here on earth. God has given each of us a free will. Most of us use our free will to do whatever we think best for ourselves. This basic selfishness of human nature leads to all kinds of problems. The tragic history of mankind is filled with poverty, hunger, war, prostitution, and exploitation of one man by another. To top it all off, many of us blame God for all the problems, violence, and unfairness we see around us. How can it be God's fault if everyone is going their own way and turning a deaf ear to God's way? The problems we have here on earth are examples of what happens when human selfishness runs its natural course. We have no case against God whatsoever.

"Blessed are the meek for they shall inherit the earth"

If we submit to the kingship of Jesus with the "meek" attitude, we will inherit the earth. God is the only one who can make truly good plans.

I spent many years thinking up great big ambitious plans for God's kingdom. I went head over heels into financial debt for the ministry feeling sure that God would pay it all back because I was doing this all "for him." It took me quite a while to learn that God wanted to fit me into His master plan, instead of me fitting him into my big, grandiose schemes. As I learned to submit even my "good ideas" to Him, I was amazed at how much smoother everything went. If we really mean it when we pray, "Thy will be done on earth as it is in heaven," the first place to start is our own personal lives.

Give us this day our daily bread

"Blessed are those who hunger and thirst for doing and being right, for they shall be completely satisfied."

When the devil tempted Jesus in the desert by asking him to turn some stones into bread because he was hungry, Jesus answered, "The Scripture says, 'Not on bread alone can man live, but on every word that comes from the mouth of God.'" As we

1

decide to enter the Kingdom of God with the attitude of being spiritual beggars, spiritually destitute, and poverty stricken, we will at first be appalled by how badly we've messed up our lives by going our own way. We are also saddened at the thought of supposedly giving up most of our present "pleasures" for the sake of God's Kingdom. Then, when we firmly decide to completely submit to Jesus' Kingship in all areas of our lives, an amazing thing happens. Jesus' thinking begins to start rubbing off on us, and we actually begin to hunger and thirst for doing and being right. We begin to start wanting what God wants. We find out that the Christian life isn't a dull, dry, monotonous, legalistic list of strict do's and don'ts seemingly designed to eliminate any chance of having fun. The Christian life becomes an uplifting, fulfilling, satisfying personal relationship with God in which He feeds us with every wholesome thing that there is. As God reaches into every remote corner of our lives, provided we respond by yielding to Him in every area that He puts his finger on, He will begin to fulfill and satisfy us in ways that would have been impossible for us to even imagine prior to entering His Kingdom.

Forgive us our debts as we also have forgiven our debtors

STOP! Could Jesus have made a mistake here? Did he really mean to imply that God won't forgive us if we fail to forgive those around us? When Jesus said,

"Blessed are the merciful for they shall obtain mercy"

Did he really mean it? The possible repercussions are enormous. Yet, there is absolutely no getting around it. Here in the middle of the Lord's prayer, we find that it is no use asking God to forgive us our shortcomings and failures if we have failed to search our hearts and forgive anyone who could be considered our debtor.

A merciful, forgiving attitude is essential not only for reaching our family members for Christ, it is essential for our own forgiveness. Let's stop right now and search our hearts.

Remember: Mercy is a decision, not a feeling. Mercy is forgiving someone else even if they don't deserve it. How does God forgive us?

Isaiah 43:25 says:

> *"I, even I, am he who blots out your transgressions, for my own sake, and remembers your sins no more." (NIV)*

If we are going to really pray, "Forgive us our debts as we also have forgiven our debtors," it will do us no good to say to those who have wronged us, "Well, I'll forgive you but I'll never forget it." When God forgives someone, He lets go of it completely and does not drag the issue back up at a later date. We must be willing to do the same.

We have just arrived at a terrible paradox. If we do not unconditionally forgive those who have wronged us, then God will not forgive us our failings. The only problem is that most of us are incapable of completely forgiving anyone else. Even if we can mumble the words, "I forgive you" to the other party, the hurt that has been done to us still seems to linger on in our subconscious, biding it's time to resurface and harm our relationship with that person once again. What if we are not dealing with isolated instances of wrongdoing against us? What if the insult and injury are still going on? What if the other person is unrepentant and is continuing to hurt us more and more each day?

I faced such a situation when I was kidnapped and held captive by Marxist terrorists for 142 days. My initial reaction to being brutally kidnapped was one of bitterness, frustration, and rage. After several days, I began to see that negative emotions and thoughts could do no harm to the terrorists! But they could harm me! For several weeks I fought an agonizing spiritual battle in my mind as I sought to respond to my captors in mercy and love instead of in bitterness and hatred. Left to my own resources, the situation was doubly hopeless. Not only was I in an impossible physical situation, but I was also in an impossible mental and emotional situation of anguish that would leave deep scars even if I were released physically unharmed.

I found, to my relief, that as a Christian I had resources available to me that I had previously not even been able to imagine. When Jesus lived a perfect life, died a perfect death, and rose from the dead victorious over sin and death, he made a tremendous power available to those of us who wish to follow him. When we enter the Kingdom of God with the attitude of the "poor in spirit," and place our complete faith and trust in Jesus Christ as King and Lord of our lives, it is possible for us to actually identify with the death and resurrection of Jesus. We are in a sense declaring ourselves dead and then rising to a newness of life with Jesus Christ in charge of our life. Jesus has faced and overcome every possible problem of life. He has made himself available to literally put his hand on our hands and guide us through the rough parts of life. The Holy Spirit, who was made available to us through the death and resurrection of Jesus, can provide us with unlimited power and resources.

As a prisoner in a Marxist guerrilla camp, I found out that even though my captors had physical weapons like machine guns, I had spiritual weapons that were much more powerful. Armed with spiritual weapons like truth, prayer, mercy, forgiveness, and a concern for the spiritual well-being of my captors, I watched God turn the tables and win a tremendous victory in a seemingly hopeless situation.

And lead us not into temptation, but deliver us from the evil one

When we reach out to others in mercy, forgiveness, and love, it influences the behavior of those around us. It also has a subtle influence on our own lives. In time, the seeds of mercy and forgiveness run full circle and affect the way God treats us. It's like giving God a license to reach deep down in our subconscious and begin a cleansing, healing process. After "blessed are the merciful," Jesus said,

"Blessed are the pure in heart, for they shall see God face to face."

As we reach out to others in mercy and forgiveness, God uses the opportunity to begin purifying our hearts. It is when we enter into the spirit of forgiveness that God will "Lead us not into temptation" and to "Deliver us from the evil one."

Upon my release after four and a half months of being tied to a tree in a Marxist guerrilla prison camp, I had no psychological scars. I have never had a nightmare or a flashback. I believe that a God given attitude of mercy and forgiveness on my part towards my captors was the key to my not suffering any permanent psychological damage.

For if you forgive men when they sin against you, your heavenly Father will also forgive you. But if you do not forgive men their sins, your Father will not forgive your sins.
(NIV)

Matt. 18:21-35:
"Then Peter came to Jesus and asked, 'Lord, how many times shall I forgive my brother when he sins against me? Up to seven times?"

Jesus answered, "I tell you, not seven times, but seventy times seven.

Therefore the kingdom of heaven is like a king who wanted to settle accounts with his servants. As he began the settlement, a man who owed him ten thousand talents was brought to him. Since he was not able to pay, the master ordered that he and his wife and his children and all that he had be sold to repay the debt.

The servant fell on his knees before him. "Be patient with me," he begged, "and I will pay back everything." The servant's master took pity on him, canceled the debt, and let him go.

But when that servant went out, he found one of his fellow servants who owed him a hundred denarii. He grabbed him and began to choke him. "Pay back what you owe me!" he demanded.

His fellow servant fell to his knees and begged him, "Be patient with me, and I will pay you back."

But he refused. Instead, he went off and had the man thrown into prison until he could pay the debt. When the other servants saw what had happened, they were greatly distressed and went and told their master everything that had happened.

Then the master called the servant in. "You wicked servant," he said, "I canceled all that debt of yours because you begged me to. Shouldn't you have had mercy on your fellow servant just as I had on you?" In anger his master turned him over to the jailer's until he should pay back all he owed.

This is how my heavenly Father will treat each of you unless you forgive your brother from your heart."

GET GOING

You have sought My face
    and asked for the grace
to turn the hearts of your loved ones back to you.
    You said, "Where do I start? And what can I do?"
Express your appreciation for the good things that they do,
    and don't be concerned with what they think of you.
You must continue to plant love's seeds
    by sowing in the soil of their needs.
It is up to Me to change their hearts,
    but you must be faithful and do your part.
If you see a wall and it seems so cold,
    just sow your seeds and watch love unfold.
As day by day you show your concern,
    eventually, their hearts will turn.
Resentment, anger, and unforgiveness will melt,
    as the constancy of your love is felt.
You will instill in them a confidence
    which will disarm them of all resistance.
You desire your family to be
    brought into unity, united in me.
Your obedience is the key
    for this to become a reality.
So get going, and be sure to do
    all the things that love tells you to.
This is a crossroads in your life.
    Right now you feel their opposition and strife,
but it won't be this way always.
    So look to Me and walk in My ways.
You shall receive a great reward—
    for soon you will all be in one accord.
I desire that you be a bright light
    to direct their feet out of the dark night.
When you determine to become live bait,
    it won't be long that you will have to wait
for them to come into My net.
    Let your goal be solidly set.

See them alive and seated with Me
    at My right hand in the heavenlies.
Eternal life is what they need.
    So get going and proceed!

Doris McLaughlin

VI.
REPAIRING THE BREACH

Our Father in heaven, hallowed be your name, your kingdom come, your will be done on earth as it is in heaven. Give us this day our daily bread. Forgive us our debts as we have forgiven our debtors. And lead us not into temptation, but deliver us from the evil one.
(NIV)

For if you forgive others their shortcomings, your heavenly Father will forgive you, too. But if you do not forgive others, your heavenly Father will not forgive your shortcomings either.

Also, whenever you fast, you must not look gloomy like the hypocrites, for they put on a gloomy countenance, to let people see them fasting. I solemnly say to you, they already have their reward. But whenever you, follower of mine, fast, perfume your head and wash your face, so that your fasting may be seen, not by men but by your Father who is unseen, and your Father who sees what is secret will reward you. (Williams)

Prayer and fasting are the traditional Judeo-Christian remedy for what-ails-you. Prayer is our traditional Christian recipe for marital troubles, rebellious teenagers, unsaved loved ones, or any other serious problem. If endless repetition of problems and names from our "prayer list" doesn't produce results, then we can always piously spend some time in actual prayer and fasting (abstaining from food) in hopes of getting God's attention. We have just studied prayer, and we have seen that Jesus teaches us that the secret of effective prayer is not endless repetition like the heathen do. Jesus places the emphasis on having a forgiving attitude and requires us to forgive all of our debtors as a pre-condition to being forgiven by God. Until our present sins have been forgiven and we are reconciled to God, how could we possibly hope to establish communication with Him and expect Him to respond to our prayers? It is amazing that sometimes God in His profound mercy responds to our prayers of desperation, even when we are not all that we should be. Prayer and fasting can be tremendously effective spiritual weapons, but only if we use them with the right attitude.

We have discovered that a merciful, forgiving attitude on our part is essential to an effective prayer life. Listen to what the prophet Isaiah has to say about effective fasting and notice how it dovetails perfectly with Jesus' teaching on family reconciliation:

> *"Is not this the fast that I choose:*
> *to loose the bonds of wickedness*
> *to undo the thongs of the yoke,*
> *to let the oppressed go free,*
> *and to break every yoke?*
> *Is it not to share your bread with the hungry,*
> *and bring the homeless poor into your house;*
> *when you see the naked to cover him,*
> *and not to hide yourself from your own flesh?*
> *Then shall your light break forth like the dawn,*
> *and your healing shall spring up speedily;*
> *your righteousness shall go before you,*
> *the glory of the Lord shall be your rear guard.*
> *Then you shall call, and the Lord will answer;*
> *you shall cry, and he shall say Here I am.*
> *"If you take away from the midst of you the yoke,*
> *the pointing of the finger,*
> *and speaking of wickedness,*

if you pour yourself out for the hungry
and satisfy the desire of the afflicted,
then shall your light rise in the darkness
and your gloom be as noonday.
And the Lord will guide you continually,
and satisfy your desire with good things,
and make your bones strong;
and you shall be like a watered garden,
like a spring of water,
whose waters fail not.
And your ancient ruins shall be rebuilt;
you shall raise up the foundations of many
generations;
you shall be called the repairer of the breach,
the restorer of streets to dwell in.
(RSV)[1]

Will you let God turn you into the "repairer of the breach" within your family? If you allow Jesus' message of mercy and forgiveness a foothold in your life and family, He won't stop there either. After God has repaired the breaches in your family and marriage, He can make you into a "restorer of streets to dwell in," and you can help bring his peace to many other suffering homes and dwellings. If you like the sound of this idea, then get ready to obey King Jesus' next command and:

"Stop storing up your riches on earth where moths
and rust make away with them and where thieves
break in and steal them. But keep on storing up your
riches in heaven where moths and rust do not make
away with them and where thieves do not break in
and steal them. For wherever your treasure is, there
too your heart will be." (Williams)

We are born into this world naked. When we die, all of our physical wealth and goods remain here. On the other hand, the

---

[1]   From the Holy Bible, Revised Standard Version, Isaiah 58:6–12

memories of the experiences we have had, and the character that we have formed during our lives here on the earth, will be ours for all eternity. If we can think and speak and act each day in a manner that allows other people to see the light of God's love in us, then we are storing up treasure in heaven each time we influence someone else for good and helping God to mold human lives into heavenly gold, silver, and precious stones.

> *"The eye is the lamp of the body. If your eyes are good, your whole body will be full of light. But if your eyes are bad, your whole body will be full of darkness. If then the light within you is darkness, how great is that darkness! No one can serve two masters. Either he will hate the one and love the other, or he will be devoted to the one and despise the other. You cannot serve both God and money," (NIV)*

Our physical eyes need light in order to see and orient our whole body towards the goals and needs of our physical lives. If we had to live as blind people in darkness, obtaining even the basic necessities of life would become very complicated. Many normal activities, such as driving a car, would become impossible. Our spiritual eyes also need spiritual light in order to see and orient our spiritual lives towards God's goals and objectives. If we are after the wrong goals and concerned with storing up treasures on earth instead of in heaven, then we are still wandering around in spiritual darkness.

As we progress in knowledge of God and God's Kingdom, many of us would like to "have our cake and eat it too." We would like to enjoy the maximum benefit of all the material things that our money can buy. At the same time we are devoting a significant percentage of our time towards seeking to serve God because we are beginning to become concerned about our eternal well-being and the eternal fate of others. Jesus says that we will ultimately run into a conflict of interest and be forced to choose between love for God and love for money. It is impossible to remain seated on the fence, forever. Notice, that the root of the problem is not the money but the making of money our master. It is only under God's direction that we can obtain any lasting satisfaction from the use of our money. Otherwise, the greater our store of material goods, the more difficult it will be to preserve them from the "rust and the moths and the thieves." More money will only mean more headaches and more worries and less real happiness.

"Therefore I tell you, do not worry about your life, what you will eat or drink; or about your body, what you will wear. Is not life more important than food, and the body more important than clothes? Look at the birds of the air; they do not sow or reap or store away in barns, and yet your heavenly Father feeds them. Are you not much more valuable than they? Who of you by worrying can add a single hour to his life? And why do you worry about clothes? See how the lilies of the field grow, they do not labor or spin. Yet I tell you that not even Solomon in all his splendor was dressed like one of these. If that is how God clothes the grass of the field, which is here today and tomorrow is thrown into the fire, will he not much more clothe you, O you of little faith? So do not worry, saying, 'What shall we eat?' or 'What shall we drink?' or 'What shall we wear?' For the pagans run after all these things, and your heavenly Father knows that you need them"
(NIV)

The two primary underlying factors that cause us to worry are selfishness and pride. Until we have honestly faced and allowed God to deal with these two issues, we will be unable to stop worrying. The more material things we obtain by giving in to our selfishness, the more are the worries that come along with them. Then pride can provide us with many more worries, as we begin to compare ourselves with those around us and worry that we are inferior to them. This develops an endless vicious circle of buying more and more "superior" things in order to "keep up with the Jones."

Worry, after not forgiving others, ranks as a primary cause of strife and friction within the family. Worry generally precedes unforgiveness and plays a major role in the development of family fights in the first place. Almost every time that we build up anger or resentment against someone in our family, it is because we are worrying that the other person is going to harm some material possession of ours, or deny us some physical pleasure.

In order to live a victorious Christian life, our entire manner of thinking must undergo a complete transformation. Jesus tells us that harboring an angry grudge against our brother is equivalent to murdering him (Matt. 5:22) and that looking at another woman lustfully is the same as committing adultery with her (Matt 5:27). The old maxim: "You are what you think," is very true. We are not necessarily what we think we are, but we are what we think. Eventually the thoughts that we allow to dominate our minds will begin to dominate the way we act also.

If we allow our minds to be constantly dominated by thoughts of worry concerning our physical well-being, our lives will become enslaved to fear, anxiety, and depression. Jesus devotes a large portion of His Sermon on the Mount to teaching us the utter uselessness of worrying. As long as we are worrying about what to eat, drink, wear, and etc., we will have trouble understanding what Jesus really wants us to do. Worrying about the wrong type of things can drown out the Lord's still, small voice and leave us drifting through the dangerous, rocky seas of life without His guidance and direction. On the other hand, if we worry about pleasing God and if we worry about being and doing right, Jesus says that God will take care of all of our physical needs.

*"But seek first his kingdom and his righteousness,
and all these things will be given to you as well.
Therefore do not worry about tomorrow, for tomorrow
will worry about itself. Each day has enough trouble
of its own." (NIV)*

This is a promise to which I can personally testify. When I was in the jungles of Colombia as a prisoner of Communist guerrilla terrorists, I was asked a question by one of the men guarding me. This particular guerrilla was one of the ones constantly pointing his assault rifle at me as he held the other end of a rope tied around my neck in a slip knot. I had been explaining my faith in God to this man and he turned to me and said, "Look where your faith in God has gotten you now. What have you got to show for it?" I proceeded to tell him that the Christian life wasn't always a bed of roses, but that God had promised to always take care of providing me with food, drink, clothes, and a place to stay, as long as I put Him first in my life.

Ironically, the guerrilla leaders had just brought me some new clothes, a new hammock, and a new mosquito net that very morning. They had made me a small split-palm table, and at the very instant that I was asked this question, the cook walked over with a steaming platter containing my lunch. I had gone out of my way to be friendly to the cook and had been complimenting him on his cooking even when it wasn't all that great. The food had been getting better and better. This day my meal consisted of fried chicken, vegetables, and even a can of Coca-Cola. I turned to the guard who had asked the question and pointed out to him the new clothes, the nice hammock and mosquito net, and the excellent meal. I said to him, It looks to me like God is keeping his promises just fine! Then I bowed my head to say grace. (Psalm 23, of course—"Thou preparest a table before me in the presence of my enemies.")

Since my release, I have been living without a fixed income, traveling all over the United States, Canada, and Colombia telling people wherever I am invited all of the wonderful things that God has done for me and spreading Jesus' message of family reconciliation. In all this time I have never lacked anything that my family or I really needed, even though we have made it a policy not to solicit finances from men or from churches so as to not detract from this message of reconciliation to God and man.

"Do not judge, or you too will be judged. For in the same way you judge others, you will be judged, and with the measure you use, it will be measured to you.

Appendix

> *"Why do you look at the speck of sawdust in your*
> *brother's eye and pay no attention to the plank in your*
> *own eye? How can you say to your brother, 'Let me*
> *take the speck out of your eye,' when all the time there*
> *is a plank in your own eye? You hypocrite, first take*
> *the plank out of your own eye, and then you will see*
> *clearly to remove the speck from your brother's eye.*
> *(NIV)*

Any fool can criticize someone else. It takes someone who is truly competent to do a job right. C.S. Lewis, the master of debate, once wrote, "Negatives are rarely useful, even when they are true."[2] I hope that you have been noticing the positive angle that Jesus is using in His sermon. He could have preached "fire and brimstone," and some people probably expected him to. Jesus would have been well within his rights to tell the crowd that he was giving them all one last chance to repent or else. Instead Jesus said,

> *"Blessed are the poor in spirit, for theirs is the Kingdom*
> *of God".*

No wonder the Bible says that crowds of people followed Him around straining to hear His every word.

When I was prisoner of the Marxist guerrillas, if I would have criticized the cook for his lousy food, I'm sure that the food would have gotten even worse. When I began to speak well of him, he became motivated to do better. Pretty soon the food that I was getting was better than the food served to everyone else. I am firmly convinced that praising the positive aspects of a person will produce much better results than criticizing the person's weak points. There is a time for constructive criticism, but Jesus says that we have to have our own act together, first. The only way that another person will willingly accept our criticism is if we have proved to them that we are competent and well qualified in the respective area of knowledge.

---

[2]   *Mere Christianity,* Lewis, C. S. Copyright 1952, Macmillan Publishing Co., Inc.

A FRIEND IS . . .

A friend is . . .
A shoulder to cry on,
An ear to listen,
A hug when you need one,
Or even if you don't.

A friend is . . .
A Godsend
Someone you trust,
Someone you love,
Someone who loves you—
no matter who you are,
or what you've done.

A friend is. . .
someone to run to when
you're afraid—
someone you open up to—
and you feel safe.

A friend is. . .

YOU!

Stephanie Summers

VII.
THE NARROW GATE

"You must never give the things that are sacred to dogs, and you must never throw your pearls before hogs, for fear they might trample them under their feet and turn and tear you to pieces. Keep on asking, and the gift will be given to you; keep on seeking, and you will find; keep on knocking, and the door will open to you. For everyone who keeps on asking, receives, and everyone who keeps on seeking, finds, and to the one who keeps on knocking, the door will open. What human father among you, when his son asked him for bread, will give him a stone? Or if he asks for a fish, will he give him a snake? So if you, in spite of your being bad, know how to give your children what is good, how much more surely will your heavenly Father give what is good to those who keep on asking him?
(Williams)

In order for a personal relationship to progress to the realm of true friendship, trust and confidence must be developed between two people. The more intimate the relationship, the more vulnerable each person becomes to the other. A true friend is one we can confide in and can be trusted to keep our most delicate secrets very confidential. A true friend will act in our best interest, even if we're wrong. With a real friend, we can be ourselves and not have to worry about how our actions are being interpreted. We know that our friend will automatically give us the benefit of the doubt, should we slip up or make a mistake.

However, if we make the mistake of confiding information that we hold to be sacred or of great value to an untrustworthy person, the results may be devastating. It would be the same as giving sacred things to dogs or throwing pearls to hogs.

Why does Jesus stress over and over the emphasis of our being persistent in order to obtain what we ask for? I believe that among other things, He wants to find out if we really are true friends of His before He trusts us with intimate "pearls" of truth that He considers sacred. It should be clear by now that Jesus isn't talking about our asking for, seeking for, or knocking for material wealth. He already told us earlier that if we seek first the Kingdom of God and His righteousness that we would receive all the material things that we need without even asking for them. Jesus is talking about asking for, seeking for, and knocking for important things like the intimate secrets and keys to His Kingdom. If we persist in honestly and sincerely asking, seeking, and knocking, Jesus will reveal Himself to us and satisfy our desire for wisdom, understanding, and power.

> *"What human father among you, when his son asks for bread, will give him a stone? Or if he asks for a fish, will he give him a snake? So if you, in spite of your being bad, know how to give your children what is good, how much more surely will your heavenly Father give what is good to those who keep on asking him? Then you must practice dealing with others as you would like for them to deal with you; for this is the summing up of the law and the prophets"*
> *(Williams)*

What are we to do with the wisdom, understanding, and power that God gives us? We are to use it to practice dealing with other people in the same manner that we would like them to deal with us.

How would you like to be treated by your spouse, by your children, or by your parents? A good exercise for all of us would be to get out a pencil and paper and write down exactly how we would like to be treated by each member of our family. Spend some time meditating on your relationship with each family member, and write down specifically how you would like to be treated by that person. Now comes the hard part. Jesus says that this is the way we must treat them. "Do as you would be done by." Over the years men have called this the Golden Rule. The Golden Rule is impossible for any of us to follow perfectly in our own strength. It is only with God-given wisdom, understanding, and power that we can put it into effect and make it work.

"Then you must practice dealing with others as you would like for them to deal with you; for this is the summing up of the law and the prophets. Go in by the narrow gate; for broad and roomy is the road that leads to destruction, and many are going in by it. But narrow is the gate and hard is the road that leads to life, and few are they that find it" (Williams)

The Golden Rule is, in a sense, a very narrow gate. All of us instinctively know how we would like to be treated, yet, it is so difficult to practice dealing with others as we would like them to deal with us. When we are treated nicely by others, it is fairly easy to respond in kind. When we are insulted or injured by others is when we need God's help in order to respond according to the Golden Rule. God must deal with our selfishness and with our pride before we can begin to instinctively respond to any situation according to the Golden Rule. Notice that Jesus' Golden Rule isn't lopsided. As we live according to the Golden Rule, we must stand up for justice as well as for mercy.

We are doing no one a favor by "letting them get by with murder." If someone else is in error or committing a crime, the most merciless thing we could do would be to let them continue down the road to destruction without trying to stop them.

Every time that we honestly confront evil, we are faced with another narrow gate decision. If we succumb to the philosophy, "the end justifies the means," it is easy to begin to hit below the belt just because the enemy is hitting below the belt.

There are people who lie, cheat, and steal because their enemies lie, cheat, and steal. These are the people who are always
complaining that they never know where to "draw the line."
These are the very people who may actually become murderers
in their zeal to not let their enemies "get away with murder."

Another school of thought says that "The world is constantly degenerating, and everything is always getting worse,
so why get involved or uptight about issues that are 'right' or
'wrong.'" Still others sit smugly back and wait for what they
feel is the "basic human good in all mankind to surface and
provide the basis for meaningful dialogue that will provide al-
ternate solutions to violence and despair."

Jesus says,

"Blessed are those who are persecuted for doing and being
right."

Therefore, we should oppose evil with every "legitimate"
means that we have at our command. We must oppose evil and
get involved with issues of right and wrong, but Jesus' Golden
Rule does not allow us to fight dirty just because the enemy is
fighting without scruples.

*"Look out for false prophets, who come to you under
the guise of sheep, but inside they are devouring
wolves. You must recognize them by their fruits. People
do not pick grapes from thornbushes or figs from
thistles, do they? So any healthy tree bears good fruit
and a sickly tree bears poor fruit. A healthy tree
cannot bear poor fruit, and a sickly tree cannot bear
good fruit. Any tree that does not bear good fruit is cut
down and burned up. So you must recognize them by
their fruits. Not everyone who says to me, 'Lord, Lord,'
will get into the kingdom of heaven, but only those
who practice doing the will of my Father in heaven.
Many will say to me on that day. Lord, Lord, was it
not in your name that we prophesied, and in your
name that we drove out demons, and in your name
that we did many wonder-works?' And then I will say*

to them openly, 'I never knew you at all. Go away from
me, you who practiced doing wrong,'" (Williams)

There are many people offering us seemingly brilliant solutions to all of our problems. Some of them sound very convincing. Marxism, for instance, looks very good on paper. It isn't until we examine the fruits of Marxism in the countries that have tried it that we recoil in horror. Reversing social injustice by force and instituting obligatory reforms sounds good until bitter experience proves that in Marxist countries, liberty and personal freedom are lost along with economic productivity. Jesus says that we should check things out first before accepting a new teacher hook, line, and sinker. This is why I believe that the Sermon on the Mount should be taken in the light of Jesus' life and of all that has happened since Jesus' death and resurrection. If there ever was a life that has produced and is producing good fruit, it is His. It was due to the great Christian heritage and faith of the men who founded America and to the grace of God that our country has become the most fruitful nation on the face of the earth.

On the last day, God's day of judgment, Jesus says that the eternal fate of each of us is going to hinge on one of two things. Either we will be among those who inherit the Kingdom of God because we "practiced doing the will of Jesus' Father in Heaven," or we will be eternally separated from Jesus because we "practiced doing wrong." The key word here is "practice." Jesus is not the kind of judge who is going to rake us over the coals with a fine tooth comb to see if He can condemn us for a few isolated mistakes. If we have been truly born again by the grace of God, our lives, should show a definite change in direction. Jesus is going to look at our goals and at the motivation of our hearts. Did we really "practice" doing what was right, or did we "practice" doing wrong? Was our goal to please God and to reflect His love to those around us, or did we curse God and refuse to honestly admit to our mistakes? The only way that any of us can consistently practice doing God's will is, with Jesus' help, by meekly submitting to His orders and by receiving the power of His Holy Spirit. This is why the Bible says, over and over, that the only way to salvation is through faith in Jesus Christ.

As we live out our lives here on earth, we get a lot of opportunities to "practice" obeying and pleasing God. The first and most obvious place to "practice" is in our own families. After Jesus' message begins to grow in our hearts, our first goal should be to demonstrate Jesus' mercy and love to our closest relatives. Then, as our families are reconciled to one another and to God, others will become convinced of the truth when they see our "good fruit."

> *"Therefore everyone who hears these words of mine and puts them into practice is like a wise man who built his house on the rock. The rain came down and the winds blew and beat against that house; yet it did not fall, because it had its foundation on the rock. But everyone who hears these words of mine and does not put them into practice is like a foolish man who built his house on the sand. The rain came down, the streams rose, and the winds blew and beat against that house, and it fell with a great crash." (NIV)*

I was taught as a child in Sunday school that Jesus was the "rock" and that if I believed on Him that my house was being built on a secure foundation. Believing on Jesus is a good beginning, but Jesus says that we must hear his words and "practice" them in order for our "house" to stand up against the storms of life. Paul told the Philippian jailer,

> *"Believe in the Lord Jesus Christ and you will be saved—you and your house." (Acts 16:31)*

Paul did not mean that the four walls and the roof would be saved. Paul meant that the jailer's entire household would be saved if one person in the household (the jailer) accepted Jesus and put His message into effect in his life by believing it. The word for believe in Greek has much more depth than our English equivalent. The Greek word means to put your complete faith and trust in something. It means much more than just a

FRIENDS & LOVED ONES REDEEMED

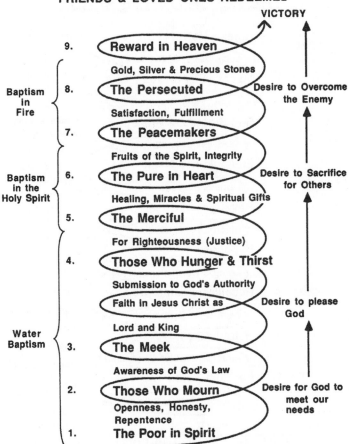

VICTORY

9. **Reward in Heaven**

Gold, Silver & Precious Stones

Baptism in Fire

8. **The Persecuted** — Desire to Overcome the Enemy

Satisfaction, Fulfillment

7. **The Peacemakers**

Fruits of the Spirit, Integrity

Baptism in the Holy Spirit

6. **The Pure in Heart** — Desire to Sacrifice for Others

Healing, Miracles & Spiritual Gifts

5. **The Merciful**

For Righteousness (Justice)

4. **Those Who Hunger & Thirst**

Submission to God's Authority

Faith in Jesus Christ as — Desire to please God

Lord and King

Water Baptism

3. **The Meek**

Awareness of God's Law

2. **Those Who Mourn** — Desire for God to meet our needs

Openness, Honesty, Repentence

1. **The Poor in Spirit**

CPP-1(1)

lxxv

THE HOUSE ON THE SAND

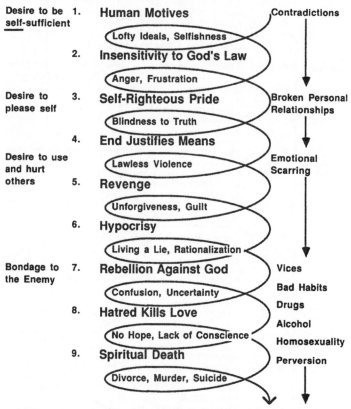

Desire to be 1. Human Motives   Contradictions
self-sufficient

         Lofty Ideals, Selfishness

2. Insensitivity to God's Law

         Anger, Frustration

Desire to 3. Self-Righteous Pride   Broken Personal
please self   Relationships

         Blindness to Truth

4. End Justifies Means

Desire to use   Lawless Violence   Emotional
and hurt   Scarring
others 5. Revenge

         Unforgiveness, Guilt

6. Hypocrisy

         Living a Lie, Rationalization

Bondage to 7. Rebellion Against God   Vices
the Enemy

         Confusion, Uncertainty   Bad Habits

8. Hatred Kills Love   Drugs

                                   Alcohol

         No Hope, Lack of Conscience   Homosexuality

9. Spiritual Death   Perversion

         Divorce, Murder, Suicide

**TOTAL DESTRUCTION OF THE FAMILY AND SOCIETY;
CHAOS**

historical knowledge of the facts. Paul was talking about putting your money where your mouth is.

Jesus uses family terminology throughout His Sermon on the Mount; words like father, son, house, brother, wife, divorce, and so on. The examples that Jesus used are right out of everyday family life such as salt, light, fish, and bread. It is very fitting that this sermon ends with an illustration of a house being built on a secure, solid rock foundation and being able to stand firm in a terrible storm. I believe that Jesus' illustration is also a promise. I believe that anyone who hears Jesus' message and decides to "practice" putting it into effect in his life will be building his household on a firm foundation that will stand against the worst storms of life. This was the guarantee that Paul was extending to the Philippian jailer. I am not just speculating when I say all of this. I have personally experienced what I am talking about. My own extended family has gone through some very difficult "storms" in the last several years. As we have concentrated on practicing Jesus' message, the "storms" have merely served to draw our family closer and closer together.

"When Jesus had finished saying these things, the crowds were amazed at his teaching because he taught as one who had authority, and not as their teachers of the law." (NIV)